杨谊 著

女儿国
The Women's Kingdom

BILLSON International Ltd.

Published by
Billson International Ltd
27 Old Gloucester Street
London
WC1N 3AX
Tel:(852)95619525

Website:www.billson.cn
E-mail address:cs@billson.cn

First published 2025

Produced by Billson International Ltd
CDPF/01

ISBN 978-1-80377-168-7

©Hebei Zhongban Culture Development Co.,Ltd All rights reserved.

The original content within this product remains the property of Hebei Zhongban Culture Development Co.,Ltd, and cannot be reproduced without prior permission. Updates and derivative works of the original content remain the property of Hebei Zhongban. and are provided by Hebei Zhongban Culture Development Co.,Ltd.

The authors and publisher have made every attempt to ensure that the information contained in this book is complete, accurate and true at the time of printing. You are invited to provide feedback of any errors, omissions and suggestions for improvement.

Every attempt has been made to acknowledge copyright. However, should any infringement have occurred, the publisher invites copyright owners to contact the address below.

Hebei Zhongban Culture Development Co.,Ltd
Wanda Office Building B, 215 Jianhua South Street, Yuhua District, Shijiazhuang City, Hebei province, 2207

目 录

CONTENTS

女儿国

1	/ 001	25	/ 049
2	/ 003	26	/ 051
3	/ 005	27	/ 053
4	/ 007	28	/ 055
5	/ 009	29	/ 057
6	/ 011	30	/ 059
7	/ 013	31	/ 061
8	/ 015	32	/ 063
9	/ 017	33	/ 065
10	/ 019	34	/ 067
11	/ 021	35	/ 069
12	/ 023	36	/ 071
13	/ 025	37	/ 073
14	/ 027	38	/ 075
15	/ 029	39	/ 077
16	/ 031	40	/ 079
17	/ 033	41	/ 081
18	/ 035	42	/ 083
19	/ 037	43	/ 085
20	/ 039	44	/ 087
21	/ 041	45	/ 089
22	/ 043	46	/ 091
23	/ 045	47	/ 093
24	/ 047	48	/ 095
		49	/ 097

50	/ 099	78	/ 154
51	/ 101	79	/ 156
52	/ 103	80	/ 158
53	/ 105	81	/ 160
54	/ 107	82	/ 162
55	/ 109	83	/ 163
56	/ 111	84	/ 165
57	/ 113	85	/ 167
58	/ 115	86	/ 169
59	/ 117	87	/ 171
60	/ 119	88	/ 173
61	/ 121	89	/ 175
62	/ 123	90	/ 177
63	/ 125	91	/ 179
64	/ 127	92	/ 181
65	/ 129	93	/ 183
66	/ 131	94	/ 185
67	/ 133	95	/ 187
68	/ 135	96	/ 189
69	/ 137	97	/ 191
70	/ 139	98	/ 193
71	/ 141	99	/ 195
72	/ 143	100	/ 197
73	/ 145	101	/ 199
74	/ 147	102	/ 201
75	/ 149	103	/ 203
76	/ 150	104	/ 205
77	/ 152	105	/ 207

The Women's Kingdom

1	/ 211
2	/ 214
3	/ 216
4	/ 218
5	/ 220
6	/ 222
7	/ 224
8	/ 226
9	/ 228
10	/ 230
11	/ 233
12	/ 235
13	/ 237
14	/ 239
15	/ 241
16	/ 243
17	/ 245
18	/ 247
19	/ 249
20	/ 251
21	/ 253
22	/ 255
23	/ 257
24	/ 259
25	/ 261
26	/ 263
27	/ 265
28	/ 267
29	/ 269
30	/ 271
31	/ 273
32	/ 275
33	/ 277
34	/ 279
35	/ 281
36	/ 283
37	/ 285
38	/ 287
39	/ 289
40	/ 291
41	/ 293
42	/ 295
43	/ 297
44	/ 299
45	/ 301
46	/ 303
47	/ 305
48	/ 307
49	/ 309
50	/ 311
51	/ 313
52	/ 315
53	/ 317

54	/ 319	80	/ 371
55	/ 321	81	/ 373
56	/ 323	82	/ 375
57	/ 325	83	/ 376
58	/ 327	84	/ 378
59	/ 329	85	/ 380
60	/ 331	86	/ 382
61	/ 333	87	/ 384
62	/ 335	88	/ 386
63	/ 337	89	/ 388
64	/ 339	90	/ 390
65	/ 341	91	/ 392
66	/ 343	92	/ 394
67	/ 345	93	/ 396
68	/ 347	94	/ 398
69	/ 349	95	/ 400
70	/ 351	96	/ 402
71	/ 353	97	/ 404
72	/ 355	98	/ 406
73	/ 357	99	/ 408
74	/ 359	100	/ 410
75	/ 361	101	/ 412
76	/ 363	102	/ 414
77	/ 365	103	/ 416
78	/ 367	104	/ 418
79	/ 369	105	/ 420

1

尚小宁沮丧透了,她对自己的改造彻底宣告失败。

她丈夫有了外遇后,她一气之下和他离了婚。然后,她就对自己的脸不满起来。她想,如果她再漂亮一点,再风骚一点,一定可以勾引并留得住丈夫。那个勾引了她丈夫的女人一定很妖媚,一定是个狐狸精,不然怎么会有那么大的魅力,让丈夫连家都不要了?所以,她也要改造自己,化悲痛为力量,重新塑造自己。

过去的就让它过去了,她要找个比丈夫更好的,气死他!所以,她赌气不要儿子,让儿子跟着他爸。她也不去看儿子,她不愿见丈夫,更不愿见那个"狐狸精"。她想等以后风光了,貌若天仙了再去见儿子;等以后有了幸福的家了,再把儿子要回来。

于是,尚小宁跑了好几家最大的医院,对医生说要这样那样整容。医生都叫她先去看心理医生,说她的相貌没问题。她认为医生是因为她把钱交到公家,自己得不到,所以懒得给她做手术,才这样搪塞她。她就跑到了广告做得最响的私人诊所,花了20万,一次把脸搞好。她做了双眼皮、填鼻梁、换肤术、磨下颌角、去眼袋、除皱、植眉毛、植眼睫毛,八大"金刚"整容手术套餐。

诊所之所以推荐她做这八大"金刚"手术套餐,是因为这样省钱、省时、省事,吃一次苦就不受二茬罪了,长疼变成了短疼,一咬牙就过去了。就如离婚一样,与其天天受苦、受折磨,不如立刻了断,这是她一贯的做事原则。

可是,手术过后,她吃了苦中苦,并没有成为人上人。她忍着术后的剧痛,天天换药,等来了拆线。但是,一照镜子,她吓得叫了起来,她已经不认得自己了。镜子里的脸肿得比猪头还大,眼睛也成了一条缝。脸上的皮肤也成了鲜红色,不像剥了皮的鸡蛋,倒像剥了皮的猫。

她立刻和医生吵了起来,医生忙安慰她,说这是手术后的正常反应,伤筋动骨一百天,手上刀割个口子都要七八天才好,何况这么多的手术一齐做了,怎么着也得过两个月,等肿消了吧?尚小宁立刻软了,觉得自己缺乏涵养,急性子。性急吃不得热豆腐,什么事都要冷静一点,放一放,也许她的婚姻也应该这样?

到脸上的肿全都消退后,尚小宁在镜子里的形象就如残雪消融后的大地,潮水退却了的海滩,隐藏在里面的真相暴露在光天化日之下了,成了一副惨不忍睹的景象。她的眼睛一大一小,鼻梁歪着,皮肤像上了一层釉,呈酱油色。如果这副尊容让丈夫看到了,还不笑死了?

2

可屋漏偏遭连夜雨，偏偏丈夫就在这个时候回来了，不，应该是前夫。前夫已经不认得她了，以为这个房子租给别人了，差点掉头就走。她以为儿子出了什么事，也顾不得脸了，就问起了儿子。前夫吓得后退了一步，惊恐地望着她。她慌乱中说自己的脸被烫伤了。前夫这才仔细地盯着她的脸看，又看她的穿着打扮，这一身的行头他应该是熟悉的。他看完了行头，把目光又转移到了她的脸上，看了半天，还是将信将疑。

"儿子到底有没有事？"尚小宁大声吼道。

"没事没事，我是来拿丢在家里的几个光盘的。"前夫似乎在噩梦中被喝醒，忙把目光移开。现在他有点相信这是他的前妻了，她的脾气他是知道的。但他并没有去办他的事，过了一会又把目光移到她的脸上。前夫对她的脸表现出的这种少有的关切，令她很难堪和愤怒，她生气地说："你要拿什么就赶快拿走！"

丈夫慌慌张张地拿着光盘逃走了，临出门前还不忘回头再看看她的脸，小心地说："你不要紧吧？"

她皱着眉头说："我没事。你不要对儿子说。"

前夫走后，她狠狠地把门关上，坐在沙发上号啕大哭。她哭的不光是她的脸，而是她的丑样被前夫看到了，她未来的家庭也成了泡影，她永远也不能去见儿子了。

哭完后，尚小宁痛定思痛，她要拿起法律的武器为自己讨回公道。起码要得到点赔偿留给儿子吧？这样心里也有个安慰。她抓起大草帽，遮住脸，出门去找那家诊所。可是，诊所变了，她见不到一个她以前见过的人，问谁都不知道。这里已经换成性病诊所了。尚小宁在那儿又哭又闹，逢人就说自己的不幸遭遇，人们只同情地望着她。有个小护士还算善良，对她说："又不是我们把你弄坏了，你在这儿哭没用，你还不如去找315。"

一句话提醒了尚小宁，尚小宁马不停蹄找到了315，可她拿不出任何证据证明她是在谁手上做的手术。315建议她报案，说这些人可能是骗子。尚小宁又去报了案，警察做了笔录，问了她那些人的相貌特征，尚小宁只能想起一句说一句。她没想到要留一手，她那时哪会想起来要仔细看他们？她只能说出是男的，女的，老的，少的，其他的都模糊了，她就是在路上遇到他们，也认不出了。

尚小宁回到家，觉得世界末日到了。她受的苦不说，主要是感到委屈，被耍了，就如她的婚姻一样。如果她没有被欺骗，没有付出太多，她不会像现在这样惨痛。这不仅仅是手术的失败，也是梦想的消失，她无法从头再来了。尚小宁把家里的白酒拿出来，喝了个酩酊大醉。她平时不会喝酒，一喝就醉。这些酒都是前夫的，他离婚时没把酒带走。

3

尚小宁醒了后再喝，喝了又醉，直到家里没有白酒了。尚小宁最后一次醒来了，躺在沙发上，不知道以后该怎么办。以前和丈夫开了个店，但是离婚要分财产，她家有2套房子，正好一人一套。她把店也卖了，钱也一人一半。现在钱也花了一半了，她觉得留在这个世界上没什么意思。于是，她开始写遗嘱，把剩下的钱和房子都给儿子，别人不得侵占。然后，在天黑以后，尚小宁出了门。她这几个月白天都不敢出门，现在，她终于可以正大光明地走在街上了。她手术后，除了换药、拆线需要到诊所戴个大草帽外，就一直躲在家里，也不烧饭，天天叫隔壁的小店送饭来。

现在她可以扬眉吐气、做个自由人了。不过，这是到鬼门关前的自由和洒脱，尚小宁不由地惨笑着。再见了，这个群魔乱舞的世界；再见了，可怕的人间。尚小宁又想起了儿子，她很舍不得。她多想见儿子最后一面？可她这副人不人、鬼不鬼的样子，不把儿子吓着了？尚小宁狠了狠心，就让儿子留下她美好的印象吧。尚小宁边走边流泪，然后坐车来到了海边。

尚小宁避开热闹的海湾，那里有许多人在游泳。尚小宁沿着海滩向远方走去，一直走向黑暗。当她走到一片孤寂的黑暗中时，又有些害怕起来。海水的哗哗声和无边的黑暗，仿佛隐藏着什么巨大的危险，一切看不见的东西都幻化成了一个无形的狰狞魔王，它正张着血盆大口，瞪着铜铃般的眼睛，悄无声息地等待着她的到来。尚小宁浑身的汗毛都竖了起来。

寻死的勇敢和对幻境的恐惧不能互相抵消。恐惧来自本能的求生欲望，寻死则是理智屈服于压力而寻求解脱。本能和理智较量的时候，本能占有绝对的优势。不然，怎么男人宁要美女蛇，也不要苦菜花？世界上的诸葛亮只有一个，他的老婆就很丑，但喜欢女人内在美的男人屈指可数。

尚小宁停下了脚步，缩起了肩膀，猛地转身，准备往回走。可抬头一看，游泳的人仿佛全都消失了，前方是更为恐怖的黑暗。这时她才知道她已经走得太远了。她环顾四周，竟没有一个小洞可以躲藏。本能是需要一个小洞来拯救的，她几乎要发狂了。

忽然，尚小宁发现远处的地平线上好像有个灯光，那灯光就是她本能渴求的希望。本能驱使着她用尽全身的力气，像上足了劲的发条，她狂叫着，不顾一切地朝灯光飞奔而去。

渐渐地，灯光越来越明显了，那里好像是个村庄。在靠近村子后，尚小宁的心稍微安定了些，她停下了脚步，大口地喘着粗气，五脏六腑都揪成了一团。在休息了好一阵后，她朝最近的灯光走去。

在快走到那座房子时，尚小宁停住了，她这是在干吗？去向人求助？向人诉说自己的不幸？别人会同情她、理解她、留她住宿，然后第二天她再回家？不，决不，她死也不再回去了。在生的欲望能够满足时，本能放心了，开始退却，理智重新占了上风。

4

刚才的恐惧和一路狂奔让尚小宁觉得好笑,她现在依然要考虑她严肃的人生问题。房子不远处有块巨大的礁石,尚小宁走了上去,一直走到尽头,然后坐了下来。她看着下面幽暗、闪着白浪,低吼的海,不由地闭上了眼睛。她又开始恐惧了,海就像个地狱张大着嘴,片刻就能把她嚼得尸骨无存。她犹豫了起来,她从小长这么大,吃这么多苦,走那么多路,就为了这一刻?她有些不甘心。

这时后面传来了脚步声,把尚小宁吓得一激灵,求生的欲望立刻抓住了她,她用手在地上摸索着,摸到了一块石头,立刻把它紧紧握在手里。她一回头,见是一个老依姆(老大妈),尚小宁吐了一口气,紧缩的心,立刻松弛了下来。

"这么晚了,你在这里干吗?"老依姆问。

尚小宁没作声。

"你不会跳海吧?"

尚小宁仍然没作声。

"这里经常有人来跳海。我昨天还救了一个依妹(小妹),她现在还在我家里。我家就在那边。"老依姆指了指离这里最近的那个灯光,那就是刚才尚小宁朝它拼命狂奔的房子。

尚小宁朝房子望去,见房里有人影晃动。那么,坐在那座房子里,应该是可以看到这里的。尚小宁叹了一口气,真是人连死都要有人来干涉。

"要不要到我家喝杯茶?"

尚小宁没动。

"有什么想不开的?是不是和丈夫吵架了?女人都想不开。"

"唉，比这个严重得多，我们离了。"

"那又怎样呢？我家里就我一个人，还有那个依妹。反正我也睡不着，你就把你的事讲给我听听，讲完再死也不迟。我也把我的讲给你听。我要跳海更容易，海就在家门口。"

老依姆的最后一句话引起了尚小宁的兴趣。一个老太婆独住着，肯定有更大的苦难，但为什么她不死？尚小宁准备跟她走了，可她突然又想起，老太婆该不会是个人贩子吧？把她卖给乡下人做老婆？这会她倒情愿做乡下人的老婆，在女人资源稀缺的地方，女人就是个宝，不会被挑肥拣瘦，而且永远也不会被抛弃。想到这里，尚小宁不由得苦笑了一下。

"你不到我家也行，我就在这里听你讲吧。讲吧，有什么大不了的事？"老依姆说着，坐在了尚小宁的旁边。

尚小宁反倒不好意思了，她断定老依姆不是坏人。坏人总是劝人做成某事，就像她的美容手术。如果老依姆想把她卖了，一定会说得天花乱坠。尚小宁站了起来，说："走，到你家去。"

5

尚小宁也需要找一个人说说自己的苦。她在熟人面前不能说,亲戚面前不能说,父母面前更不能说。父母会痛心,旁人会嘲笑或幸灾乐祸,有什么比一个女人婚姻不保、遭丈夫抛弃更让人瞧不起?不发生在自己身上,谁都不能体会个中的滋味,谁都可以说是她的责任,什么不够温柔啦,不够美丽啦,不会培养爱情啦,不会做菜留住丈夫的胃啦,其实什么都不是。

谈恋爱时她就是现在这样的一个人,丈夫怎么就那么苦苦地追她呢?她那时还不如现在,那时还是个娇惯的丫头,不知道体贴人、操持家务、心疼丈夫,而现在的她是个更出色、更完美的女人。那时她很自信,认为全世界的男人都变心了,她的丈夫都不会,她的婚姻是铜墙铁壁,这全是因为她是个好女人。

可是,一切说变就变,与她无关。男人对女人可以有审美疲劳,可是女人为什么对男人就没有呢?这不过是男人为自己的花心找借口。你就是今天给他个18岁的大姑娘,明天再给另一个,他照样对今天的大姑娘审美疲劳。这正是,男人结了婚就开始花心了,女人结了婚就开始安心了;男人结了婚就从奴隶到将军,女人结了婚就从公主到奴婢。将军嘛,身后的女人当然是韩信带兵,多多益善。

有时苦恼对一个陌生人反而更容易说,谁也不认识你,听完了,议论几句,表示同情,过后各走各的路。

尚小宁跟着老依姆来到了她家。这是一座旧木屋,一间客厅,一间卧室,一间厨房。门窗都开着,卧室里坐着一个姑娘。这大约就是那个要自杀的姑娘吧?尚小宁见到她有一种像见到亲人般的感觉。她竟忘了自己恐怖的面貌,姑娘见了她也没有什么吃惊的表情。容颜的更改只对熟人产生效应,陌生人谁知道她原来是个什么样呢？大不了以为她天生是个丑八怪罢了。

老依姆给尚小宁倒了茶，尚小宁喝了后，就讲起了自己的故事。姑娘叫白菊花，也讲了自己的故事。她从家乡出来打工，和男友同居2年，为他打了胎，可就在她躺在床上备受身心煎熬，觉得是自己杀死了孩子时，男友失踪了一个星期，手机关机。后来男友出现，她和他吵，吵到最后，男友说出了真心话："瞧你的胸部，跟男的一样，谁对你有兴趣？"白菊花感到羞辱，极度羞辱！就像遇到吃白食的，吃完了不给钱，还说："你这什么烂饭菜！"所以，白菊花要死，要让男友内疚一辈子。是他的话害死了她！

"哼哼，他才不会内疚呢。你死就白死了。他要内疚，就不会说出那样的话。"老依姆也说了自己的故事。一个简单得不能再简单的故事。她在新婚之夜，新郎跑了，原因是她是石女（天生没有阴道）！她一辈子就一个人过，靠给别人打短工，做些手工活，在海滩边捡些海鲜卖了过活。

6

"一个人也不错,自在。我不想男人,才活到现在。到这里来跳海的女人都是为了男人,我救过了多少?这些女人真傻,我们女人又不是为男人生的,没他还过得更好。"

是啊,尚小宁听了这话,忽然觉得她那点事不算什么事,不就为了个男人吗?犯不着搭进去一条命。而且他也不会觉得她的命值钱,可她还当它是个宝呢。难怪白菊花不死了,想开了就是这么回事。

然后老中青三个女人就敞开了聊,直聊到东方发白,才挤到一张大床上睡了。

一觉醒来,尚小宁发现老依姆不见了,白菊花还正睡得香呢。她忙起来跑到厨房,见老依姆正在做饭。尚小宁很不好意思,要帮老依姆做点什么。其实也没什么好做的,老依姆已经煮好了稀饭,煎好了小咸鱼。

尚小宁这顿饭吃得好香,不知道是心情突然好了,还是这饭菜真的这么香,尚小宁爱上了这里的生活。难怪白菊花不死了,还赖在这里不走,这里真是神仙般的日子,没有世间的一切烦恼。尚小宁把这当成了家,跟着老依姆做这做那。她没带多少钱来,只有拼命多干活,多挣钱,不能白吃老依姆的。

三个女人在海滩的沙里挖着躲在里面的海螺、贝类;海水退潮后,许多坑里都留着来不及逃走的鱼、虾、螃蟹之类,她们捡了,大的就拿到饭店去卖钱,小的留着自己吃。每天的凌晨、下午两次退潮后,够她们忙一阵的。岩石上还长满了海蛎、淡菜,都指甲盖大小,稍大一点的她们就用铲子铲下来煮汤吃。

尚小宁愿意花一辈子的钱来过这样的生活。在这里只为生计操劳,完全是原始的生活，困了就睡，饿了就吃，没有镜子、化妆、时装、逛街、电视、广告等等的时尚东西，没有外界的东西可以左右她们的生活。尚小宁都忘了自己的脸，她准备过几天就回去取点钱，把家安在这里，在这里过一辈子。老依姆说得对，吃饭、睡觉才是生活的根本，爱情都是吃饱了撑的。

可是尚小宁还没来得及细细体验这美好的生活，就被白菊花劝着登上了渔船——出海打鱼。白菊花看渔船回来打了那么多的鱼虾，就羡慕得不得了，非要到渔船上去体验生活。渔船不愿意带她，因为女人一般都不出海。白菊花好不容易找到一个夫妻出海的渔船，说帮他们打工不要钱，就是想出趟海。渔船同意了，白菊花就拖着尚小宁一道去了。

两人做了好一番准备，吃的喝的都带了，还买了许多晕船药，没上船就吃了。幸亏她们做好了这样的准备，才可以在船上没有吐得死去活来。渔船上远没有她们预想的好玩，船在海上颠得很厉害，几乎站不稳，她们吃了太多的晕船药，迷迷糊糊，老想睡觉，也做不了什么。

7

到了渔场,是夜里下网,夜里起网,两人不行了,一点新鲜感和刺激感都没有,两人穿着救生衣,半睡半醒地机械地干着活。要不是一开始求着人家来打免费的工,两人就去睡了,什么也不管了。

到忙完了,天也亮了,两人不顾一切地躲到舱里去睡了。不知过了多久,巨大的摇晃把她俩弄醒,她俩还没明白是怎么回事,就被抛到了地上。尚小宁本能地想抓住一个东西,可没东西可抓。白菊花尖叫着,抱着头,像强盗来了一样。尚小宁找准了一个机会,一把抓住白菊花,白菊花也像抓住了救命稻草一样向她扑来,两人紧紧地抱在一起。

然后两人就像一个玉米一样在地上滚来滚去。不过重量增加了,起到了一定的稳定作用,而且两人合成了圆柱形,比较便于滚动,减少了碰撞,虽然这会儿身上已经被砸得青一块紫一块的,但她们没感到痛。

她们一直保持着这个姿势,直到晃动平息下来。两人一骨碌爬起坐着,互相望着。

"一开始我还以为是地震,后来一想这是在船上。"白菊花说。

"肯定是遇到了风暴。"尚小宁说,然后又惊跳起来,"哎呀,他们呢?不会掉到海里去了吧?"尚小宁说着就要往外冲。

跑到甲板上一看,人都还在,女人在弄缆绳,男人在驾驶室里。两人松了口气。尚小宁对女人说:"刚才把我吓死了,是不是有风暴?"

女人心事重重地点了点头。尚小宁抬眼一看,天空要多恐怖有多恐怖,翻滚的乌云像十万天兵天将,马上就要逼到眼前了,压得人透不过气来;海浪像无数个妖怪正举着尖刀跳跃着,像随时要把船撕碎。船还是摇晃得厉害,尚小宁几天来已经习惯了这种摇晃,不然根本站不稳。

"我们赶快回去吧,鱼都打到了?"尚小宁惊恐地说。她已经后悔上船了。

"是要回去,但是船一直顶着风开不了。"

"那怎么办?"

"我们先顺着风到哪里躲一躲。"

"有地方躲吗?"

女人点点头。

尚小宁放心了,渔民肯定有经验,不然也出不了海。

8

"有什么事我们来帮帮忙。"

"你们还是回舱里,不然容易掉到海里。"

尚小宁望望白菊花,白菊花点了点头。两人又回到了舱里。还没等她们喘口气,剧烈的晃动又开始了,这次她们有经验了,立刻抱在了一起,滚到地上。

天昏地暗,地动山摇,两人好像是筛子里的豆子,随着主人的手而滚动着,没有一点自己的主张。

尚小宁断定自己这次是回不去的了,她头脑里一再闪过儿子的形象。她好好的离什么婚?丈夫有外遇就有外遇好了,起码她还可以过安稳的日子,天天和儿子在一起。整容失败了就失败了,寻什么死?活着就好。本来和老依姆活得好好的,上什么船?这个白菊花害死人。不过也怪自己不坚定,就是不上船,她也没办法……

仿佛过了几千年、几万年,她们已经忘了吃饭、睡觉,忘了世界上还有别的生活,只希望风暴赶快过去。

在船恢复了常态后,两人也垮了,躺着动不了了,极度困乏又极度兴奋,想睡也睡不着。过了好久,尚小宁说:"不行,我要上去看看,不知道他们怎样了。"

"我也去看看他们,现在变得像亲人一样了。"

两人艰难地爬了起来,扶着船壁,走向甲板。甲板上没人,她俩正要到驾驶室去找,突然船猛地一歪,她俩都掉进了海里。

尚小宁在一阵迷乱,喝了好几口海水后,又浮出了海面,她这才想起自己穿着救生衣。幸亏穿了,不然就死定了,她不大会游泳。不过现在也基本死定了，不会有人来救她的，即使有人来救，她能等到那一刻吗？她就像是一个孩子手边的蚂蚁，随时都有可能被碾成粉末。

突然，尚小宁看到不远处有个红点，那是白菊花！尚小宁一阵兴奋，就像看到了救生人员，她拼命喊着，挥舞着手，白菊花也看到了她，也同样兴奋。两人四肢并用地向对方划去。

不久，她们在海里胜利会师了，两人紧紧抱在一起。她们想起了船，再去找，发现船虽然离她们不远，但船上没人。她俩用力向船划去，但船好像总和她们保持着等距离，永远不可接近。她俩渐渐垮了，再也没力气游了，一天没吃东西，又没睡觉，她俩渐渐失去了知觉。

尚小宁醒来时，发现自己在一个很小的房间里，根据这间房间的结构和摇来摇去的感觉，加上一股强烈的鱼腥味，尚小宁断定自己是在一条船上，她看到周围全是陌生的面孔，知道自己得救了，瞬时流出了眼泪。人们拿来了水和面包，尚小宁才觉得自己太渴了，太饿了，忙吃喝起来。

人们又叫她到卫生间冲个淡水澡，换上衣服。

9

到尚小宁稍稍恢复了元气,可以讲话时,她讲了自己的故事。讲着讲着,她想起了白菊花,问她们有没有救起另外一个姑娘。她们说没有。尚小宁又哭了。

"喂,女儿有泪不轻弹。"

听到这个奇谈怪论,尚小宁吃了一惊,她发现说这话的是一个和她差不多大的女人。尚小宁又看看周围,这才发现自己的身边全是女人。

"你们都去干活吧,我陪着她就行了。"那女人对其他女人说。

看着女人离开的身影,尚小宁疑惑地问:"不是女人不让出海吗?"

"是男人不让出海!"

"什么?"尚小宁明明记得她们要上渔船人家不带她们的,难道真的是她头脑坏了,记错了?

"男的上船忌讳。你想想,他们上了船做不了什么事,还尽添乱。"

"你们这船上没有男人?"

"没有。"

"那船长呢?"尚小宁又看看周围,这是条不小的船,应该属于远洋渔船一类的吧。对于远洋渔船,尚小宁是这次到海边才知道的。具体的她说不清,反正就是要足够大,能抗大的风暴,能装很多的鱼,可以带很多吃的、用的。

"我就是啊。"那女人笑着说。

"呵,真了不起。"尚小宁由衷地佩服着。她想起了女列车长、女乘务长、女部长,"我就不是这块料。"

"女人应该做出一番事业。"

尚小宁听了，想了想，点了点头。她喜欢上了这个女船长。

"不是我说你，你看你，为了个男人，差点毁了自己。女人重要的不是相貌，而是事业。你事业有成了，有房有车了，男人还不蜂拥而上？你什么样的男人找不到？"

对呀，女船长的这番话，简直就是醍醐灌顶，击中要害，令尚小宁幡然猛醒。尚小宁感叹自己没有早一点遇到女船长。

"所以我对她们都很严厉，不允许有感情的纠葛影响到工作和事业，也不许追星。你看我这条船上，没有一张明星照，那些虚华的东西没意思。"

尚小宁不住地点头，觉得女船长的话很有道理，其实想想也就是这么回事，感情和一生的大计来比，算不了什么。但这话要是以前，她是听不进去的，她受了挫折，又在海边生活了一段时间，现在由这个女船长把意思总结出来，就觉得精辟。

10

尚小宁想起刚才看到的那些依妹、依姐，包括这个女船长都是短发、本色，没有一个是浓妆艳抹的，皮肤也没有很好地保护。怎么说呢，像是30年前的中国女人。不过，即使是那个年代，女人也会利用一切可以得到的手段来装扮自己的；就是样板戏里的女英雄，也会在前额卷起一排刘海，以让自己显得漂亮些。

这些女人完全是天然去雕饰，还有一种硬朗和沉稳，让尚小宁耳目一新。她想起了以前战天斗地的铁姑娘队，她小时候是很羡慕这些能干的姑娘的。可能风里来雨里去吧，这些女人多了朴实，少了娇气；也许是女船长的做派吧，其他人也就都和她一样了。尚小宁很喜欢这样的作风，除了工作上的要求，女人在这里可以很随便。

"你再休息休息，我去忙了。等船靠岸了再到我家去玩。我喜欢交朋友，在海里捡到个朋友不容易，缘分。主要是我喜欢你的气质，文静。到你什么时候你不想住我家了，我再送你回去。"

尚小宁第一回听人这样说她，她总觉得自己不够温柔，不够女人味，不够会撒娇。如果一般人这样夸她，她还以为是在讽刺她，可她在女船长面前，确实够女人的。

女船长站起来走了。尚小宁又吃了点面包，喝了点水，吃了点水果，就迷迷糊糊地睡了。以后女船长再也没有露过面。尚小宁虽然醒过好几次，但她都懒得动，想着心事。到女船长再次露脸的时候，船已经靠岸了，天也黑了。

"这是你的衣服，已经洗干净了，换上吧。"女船长手里捧着一叠衣服，递给了她。

尚小宁拿着自己干净的衣服，很感激，说："谢谢，谢谢。"既然女船长叫她换上，她就没理由再一直穿着别人的衣服了。

女船长出去了一会，等她换好了衣服才进来。看着尚小宁穿的衣服，女船长微微皱了皱眉："你的衣服怎么这样？"

尚小宁赶紧低头检查自己的衣服，没有扣错扣子，也没有走光，她疑惑地望着女船长："……还好啊……"

"不，我是说你的衣服怎么这么紧？把胸部完全都暴露了出来，这有多难看？还有你的裤子，也包得这么紧，屁股都看到沟了。也不戴个围脖。"

尚小宁看看船长，她真的戴着个围脖。其他的船员也是。

"暴露？"尚小宁第一回听人家说她穿衣服暴露。

尚小宁又低头看自己的衣服，没有啊，这能叫暴露？她就穿了件普通的花衬衫啊，不过是收了腰的，非常合身；她又摸了摸自己的裤子和屁股。裤子是有点紧，它是牛仔裤，现在不都流行紧身的牛仔裤嘛。这是尚小宁最喜欢的衣服，她才穿着它准备跳海寻死的。既然没死成，她又在老依姆家住着，没衣服换洗，她就索性穿着老依姆的衣服，反正夏天，简单。

11

老依姆的衣服有不少，够穿，白菊花也穿着老依姆的衣服。是不是她经常救那些想自杀的人，留她们过些日子，就多准备了些衣服？尚小宁想，应该是这样的。后来她的衣服洗干净了她也没穿，她想和旧的生活告别，不想再看以前的衣服了。

这次出海前，白菊花劝她还是穿自己的衣服，别弄得像要饭的一样。

"那自己的衣服就一套也不够换啊。"尚小宁说。

"那不能白天穿自己的衣服，睡觉穿老依姆的衣服，把它当睡衣？"

后来她们在船上就真的这样穿了。到自己的衣服脏了，就晚上洗洗，晾干了，白天穿，一套衣服也够了。

但是自从到了渔场后，这个规律就被打乱了，也不分白天、黑夜，衣服脏了就换干净的，也懒得洗，实在洗不动了。到她们被抛到海里之前，都一直穿着自己的衣服，白天、黑夜。她们累瘫了，倒头便睡，还洗什么澡，换什么衣服？要换也没得换，都是脏的。

假如她没有被抛到海里，在海水里浸泡，被暴风雨全自动地搓揉，在一望无际的、世界上最大的洗衣机里经过数天的漂洗后，她的衣服一定是臭不可闻的。现在这身衣服经过大自然的清洗，人工的清洗，已经又恢复了它的本色，正散发着特有香味。

尚小宁觉得听到了自己已经过世的外婆的声音。外婆最反对她穿这样的衣服的。她认为女人把胸部的曲线弄出来很不雅，裤子包在身上很不成样子。这个女船长看来年纪也不太大，和自己差不多，怎么这么老古董？

尚小宁回想起这个船上的特点，觉得女船长也太封建了，这种衣服还叫紧身？那她看到姑娘们穿的吊带、背心、超短裙、下面露出一点屁股的短裤、挂在胯部、一弯腰就露出屁股沟的长裤、三点式的服装，还不晕过去了？也难怪，大概整天在海上漂吧，工作忙，不着家，不逛街，也不知道现在是什么时代了。尚小宁也没工夫逛街，但她守着小店，没事时候，看街上来来往往的人，也会注意到这些姑娘的装扮。

"你就是这身衣服难看，简直是奇装异服。站在男人面前多那个？好，我们走吧。一个人一个习惯。"

女船长带着她下了船。女船长已经在岸边的车库里取了车，开了过来，停在码头，要接她到她家去。尚小宁甚至都没来得及看一眼这个陌生的地方，就上了车。在车上尚小宁想看看街上的夜景，可女船长把车开得飞快，几乎要成了赛车了，窗外的景色都花成了一片，尚小宁的心也提到了嗓子眼。

12

在一座小洋楼前，车子停下了。"这是我家。"女船长自豪地说。尚小宁下了车，女船长把车开进了车库，然后领着尚小宁进了家。

开门的是个非常漂亮的年轻男人，他扎着马尾巴，下巴上留着长胡子，唇上的胡子剪得与上唇平齐，也戴着围脖，这怪异的打扮，令尚小宁大吃一惊。他还穿着件粉红的睡衣，而且温柔、腼腆，是个典型的白马王子加新好男人。尚小宁差点晕倒了，晕倒在这个神话前。

尚小宁如腾云驾雾般地、不真实地进入了这个豪华的家。两个孩子扑了过来，女船长搂着他们亲了半天。男人给她们倒了茶，又把女船长的旅行包打开，把里面的东西拿出来放好，又把脏衣服拿到阳台的洗衣机里去洗，接着又进了厨房。

"这是你儿子？"

"哪里，是我丈夫。他叫温碧玉。"

尚小宁不相信似的瞪大了眼睛，看了看女船长："他好像比你小很多。"

"是小很多，小 18 岁。我们结婚的时候他才 18 岁。"

"什么？"

"我因为要搞事业，36 岁才结婚。"

"那还能结到婚？"

"怎么结不到婚？我不是说了吗？有了事业，有了房子，有了车子，什么样的男人找不到？"

"但是女人太大了，生孩子困难……"

"我在 20 岁的时候就把卵子冻起来了，提前做好了计划。我事业心很强，哪会因为家庭和孩子拖后腿？"

"你说什么？什么卵子'冻起来'？"

"这个你都不晓得？你也太孤陋寡闻了。难怪你那么早生孩子。"

"我生孩子也不早啊，28岁。"

"那还不早？我24岁才大学毕业，要当5年水手，5年大副，当上船长2年才可以结婚。每升一级，竞争都非常激烈，都要经过严格的考试，笔试和操作。不是每个人都可以当上船长的，许多人当一辈子水手。"

"那她们就一辈子不结婚？"

"不不，考试只有一次机会，考得上就上，考不上就不上，然后她们就可以结婚了。婚假都是3年，包括产假。反正我是要干大事业的，所以就把卵子放到卵子银行去冻起来。如果考不上也没关系，那我就自己生，不要那些冷冻的卵子。"

"什么是卵子？"

13

"嗨呀,男人的那个是老百姓说的睾丸。我们说的是女人真正的卵子。我们体内不是有子宫吗?那是长孩子的地方;还有卵巢,是长卵子的地方。没有卵子,怎么会长出孩子?卵子就是很小很小的'鸡蛋',我们肉眼勉强能看见。我们有两个卵巢,每个月它俩交替排卵。排卵就是'下蛋',这个月这个下,下个月另一个下。有时一道下了,就生双胞胎了。不过这种双胞胎不太像,其实就是普通的兄弟姐妹。那种很像的双胞胎是一个卵子分裂成了两个人。"

"啊?我们人也会'生蛋'?"

"怎么不会?是女人都会'生蛋',就和母鸡一样,只不过蛋没生到外面,而是生到子宫里去了,蛋就在子宫里长成了小孩。"

"哦——是这样的哈,那……为什么非要结了婚,蛋才能长成小孩?"

"还不是一样的道理?没有公鸡,母鸡生的蛋也孵不出小鸡。"

"对对对,哈哈哈……你又不是医生,怎么懂这么多?"

"这是起码的常识,我们在学校都学过。不知道这些,我怎么会把卵子保存起来?"

"哎哟,我们都没学过。不过我也没念几年书,家里太穷……你那时候不是没结婚吗?卵子怎么能长成小孩?"

"这就是试管婴儿啊,在外面弄好了,再种到肚子里去。不过我用的还是我身上新鲜的,没用冷冻的卵子,我还没老到那个程度呢。50岁以后才没有卵子。老母鸡下了几年蛋后,就下不出来了。"

"呵呵,你讲话真有意思。那……以前没有这个技术怎么办?"

"那就大学毕业后,先结婚、生孩子,到孩子上幼儿园了,再工作。"

"嗨,我们哪懂这些?到时候就晓得谈恋爱、结婚,不懂得这样安排。这些都是你们单位规定的吧?"

"可能,不同的职业可能有不同的规定。"

"所以讲,有单位,也好也不好;不过像我们这样做生意的,也都被生意拴住了。不做,钱就损失啊,过年过节的时候最好赚,想歇都歇不下来。"

"还不一样?我们出一趟海,哪有什么周末、节日?"

"不过你有个这么好的丈夫,也很幸福。"

尚小宁有点酸溜溜的,觉得命运太不公平了,她自己如花似玉,却找了那么个丈夫,她倒是想安安心心过日子了,可丈夫又要作怪。唉,人比人气死人。这女船长的命怎么这么好?不过这男人是真的爱她吗?不过是靠着女人吃软饭吧?自己可以不劳而获,当个小白脸。现在时兴这个,找个有钱的老女人,等于被包养,然后熬不住自己再找个情妇。

14

就在尚小宁暗自神伤，受着与其说是羡慕不如说是嫉妒的折磨时，饭菜好了。温碧玉笑眯眯地喊他们吃饭。尚小宁端起饭碗，品尝着连她自己都做不出来的非凡的美味菜肴时，忍不住地赞扬起温碧玉来。

温碧玉得意地笑着，女船长很满足的样子。

"来来来，喝酒。"女船长已经给尚小宁倒了满满一杯白酒。

"我不喝酒的。"尚小宁忙推辞着。

"哪有女人不喝酒的？不行，一定得喝。"

"我真的不喝，你俩喝吧。"

"他不喝酒，我不让他喝。"

"我从来不喝酒，她说男人喝酒不像样子。反正我都听她的。"温碧玉应道，一副乖巧的样子。

尚小宁觉得这男人什么都好，就是太软了点，不太像个大男人。尚小宁只得硬着头皮喝。

"嗨，我还没说我叫什么名字呢，你以后可别喊我船长，那是下级这样喊我。既然我们成了朋友，你还是喊我名字。我叫严花生，不是腌花生，是严肃的'严'。"

"哈哈，那花生是吃的'花生'吧？这个名字好玩。"

"嘿嘿，就是吃的花生。这里面有几个意思。我妈妈姓花，我当然就是花生了。另外，我家的兄弟姐妹都是"插花生"的，也就是一个男孩，一个女孩，隔开的，很有规律。我是老四，就叫花生。还有，花生的生命力很强，又把果子结在地下，不虚，很实在。我也就是这样的一个人。"

"这样看来这个名字确实起得很好。人像名字，也有人说，字也像一个人。我的字就写得特别大,特别草。"

"可能,小心谨慎的人字总是写得很规矩,古怪的人字也写得古怪。"

"我,我,我的字也写得很好看。老师都表扬我了。"两个孩子也在欢快地吃着,大一点的插嘴讲着。他们也戴着围脖。反正尚小宁看到的所有的人都戴着围脖。

"你很乖,很能干。"尚小宁夸着孩子,不禁又想起了自己的儿子,一股柔情使她仔细打量着他们。

"你女儿好漂亮,像爸爸。"

"不,他不是女儿,是儿子。那个是女儿。"

"不,我说的是她。"尚小宁指着身边梳着辫子、穿着裙子的孩子说。

"没错,他是儿子,这个才是女儿。"女船长指着自己身边的男孩模样的孩子说。

"什么?"尚小宁简直不敢相信自己的耳朵,她又看看温碧玉。现在连儿子都这样打扮,而女船长和女儿都像男的一样,这让尚小宁很不舒服。

15

"我……我觉得，还是男孩有男孩的样子比较好。"尚小宁小心翼翼地说着，同时瞥了温碧玉一眼。

"就是嘛，我也这样认为。人就应该本分。现在风气太坏，我家都不放电视，怕那些广告毒害孩子。"

话说到这份上，尚小宁就不好再说什么了，只得低下头去吃菜。女船长又劝尚小宁喝酒，尚小宁只得硬着头皮喝了。女船长自己也喝了几杯酒，然后，点了支烟抽着，把手搭在温碧玉肩上，说："我有个好丈夫，心灵手巧，又漂亮。许多人都羡慕我。我很幸福。不过我对他也不差，我出去挣钱，回来都交给他。他也好，家里都不要我操心的，他也很辛苦，拉扯着两个孩子不容易。但是，我也对得起他，在外面都很正派。来，干杯。"

尚小宁和女船长干着杯，"我要过上你这样的日子一天，死也闭眼睛了。"

"会有的，你条件比我好，会找到好男人的。干了这杯就能找到。"

"好，托你吉言，干！不过我还是劝你少喝点酒，尽量不抽烟，这两样东西对身体不好。"

"哈哈，我是烟酒茶都来，没办法，在海上不喝不行。不过我不赌、不嫖。"

停了一会，船长又说："你的长发应该剪了，留着个马尾巴像什么样子？"

尚小宁对女人剪短发最为反感，认为女人就应该留长发，对剪男人头，甚至剃光头的女人简直不能容忍。

尚小宁尽管那些日子在家里天天醉酒，但她还是不会喝酒，喝了几杯后，头一下晕了起来，女船长扶着她来到客房的一张大床上睡，"这是你的房间，你就住在这里，爱住多久住多久。"

尚小宁躺到床上后，很快就睡着了。

到尚小宁一觉醒来,都第二天中午了。女船长打高尔夫球去了,要很晚才回来,孩子到幼儿园去了。尚小宁洗漱好了后,温碧玉已端出了饭菜,喊她吃饭。这弄得尚小宁很不好意思。

"我来吧,一直要你伺候我,真是不好意思。"

"这有什么?做惯了,不费事的。"

"你真好。我家的家务都是我做。"

"是吗?"那男人睁大了眼睛,"像你这样的人不多见。"

"什么?"尚小宁笑了起来,"像你这样的人才真是不多见。"

"也难怪,我小时候,我爸爸就教育我,要懂事,要体贴女人,管好家,让女人在外面干好事业。"

"你爸爸也真是个好爸爸。我怎么就遇不到这些好男人?"

"是啊,虽然现在观念变了,但是我家很传统,我家的她也很传统。"

16

"这样最好,两个人互相关心,互相体贴,日子过得才有意思。"

"是吗?你觉得有意思吗?可是我却觉得乏味得很。"

"什么?"

"你想,我整天关在家里,孩子,家务,她又经常不在家,我闷得很。我渴望到外面去,渴望工作。"

"那就去工作好了,家务和孩子交给保姆。"

"不行,她不肯,她只希望我做个全职丈夫,照顾好家,照顾好她。"

"这也太自私了。"尚小宁脱口而出,说完又有点后悔。女船长待她不薄,把她当自己人,她吃了人家的,喝了人家的,住在人家,还说人家的坏话。

"其实她也挺好的,各方面都不错。找到她也是我的福气,有多少人羡慕我。她正派,有学问,经济条件也不错,顾家。现在这样的好女人不多见,女人都太花。像我也没学什么东西,从小成绩又不好,不过,漂亮的人总是有人要的。"

没出息!尚小宁想着,一个大男人靠相貌娶老婆,真是头回听说。也难怪,夫妻间总是要达到某种平衡,要么是旗鼓相当,要么是金钱、地位和相貌的交换。这也就不奇怪了,她尚小宁要是找个花一样的白痴男人也找得到,但她不愿意。

吃过饭,尚小宁赶紧收拾桌子,洗碗,把温碧玉感动得什么似的,"你真是个好女人。"

"是吗?"尚小宁笑了起来,"这算什么?我在家什么都做,和你一样。"

"我家她什么都不做,有点大女子主义。"

"我以后来好好开导她,女人嘛,哪能什么都不做呢?"

洗好碗，两人又坐到沙发上聊，还没聊几句，传来了钥匙开门的声音，尚小宁以为是女船长回来了，望着门，正要准备和进来的女船长打招呼，结果来的是个花枝招展的女人。

女人见到尚小宁显然愣住了，不知道进好还是退好。尚小宁回头看看温碧玉，温碧玉的脸腾地红了，局促不安的样子。尚小宁明白了，果不出她所料，这样年轻美貌的男人会守得住一个老女人？不出事才怪！她又为船长鸣不平起来，想得起来找这样一个嫩男人，那样对他好，结果全不知他在背后是这样的。这不和人家包二奶一样？老头子不在家了，二奶就和情人幽会。女船长啊，女船长，你怎么也和那些老头子一样犯傻呢？二奶靠得住吗？小白脸靠得住吗？

进来的这个女人，一定是一个可以满足男人心灵空虚的女人。尚小宁想到自己的婚姻。狐狸精！她不由得怒火中烧，好像这个女人就是那个勾引她丈夫的狐狸精一样。

17

女人叫肖天鹅。这时,她经过片刻的调整后,倒大大方方地进来了。她梳着大波浪的头,也戴着围脖。紧身的衣裤勾露出曲线。"家里来客人啦?你家钥匙怎么在门上没拿下来?"然后又朝尚小宁笑笑说,"我是他家邻居,过来坐坐。"

"哦,"温碧玉立刻明白了肖天鹅的意思,马上接过话来说,"我刚才出去回来忘了拿下来。"

但他显然是在说谎。他的声音空洞而干涩,而且音调提高了半度,这就是说谎的特征。尚小宁就是根据这个特征而断定她自己丈夫说谎的,而事实上她丈夫就是在说谎。一个人为什么要说谎话呢?比如没去一个地方说去了,去了一个地方又说没去,他必然是要隐藏什么,而一个男人有事为什么不可以对妻子说呢?尤其是对她这样一个好妻子,那就是他有另一个女人!因为丈夫在家里是自由的,无论到哪里去,交什么样的朋友,花多少钱,她都从来不过问,所以丈夫没有任何一件事有必要瞒着她。

也许尚小宁根本就不该做个贤妻良母,这样的教育害死人,她就是在这样的教育下,立志做个好女人的。也许她真应该对丈夫严加看管,搜走他身上所有的钱,不让他离家一步,他要不从就和他没完没了地拼命。那些怕老婆的男人,家里不都有这样一个胡搅蛮缠的"母老虎"?那些男人有多乖?唯一的心愿就是老婆别吵,过个安心的日子。她虽然很同情那些男人,但很多男人都是"下流胚",不这样不行,她现在知道了这一点,但迟了,她已经失去了丈夫。

肖天鹅还没靠近,一股刺鼻的香味就飘了过来。

这女人简直就是交际花,一头乌黑卷曲的头发,脸上化着淡妆,皮肤保养得很好，衣着十分得体。如果没有敌意地去看她，她应该是很漂亮的，像香港的超级美女章小蕙。除去年龄不说，她应该是和温碧玉很般配。

"来，坐坐，我去倒茶。"温碧玉慌慌张张地跑到厨房去了。

尚小宁没好气地不去理肖天鹅。女人很难和比自己漂亮的女人交朋友，更何况尚小宁的丈夫就是被这样的"狐狸精"给拐跑了？这两种敌意让她义愤填膺。可交际花并没有介意她的态度，而是在她身边坐了下来，对她很欣赏的样子，又很亲切。不知是真的欣赏，还是因为她来偷情，被抓了个正着而讨好于她。

"你是我见过的最有品位的女人。单单就凭这发型和服装。"

"啊？"

同样是这身服装，女船长就那么反感，可这个女人就很欣赏。这下轮到尚小宁局促不安了，她脸红了，不禁摸了摸自己的头发，又低头看了看自己的装扮，这是很普通的衣服啊。女人是经不住夸奖的，她当初就是听信了丈夫的甜言蜜语后，才向他投降的。

18

尚小宁想起了自己有好多日子没有照镜子了，也没有打扮，头发乱蓬蓬地胡乱扎在脑后，脸上什么也没抹。她已经忘了她是个女人了。美容的失败让她差点去死，都不敢见人了，现在她竟然得到了这位超级美女的赏识。尚小宁以为自己听错了，心虚得不行，但她宁愿自己听错了。

尚小宁对她所有的敌意立刻土崩瓦解，女人并不是对比她漂亮的女人有敌意，而是对比她漂亮，又瞧不起她的女人有敌意。如果比她漂亮的女人觉得她漂亮，那么什么敌意就都没有了。尚小宁第一次有了这种体会。

"不是我批评现在的女人，她们太随便，太不拿自己当人，没几个会打扮的。"

温碧玉已经端出了茶来，递给了肖天鹅，同时又低低地对她说，"我太太出海回来了。"

"我知道，我看她出去的，打高尔夫球去了。嗨，不过她不在家也没关系，这不是还有个女人吗？女人跟女人话更多。"

"就是。"

"同一性别的人在一起更有得谈。"

"嗯。"尚小宁点了点头。

"你在哪里工作？"

"我本来开个小店。"

于是尚小宁就把自己的事简单地说了一下。女人容易对人产生好感，一有好感，就会把什么事都说出来。她都忘了她刚才的愤慨和正义感，忘了这女人是来找女船长的丈夫私通的。她倒过来还把她当成了朋友，就因为她赏识她！

"你呀，真是太痴情，犯得着吗？三条腿的蛤蟆难找，两条腿的男人还怕找不到？你怎么就盯着他一个，别的都看不到呢？还为他死,真不值得。你要知道，人生是多么美好，我们还没享受够呢，怎么要去死？"

肖天鹅架起了二郎腿，从怀里掏出了一盒莫尔烟，翘着兰花指，从里面抽出了一支。温碧玉马上拿起打火机，给她点上了。温碧玉现在低眉顺眼地插不上话。相比之下，肖天鹅倒有一股豪气，像女中豪杰，又不失女人韵味。不像女船长，太男人化了；而这丈夫，又太女人化。

"是啊，我那时还没这么开通，现在我也不死了。"

"你还不开通？都整容了，够新潮的，够大胆的。就我这么时髦，想过整容，也还没行动呢。"

"你这么漂亮还要整容？我那还不是一时之气，被逼的。"

19

"漂亮，人都有对自己不满意的地方，都想达到十全十美的境界。你呀，除了感情上放不开，样样都好。"肖天鹅又对尚小宁从头到尾看了一遍，"你哪要整什么容？这不好得很吗？天生丽质。"

"真的？"尚小宁摸了摸自己的脸，"不过，我以前也是不丑，不然老公怎么会追我？"

"我还没见过有你这么漂亮的女人。不管你以前是什么样子，起码你现在给我的就是漂亮的感觉。"

"真的吗？"尚小宁的眼睛里充满了疑惑。

"难怪你的老公要变心。人不在乎自己是不是绝色美人，而在乎是不是把自己当作绝色美人看。不过这要有个大的前提，就是相貌还过得去。丑八怪要是这样了，就会被人笑掉大牙。"

"嘿嘿，这倒也是。"尚小宁满脸的尴尬，因为她现在已经沦为丑人了，要丑人自信是很困难的。

"你从来都没认为自己是个绝色美人吗？"

"没有。从来就没有过，现在就更没有了。"

"你看你呀。"那女人用手指点了点她，"你简直就是埃及艳后嘛。"

"什么埃及艳后？"

"古代埃及有个女王，非常漂亮，后来嫁给了恺撒大帝。现在人一说美女，就把她比作埃及艳后；说男人漂亮就说他像潘安、宋玉。"

"我像埃及艳后？"

"什么不像？你看，鼻子高高的、古铜色的皮肤像缎子一样光滑、丹凤眼、性感的嘴唇、蓬松的头发。难道你就不照镜子？"

"不照，我照镜子？还照什么镜子，这张脸我想起来就怕。我现在只想过过一般的日子，忘掉这张脸。你这是安慰我吧？怕我难过。"

"你呀，哼！我非要你照照镜子。"肖天鹅站起来，把烟放在烟灰缸上，然后像拖死猪一样，拖着尚小宁就往卫生间走；尚小宁也像死猪一样赖着不肯走。

"你就饶了我，求求你。"

"不行，你非要看上一眼，如果不像我说的那样，你就打我，骂我，我都认。"

话都说到这个份上了，尚小宁只好硬着头皮随肖天鹅进了卫生间，但她站在镜子面前低着头，还是不敢看。

"你给我看。"肖天鹅把尚小宁的头扳起来，强迫她看着镜子。

20

尚小宁不得不看了一眼镜子里的自己,这不看不要紧,一看还真吓了一跳。镜子里的自己确实如肖天鹅所说的那样。鼻子怎么不歪了呢?一大一小的双眼皮已经恢复到了以前的丹凤眼;植的眉毛、睫毛也都掉了;下颌角可能根本就没磨,因为脸型还是原来的样子;海边的太阳把全身都晒黑了,所以脸上酱油样的颜色也被掩盖了;人也胖了。她一贯瘦得皮包骨头,不长肉,在老依姆家住一阵子,竟胖了。

她不但不是丑八怪,毁容的地方荡然无存,而且还比以前更漂亮了,年轻了,起码年轻了20岁!尚小宁简直不敢相信这张脸就是她的。她有一阵恍惚,以为是在做梦。要不就是这个镜子有魔法。

她记得有个故事说的是,一个奇丑无比的女王,手里拿个小镜子,喜欢天天照。在她死后,人们发现,原来这个镜子有魔法,把美人变丑,丑人变美。她现在照的就是这个镜子吗?但她分明在镜子里看到肖天鹅依旧那么漂亮。

"你看,我俩刚好是黑白配。一对绝色佳人。"肖天鹅把脸凑过来,和尚小宁紧挨着。

尚小宁看了好久,在确信了既不是做梦,又不是魔镜后,突然爆发出了欢呼,"我变漂亮了,我变漂亮了!"然后转过身来,一把抱住肖天鹅,蹦着,跳着,"我再也不是丑八怪了,我再也不是丑八怪了!"

"怎么样?我没说错吧?"

"哈哈,太好了,太好了。你没说错,我现在就是这样。"

"现在有信心了,可以出去了吧?"

"出去?到哪里去?"

"出去玩玩啊。有一个时装表演,你看不看?"

"看!我现在巴不得出去,让全世界都看我。"

"那就走?"

"走啊。"

两人出了卫生间,欢天喜地地,却见温碧玉噘着嘴,闷坐在那里。

"干吗不高兴啊?"肖天鹅随便问了一句。

温碧玉哀怨地瞟了她一眼,扭了一下。

"我和她先走了,以后有空再来玩。"肖天鹅有点心不在焉。

"你哪会记得我?"

尚小宁看到这种场面很不舒服,她怕他们再会做出什么吓人的举动来,让她难堪,就忙打岔说:"船长也不带我出去玩玩,我只好跟她出去玩了。"

"船长会带你去的,你不是醉了吗?"温碧玉有点怪罪尚小宁的样子。

"快走吧。"尚小宁也顾不得那么多了,催促着肖天鹅,头也不回地朝门外走去。

肖天鹅也转身朝门外走去。

"你的烟还没抽完呢。"温碧玉在背后喊道。

21

"不抽了,不抽了。"

肖天鹅头也没回,追上了几步,把手搭在尚小宁的肩膀上。

"你知道我为什么叫肖天鹅吗?就因为我小时候长得漂亮,又很白,所以大家都叫我小天鹅,后来这就成了我正式的名字。"

"你现在也很漂亮。"尚小宁转过头来看着她的脸说。

"嗨,现在不行了,老了,差远了。正因为她们太丑,所以才显得我漂亮。"

"她们不丑,也显得你漂亮。"

"嘿嘿,跟你比,就比不过你了。"肖天鹅嘴上谦虚着,心里却很得意。

"我们是两个不同类型的,你比我漂亮。"

尚小宁现在也敢于承认自己漂亮了,因为她确实漂亮了嘛,人自然就有了信心。哪个美人不充满了自信?周围的人都是镜子,可以折射出她的美丽。再加上尚小宁受到了肖天鹅的蛊惑。她还从来没见过这么敢于承认自己漂亮的人。

人嘛,总是喜欢挑别人的毛病,特别是当这个人喜欢自夸时。网络红人"芙蓉姐姐"就是因为自夸美貌才遭人攻击的,大家都说她极度自恋。专家说,极度自恋来自儿时的不安全感,先受宠,后失宠,导致心理失衡,产生自卑,为引起别人的注意,便开始自夸,最后走向极度自恋,不能自拔。但是她也因为被攻击而出名了,后来人家还要请她演电视剧呢。俗话说得好,"跟好的学好,跟叫花子学讨。"尚小宁这时也觉得自己的美貌应该可以夸夸的。她已经完全站在"芙蓉姐姐"这一边了。

"我很重视我的相貌,也珍惜这种美丽,自我欣赏嘛。你看看她们,一个个蓬头垢面。所以她们就对我看不惯,说我另类。"

"哪里另类,一点也不。就这样好,像个女人。你看船长,不是我说她们,人家救了我,又招待了我,我真不应该说人家坏话。"

"就是,我也这样觉得。船长太古板,太封建。"

"倒不是古板的问题,我觉得……"

尚小宁在脑海里搜刮着词汇,想用一个准确的话来形容船长的一家,但是她找不出来,她从来没见过这样的家庭,她的知识和经验让她对理解这样的问题有些吃力。她不是个敏感多疑的人,甚至还有点马大哈。不然她丈夫有个狐狸精她怎么不知道?到了人人都知道的时候已经迟了。

"我是看小温可怜才去找他的。船长常常不在家,一个如花似玉的美丽男人整天守在家里,白白浪费了青春和美貌,浪费大自然的资源,白费了大自然的一番苦心。大自然为什么要造出多姿多彩的花儿和蝴蝶呢?就是要让它们的美丽被人享用。如果把花儿和蝴蝶都关在一个小房间里,它们就失去了生存的目的。这就叫审美浪费。"

22

"话是这么说,可是他已经名花有主了,结了婚了。他俩再不般配,有了孩子了,还是应该一心一意地过下去。而且他俩的感情还是不错的。"

尚小宁又想到了自己的家,心里一阵痛楚。她现在怎么会跟这个破坏别人家庭的人搞到一起?应该坚决地站到她的反面,站到船长一边。船长还不是像她当年一样,被蒙在鼓里,觉得无比幸福呢。她应该向船长揭露这一切的。

不过,揭露的结果是什么?家破人亡,永远痛苦。谁都不希望家人背叛自己,谁都希望有个永远稳定的家,哪怕自己在外面翻了天,还是要回家的。一个没家的人,就是失败的人,不论他自己多么飞黄腾达。

如果不知道呢?那就还是幸福的,尚小宁如果不知道,她还是原来的她,还在过着原来的生活,不至于走到这一步。丈夫死活都不肯离婚,口口声声说爱她,大概也是舍不得自己的家吧?她听了都恶心,简直要吐出来。爱妻子还能和别人上床?这在她简直想都不能想象。真不知男人是个什么动物。

不过肖天鹅还有大丈夫气,敢于承认自己是主动的,不像尚小宁的丈夫,敢做不敢当,硬要说是那个狐狸精勾引他的。勾引?一个碗不响,两个碗叮当!别人来勾引她尚小宁试试!她就不信别人能勾引得了她!

家庭出了这种事,她是不会忍着过下去的。以后丈夫只要一和她亲热,她就会想到他也曾和那个狐狸精这样过;在一起吃饭,也会想到他和狐狸精一起吃过;一起上街,她也会想到他和狐狸精一起逛过。反正她和丈夫所做过的一切,丈夫都有可能和狐狸精做过。一想到这个,她就会一阵恶心,浑身起鸡皮疙瘩。丈夫在身边就等于无时无刻不在提醒她这一事实,她将时时刻刻不得安宁，永远痛苦下去。所以，离婚，眼不见为净。丈夫不是她的丈夫了，随便怎么做都行，与她无关。

"到啦，你在想什么？"

"啊？"尚小宁慌忙抬起头。

"这就是我家。我们回来再玩，先去看时装展览。"

这也是和船长家类似的一座小洋楼，有着很大的花园和草坪。肖天鹅确实和船长家是紧挨着的邻居，不过这个紧挨着也还是隔了两个花园。不像她家的单元房，紧挨着，两家共用一堵墙，讲话都能听得见。唉，有钱就是好啊，她尚小宁虽然做个小生意，但也只能买得起单元房。

23

肖天鹅打开车库的门,开出了车子,招呼尚小宁上车。尚小宁很自然地就上去了,也不站在船长的一边了。原来看到别人的第三者并不如看到自己的那样恨。唉,随它去吧,温碧玉也有不好。尚小宁心里想着别人的事就像看电影,别人打架毕竟自己不疼。

肖天鹅一边开着车子一边和尚小宁聊。尚小宁则边和她聊,边从车窗里东张西望地往外瞧,想知道这是在哪里。她一直都认为这就是自己居住的那个城市。因为这里的人讲话、生活习惯都和她一样,只不过到目前为止,她还没发现她所熟悉的街道和房子。现在城市建设得很快,她几天不出门,就认不得路了。她也就不问了,问了惹人笑话。

她天天守着个小店,以店为家,就晚上回去睡一下,外面的事情确实不知道。像水手、船长、婚假、冷冻卵子这样的事她听都没听说过,她就像生活在外星球上一样。

肖天鹅优雅地开着车,尚小宁从侧面看着她,觉得她很了不起。尚小宁很羡慕女人会开车,女人一开车就有了一股英气。船长那个车开得……人家说女人要野起来,比男人更野。尚小宁家里有一辆很小的运货车,那都是丈夫开着车装货的,她摸都没摸过。车子好像只属于男人,赛车也都是男人开的。她只要看到的士上、公交车上的女司机,就会对她们多看几眼,觉得她们很有男子汉气概。

肖天鹅的车开得也不慢,呼的一下就过去了。尚小宁光看到商店的名字一晃而过,就是看不清写的什么。看了一会尚小宁的眼睛就花了,她眨巴了几下眼睛,不再去看外面。心想随它去吧,反正又不是在外国,等过几天厌了就回家。这下死也不走海路了,情愿坐大巴,还能在上面睡睡。

肖天鹅告诉尚小宁，她是搞时装设计的，为了这场表演，她花了不少工夫。昨天晚上很迟才回来，上午一觉醒来还得要去。她本来准备喊温碧玉一道去看表演的，带他出来散散心，他在家里太闷，没想到碰到了尚小宁，她就临时改变了计划。

　　"哎哟，那你还是应该把他带出来，我们一道看嘛，又不多他一个。"

　　"哎，算了，他在，有许多话不好讲的。反正他过这种日子也习惯了，不在乎一次两次没带他。"

　　"嗳，那样总不大好，不是我影响了他？"

　　"没事，现在你更重要。"

　　车子拐了几个大弯，把尚小宁摇来晃去的，幸亏她套上了安全带，不然就要撞到车玻璃上了。刚才肖天鹅要她套安全带她还不干呢，还是老开车的有经验。

　　"我还没问你呢，你小孩多大了？"

　　"小孩？我的小孩？哦呵呵呵呵……"

　　"你笑什么？"

24

"我干吗要有小孩？我连丈夫都没有啊，哈哈哈……"

"什么？你没结婚？你这么漂亮还没人要？要不，你离婚了？"

"我干吗要结婚？我顺便纠正一下，不是我没人要，而是我根本就不想结婚。"

"为什么？"

"单身贵族，快乐，自由，要干什么就干什么。我结婚不是自讨没趣？"

"可惜了，你有才有貌。"

"我的才和貌不是为别人而生的，是为我自己而生的。我自己应该充分享受才对，为什么要和别人分享呢？"

"总而言之，是比较可惜的。"

"其实我结过一次婚，就几个月，受不了。可能我这个人不适合结婚。离婚后我就解脱了。"

"那我离婚就很痛苦，等于脱了几层皮，死了好几次。我不想离婚。离婚就是一个女人的失败。"

"怎么能这样说？离婚是我们把自己释放出来，从笼子里逃出来。要我再回笼子？绝对没有可能。"

"真是怪事，还有女人不想结婚的。"

"一点也不怪，单身女人才有真正美好的生活。"

车子来到了一个剧院前。肖天鹅把车子停好后，就领着尚小宁进入了剧院。

台上的布景已经搭好了，但人们都还在忙，乱哄哄的。有几个人见到肖天鹅来了，都和她打招呼。但她们都很奇怪地看着尚小宁。男工作人员也都和女船长的丈夫一样，留着长胡子，扎着马尾巴。

"今天我带了个最最漂亮的美女来了！"肖天鹅大声地对他们喊着。

尚小宁感到有些不好意思，只看了他们一眼就低下了头，跟在肖天鹅后面匆匆地走着。肖天鹅把尚小宁带到后台的化妆室里。这里更乱，许多高大漂亮的男青年正在化妆，换衣服，走着台步。所有的人都戴着围脖。

"肖小姐来了。"

"肖小姐好。"

青年们和肖天鹅打着招呼，但眼光都齐刷刷地盯着尚小宁。

"这是我带来的大美女，让你们见见。"

青年们一片啧啧称赞，都围了过来。

"哇，好漂亮啊。"

"从来都没见过。"

"都快赶上肖小姐了。"

25

尚小宁没见过这种场面,只得硬着头皮对大家笑笑。她不太敢看这些青年的眼睛,虽然她都可以做他们的妈妈了,但他们的眼睛太热辣辣的了,有点叫人受不了。如果倒回去 20 年,尚小宁一定会非常陶醉的。

尚小宁有点逃避似的转过身子,到处看看,摸摸化妆台,摸摸镜子,又摸摸衣服。然后看人们化妆、试衣服、走台步。她对这一切都感到好奇。

"他们也很辛苦,都住在这里,早上要很早起来。"

"这里有宿舍?"

"哪里,就随便找个地方睡一下。一整天都不敢吃什么东西,怕胖。"

"那也太可怜了。"

尚小宁看了看周围,突然想起来似的说:"咦?我怎么没看到女模特?"

"你说女模特?干吗要女模特?女人有多难看呐。"话还没落音,肖天鹅突然用力打了一个响指,像发现了新大陆,脸上洋溢着激动和兴奋,用手指点着尚小宁,"对,你启发了我。来来来。"然后拉着尚小宁,来到一排衣服前,拿着各种衣服在尚小宁身上比试着。

"干吗?要我做模特儿?"

"对呀,还有我!既然她们都那么难看,我们为什么不上?我从来没考虑过这个问题。嗨呀,这真是一个太好的创意!"

然后肖天鹅就打量着尚小宁的全身各个部位,又把她转过来看看后面,看够了,就一手抱在胸前,一手托着腮,想着问题。

这时,一个女工作人员拿了两个盒饭过来说:"吃饭了,吃饭了。"说着把两个盒饭递给了肖天鹅。

"都吃午饭了？哈哈，我还没吃早饭呢。"肖天鹅递一个盒饭给尚小宁。

"我起得迟，早饭吃了还没多久。"

"吃吧，不然下午饿了没点心。要一直弄到很晚。"

"你们做这工作也很辛苦，生活没规律，胃要搞坏了。"

尚小宁接过了盒饭，然后她俩找了个地方坐了下来，边吃边聊。

肖天鹅又提让尚小宁当模特的事，尚小宁见她那么认真，就笑着说："你不会跟我开玩笑吧？我哪是那个料？一上台就慌，路都不会走了。我根本不会唱歌跳舞。"

肖天鹅摆了摆手，制止她说下去："没有人一生下来就是模特，在当模特前都是一般的老百姓。不要先给自己定位，我不能做这个，我不是那个料。我马上叫你当总统，你照样当得好得很。"

26

  这话让尚小宁有点吃惊,也很不习惯。她从小就被父母骂笨啊,蠢啊,丑啊,没出息啊什么的。如果她和别人吵架,那肯定是她不好,所有的孩子都比她强。但她真要有点什么想法,做点什么的时候,父母又嘲笑她,把她看成是头脑不正常。她做任何事,父母都要说她做得不对,教她应该怎样怎样做。反正她没得过父母的夸奖,她在父母的眼里就是个傻瓜。但是父母是不是就那么能干,那么正确呢?父母俩自己也天天吵架,和邻居吵架。天天埋怨,过日子比上刀山还难,还老说人家欺负他们,就因为他们穷、老实。

  尚小宁小时候非常自卑,觉得自己是世界上最难看的女孩,最没本事。学习不好,又不虚心,还犟,脾气急。直到有小伙子有事没事地找她,有人向她求婚,她结了婚,才知道自己还可以,没那么难看。再后来又觉得过日子很简单,没那么复杂,和人也很好相处。然后她再以成人的眼光来看待父母时,觉得他们过得一塌糊涂,他们的有些事都幼稚可笑。

  但她还是烦他们的埋怨,来自亲人的埋怨是最让人受不了的。她不求别人夸奖,只求别人别批评。所以她离婚的事还没告诉父母。她知道告诉的结果,那就是她没本事,连个丈夫都拴不住;她太没魅力,太干巴,太不丰满,太不温柔,太不会搞那一套,所以丈夫才有外遇了。总之都是她的错。

  她曾经也隐约地跟他们提过,男的在外面花,不能都说是女的不好;女的就是天仙,男的要花也照样花;女的是个丑八怪,男的要她照样要她,不能说这个女的就是有本事。那还有残疾人呢?瘫痪的呢?植物人呢?神经病呢?那不全都要离婚了,丈夫全都在外面花了?人嘛,又不是个猪。

就是养个小猫、小狗，把它扔了，还老大的舍不得。

现在肖天鹅这样地器重她，这样地夸她，她都想哭。她知道肖天鹅不是假的，她没有必要巴结她，故意讲好听的。从肖天鹅一见到她开始，就一直这样夸她，把她看成了了不起的美女，而且还相信她的能力。说实话，尚小宁的能力不差，但是从来就没有人告诉过她。尚小宁觉得跟肖天鹅在一起，她才是真正地被看成了人。

"也许我真的是这块料？不过我愿意试试。"

肖天鹅说："我这人就是胆子大，肯吃苦。只要我喜欢的，我会不惜一切代价。怎么样？这就是一个成功人士的气质。我是不会看错的。我见到过多少人？你呀，就是缺乏一个环境，缺乏培养。"

"还培养呢，不骂就是好事了。我到现在见到我父母都会紧张，因为我总是不对。"

"你看看，有多少孩子的自信和能力就是这样被父母扼杀了，变成了混吃等死的酒囊饭袋。"

"我要有你这样的妈妈，我就睡着了笑醒了。"

27

"现在也不晚,你就等着我来挖掘你这个人才吧。"肖天鹅吃得很快,不知是饿了,还是就这个习惯。尚小宁也加快了吃饭的速度,不讲话了。两人吃完后,肖天鹅说:"这样,我俩的事现在就暂时不谈了,还有很多事等着我去处理,演出前是最忙的。"说着从口袋里掏出一张票给尚小宁,"你先到这个座位上去坐着,等着看演出。你要瞌睡了,就在座位上睡一会。要不给你一本什么杂志……"

肖天鹅到处张望着,一眼看到刚才送盒饭的那个女工作人员,她正斜躺在一个纸箱子上,抖着腿在看杂志。

"小张,还有没有杂志啦?给一本给他看。"

"有呃,有好几本。"小张在纸箱子上面拿了几本过来。

尚小宁接过了杂志,说:"谢谢。我看完了就还你。"

"不客气,这些都是我看过的。我也不要了,买了看着玩的。你看完了就随便处理吧。"小张说完了又懒洋洋地回到了纸箱子上,接着看她的杂志。

"那我就先到座位上去了?"

"哎,你去吧,我要去忙了。哦,对了,你记住,演出结束后你不要走,就坐在那里等我。千万别走啊,我们还有事。"

尚小宁找到了自己的座位。她想看看杂志,但看不下去。这里的一切对她太有诱惑力了,特别是她以后也要成为模特,这里也将是她的舞台。她不由得思绪联翩,想着各种事情,然后又看工作人员忙,看他们试灯光,试音响,跑来跑去、爬上爬下的。她从来没见过这种场面,觉得他们就像一群蜜蜂一样嗡嗡乱转。原来演出还这么麻烦,她以为演出就是演员的事。

不知过了多久，渐渐地有观众来了，都陆续坐在自己的位子上。尚小宁的左边也坐着个男人，尚小宁只瞥了他一眼，觉得他大约和她年龄相仿，剃光了胡子，剪的短发。她并没有过多地去注意他，她目前对男人还没有兴趣，她被男人伤得太狠了，见到男人都有些怕。她不自觉地往右边稍微移了移，右边坐着的是一个姑娘。长发。2人都戴着围脖。

这时灯光暗了下来，音乐渐渐响起，柔和的灯光亮了起来，打在狭长的T型台上。尚小宁也就注意看着T型台，她对着T型台正中央。

一队打扮得光怪陆离的男模特款款从台后走了出来，他们全都剃光了胡子，头发也都剪成了寸板头。他们踩着音乐的节拍，做着姿态，却故意装得轻松地一扭一摆地向前走来。当他们稍稍走近，尚小宁还没来得及仔细欣赏他们的身材和面孔时，吓得倒抽了一口冷气，然后紧紧地闭上了眼睛，再也不敢睁开。

28

男模脖子上都围着透明的纱巾，但是，他们的身上也都是用同样透明的纱巾做的各式服装，内裤都没有穿！尚小宁知道现在流行透视装，她也在电视上看过女模特的表演，她们也是不穿内衣的，肉都在衣服里面晃荡；而且现在什么表演都穿两段式的衣服，只用布最节省地围住女人身上两段要害部位，男人只围住下面。她非常不习惯看这些东西。

"真是太不像话了！"左边的那个男人用力拍了一下座位的扶手。尚小宁不由得对这个男人多了一些注意，她仔细听着他在说些什么。

"哇，全是美男，太美了。"右边的姑娘边拍着手叫着，边和她另一边的姑娘说着，"男人就是漂亮，无论他怎么走，怎么穿，都美。人体本来就是美的，为什么要觉得它丑，遮遮掩掩的呢？这样才不辜负大自然的造化。"

另一个姑娘倒是不大讲话，只听这个姑娘不停地称赞着男模，"男人都是水做的，都有灵性，你看看他们，一个个天生就是尤物，令人陶醉，爱不释手；女人都是泥做的，都那么肮脏、混沌……"

音乐换了，尚小宁估计这队表演已经下去了，才又睁开了眼睛，吐出了一口气。

左边的那个男人也一直在嘀咕着，"干脆脱光了算了，什么也别穿，那才最美！这些主创人员自己怎么不脱？全都脱光了最好！连灯光、舞美也都什么别穿！"

现在男模都一个个地上台了，有时也有两个一道走出来的，但衣服还是那个套路，尚小宁还是不敢看，又闭上了眼睛。

尚小宁就这样，一会睁眼，一会闭眼，紧张得像在偷看人家洗澡，身上直冒汗。但是观众的气氛是很热烈的,有的鼓掌,有的尖叫,闪光灯也在不停地闪烁着,一群记者、摄影师、录像师忙个不停。

要不是肖天鹅叫她千万别走,尚小宁这时一定走了,她非常不舒服,但又得忍着,没地方躲;想看看手上的杂志打发时间,灯光又太暗,看不见字。尚小宁如坐针毡般地在座位上不停地挪着,一副焦躁不安的样子。

"你哪里不舒服?"左边的男人说。

"嗬,没有……我只是……不太习惯看他们。"

"你也不习惯吗?那你一定是个正派的人。"

"嗳,倒不是这样讲,可能是第一次看到,不习惯。"

"不正派的人第一次看到都会习惯的。"

"可能我太落后了,赶不上时代潮流。我比较老土。"

"这样的土才好。如果大家都能老土,社会风气就一定比现在好。你看看现在都成了什么样子,电视、广告、表演都不能给孩子看。孩子生活在这样的环境里,怎么能不变坏?"

29

"我也有这样的看法。一个普通的电视剧,没说儿童不宜,男女一好了,就急吼吼地脱衣服。"尚小宁刚一说完"脱衣服"就有点后悔,不禁脸一红,这人到底是个男的。好在场子里很黑,没人看见。但尚小宁还是不好意思地低下了头。

"是啊,小孩子不是学吗?既然大人男女在一起就要脱衣服,那他们也脱。太小的不懂事的,大人还觉得他们好玩,可是再大一点呢?十一二岁呢?十五六岁呢?"

看到有人也和她观点相同,尚小宁就不觉得自己少见多怪了。这时她觉得这场演出的服装设计肖天鹅有问题,不是她太时尚了,而是太另类了。尚小宁还从来没看过哪个时装设计师敢拿男人开刀,让男人穿透视装!肖天鹅的胆量已经远远地超过了一般的人。

呀,肖天鹅该不会将来也要她尚小宁穿这样的透视装吧?那打死她也不干!别说透视装,要她露肚脐眼她都不干!她还没到那个要靠展览自己的身体过活的地步。要她穿漂亮衣服上台可以,但衣服必须不透明!

"我还很少见到有像你这样知道羞耻的女人。知耻者,近乎勇。"

"不知耻者才近乎勇。",右边的姑娘倒接上话了,她留着长发。"知耻者怕难为情,不上台,就不勇啦;无知者才无畏,哈哈哈哈……"

灯光突然大亮,演出结束了,尚小宁这三个人也停止了论战,都看着台上。一群花里胡哨的男模簇拥着肖天鹅从后台走了出来。肖天鹅经过了精心的化妆打扮,如一颗闪亮的钻石,在一片珍珠中发出璀璨、耀眼的光芒。不要说男人,就是尚小宁,也被她的光芒刺得睁不开眼睛。

肖天鹅穿着白缎子的晚礼服,上面缀满了亮片,头发高高挽起,头上戴着皇冠。她手捧白色的百合花，微笑着，仪态万方地走了出来，像个女皇。

全体观众都站起来向她欢呼着，热烈地鼓掌。掌声经久不歇。

肖天鹅优雅地向着观众鞠躬，再鞠躬。

演出结束了，许多人跑到台上要和肖天鹅合影，找她签名。肖天鹅也都不拒绝，微笑着满足他们。也有的人找自己喜欢的男模签名、留影。

紧接着，工作人员小张等人护送着肖天鹅走向后台。尚小宁左边的男人和右边的姑娘也都朝后台跑去。尚小宁不知道发生了什么事，也就不自觉地跟着去了。

尚小宁随着他们进入了剧院侧面的一个不太大的厅内。厅内迎面的墙上贴着"记者招待会"几个字。一排长桌上放满了鲜花，鲜花丛中有几个话筒。肖天鹅也正被人簇拥着进入了厅内，坐到了长桌前。

长桌的对面有许多椅子，记者都纷纷坐下了。尚小宁也在最后一排找了个位子坐了下来。在主持人做了一番介绍后，记者开始提问。

30

"我来先说。"一个姑娘站了起来,她留着长发。"我是海滨大学广播站的特派记者李白玉,我想问的是,这次模特的风格大变,以冷峻、怪异的面貌出现,一改以往的清纯、柔美。是不是意味着你在转型,以后就要沿着这种风格走下去?我的话完了,谢谢。"

尚小宁只看到这个姑娘的后背。但尚小宁根据声音,可以推断出她就是刚才坐在她右边的那个姑娘。

肖天鹅微笑着说:"艺术没有一定的模式。今天可以这样,明天可以那样。如果我总是只有一种风格,那就说明我老了,已经没有创造力了。谢谢。"

"你认为男人完全暴露出自己的身体就是一种美吗?谢谢。"

尚小宁循声望去,也只是看到一个男人的后背,但她肯定这就是刚才坐在她左边的那个男人。

肖天鹅扬起了眉毛,带有挑衅意味地说道:"啊,焦亮记者,我们是老朋友了。你的那些观点还是一点儿也没改变吗?关于什么是美的问题,我在这里就不说教了,我想大家也都知道。不过我要强调的是,人性的挖掘和解放,和谐的突破和创新。这就是艺术。请你务必记住这一点。"

众人全都笑了起来。

"请问你的私生活也是这样不检点吗?"

"是的,我在家全裸,不可以吗?和男朋友在一起也这样,违法吗?"

众人哄笑。

"我是台风电视台的记者金瓶梅,我能问几个与您本身有关的问题吗?"

"请便。"

"您这次自己也改变了以往的风格，穿起了裙装，这意味着什么？"

"这才是我最感兴趣的话题。"肖天鹅笑着说，"给我这次灵感的是一位特殊的人物，谁都不会想到的。她这次也来观看这次演出了，我叫她留在座位上别走……"肖天鹅低声对旁边的工作人员小张说，"你到场子里去把她找来。"

"我在这里，我跑到这里来了。"尚小宁站起来，扬起了手，招呼着肖天鹅。

31

肖天鹅看到了她,也对她招着手,"来,到这里来,让大家见见。"

"不不,你忙你的,我就在这里等你。"尚小宁吓得连忙摇手。这种阵势她也是头一次见,新鲜还来不及,要她上台哪行?但小张已经走过来了,硬把她拖了上去。

尚小宁站在长桌前,面对着眼前的人群,她手足无措。眼睛光会盯着那些鲜花看,不敢抬头。刚才看肖天鹅那么应对自如,摆着架子,她还觉得肖天鹅换成了另一副面孔,和她在一起时完全不一样。和她在一起时,才是肖天鹅本来的样子。要是她尚小宁将来大红大紫了,应该摆出什么样的姿态?这些问题还没来得及想好,她就被拎到了台上。

"就是她,尚小宁,这位大美女,启迪了我的思维。我的下一次的时装表演,将会是以我们为主的空前绝后的表演。我今天以这样的装束出场谢幕,就是等不及到那一天了。我恨不得马上就进行这样的表演。"

闪光灯嚓嚓地响起,有几台摄像机的镜头对准了尚小宁,弄得尚小宁眼都花了。她想抬起头正面对着摄像机镜头,笑一下,但眼睛被灯光刺得老要眨,脸上的肉也不听指挥了,全在抽动。她勉强咧开了嘴,做出笑的样子,但嘴唇却抖得厉害,她只好用牙咬住下嘴唇,维持着颤抖的微笑。她的眼睛什么也看不见,耳朵什么也听不见。

不知过了多久,眼前晃动的人影退去了,嘈杂的声音也小了,尚小宁才似乎从梦游中醒了过来。她跌坐在椅子上,全身酸软,后背发凉。原来衣服都湿透了,她出了一身的冷汗。

"走吧,我们去开庆功会去。"肖天鹅挽着尚小宁的胳膊,又回到了平时和她在一起的状态。尚小宁这才觉得肖天鹅真的了不起,在那样的场合这样应对自如，还反击一切攻击的言论，快速做出反应，解答各种问题，不出丑，不给人留把柄。尚小宁说："你真是太不简单了。乖乖，我一到人面前就发慌。"

"没关系，一开始都这样，慢慢就好了。"

"恐怕我一辈子都不行，我不是这块料。"

"又来了，有我在你怕什么？走吧。"

"到哪里？"

"当然是去吃饭啦。我不是告诉你中午一定要吃吗？你要是中午不吃哪能撑到现在？"

尚小宁跟在肖天鹅后面，像跟在老大姐后面，其实她俩的年龄也差不多，说不定肖天鹅比她还小呢。这就是能力的问题啊，不服不行。

32

上了车，肖天鹅依然精神饱满，优雅地开着车，好像刚起床一样；尚小宁就不行了，经过了刚才的折腾，她就像打了败仗，浑身提不起精神来。

车子停在了一家豪华酒店的地下停车场里，两人坐电梯直接升到了9楼的大厅外。步入大厅，大厅正面的舞台上挂着猩红色的鹅绒幕布，幕布上有3个白色的泡沫刻出来的字"庆功会"。大厅的中央和四周都摆满了桌子，桌子上全是美味佳肴、各色水果和酒水。已经来了不少人了，人们都在忙着端着盘子，找自己喜欢的食物。

自助餐尚小宁以前也有吃过，但这么大规模的还没见过。工作人员小张过来和她们打着招呼。

"尚姐——"一声女人的尖叫吓了尚小宁一跳，这里哪有人认得她？就是船长也老大不小了，不会像一个小姑娘的声音。猛然，尚小宁的心一跳，是她？她没死，也到这里来了？

果然不出尚小宁所料，白菊花冲了过来，一把抱住尚小宁。两个人像失散多年姐妹，抱在一起亲着、揉着、哭着、笑着。

到她们可以安静一些的时候，肖天鹅说："这就是白菊花吧？瞧你们亲热得，我都嫉妒了，你还从来没对我这样过呢。"

尚小宁有点不好意思地说："我太激动了，我以为一辈子都看不到她了。我自己不也差点死了？"说着不禁悲从中来，又哭了起来。

"好了，这不都活着吗？"肖天鹅替尚小宁擦去了眼泪，又帮她理好了头发，整理好衣服，"来，我们去吃吧。"然后又招呼服务员弄张桌子和几个椅子来，放在一个角落里。

"这里的服务员很讲卫生啊，还戴口罩。"尚小宁说。

"是啊,这是最高级的酒店,当然要注意这些,不然胡子掉到菜里去了,客人有意见。"

三人坐下后,肖天鹅又叫服务员随便装一点吃的来,然后尚小宁和白菊花各自说着自己的经历。原来白菊花在海里也被一个船长救了,她现在就住在这个船长的家里,还和她的女儿结成了干姐妹。

"她也来了,我去找她来。"白菊花说完,慌忙站起来走了。

这边尚小宁和肖天鹅还没感叹够人生的不幸与巧合,那边两个姑娘已经来了。

肖天鹅一抬头,略微顿了一下,"这不是大记者李白玉小姐吗?来来来,坐坐坐。"

李白玉惊喜地说:"你怎么还记得我的名字?我只是特约记者,临时的。"

33

"哎呀,我有练过。再说,开记者招待会之前,我就已经知道了哪些部门要来,派谁来,都把这些人名字背熟了,以显示自己有惊人的记忆力。其实完全不是那么回事,你当是真的?政治家喜欢搞这一套。当然我也不例外啦,顺便表演一回。还有什么即兴演讲,哪个不是事先写好、背好的?还有回答的问题也都事先准备好的,不就这些问题吗?还能问到外国去啦?"

"哦——原来是这么回事。"尚小宁又觉得肖天鹅没那么神了。

"我比较不喜欢作假,但在那种场合,没办法。人们需要这些。"

"刚才我在记者招待会怎么没看到你?"尚小宁问白菊花。

"玉姐姐叫我在这里等她,说那是一个很重要的会,我没有记者证,不能进去。"

"那你又怎么进到这里来的?"尚小宁又问。

"玉姐姐给了我一张餐券。"

"我进来也要餐券?"尚小宁问肖天鹅。

"当然,我已经替你给了。"

四个女人叽叽喳喳、嘻嘻哈哈地吃着、聊着。到她们吃完了,大家早都吃完了,全部到隔壁的舞厅去跳舞去了。肖天鹅也领着她们来到了舞厅。舞厅里很暗,她们去了一时还不适应,就找了个座位坐了下来。

震耳的音乐吵闹着,彩灯闪烁着,人们旋转着,尚小宁眼花缭乱。她不会跳舞,也看不出门道,就不停地喝茶、吃瓜子。

"啊,灯光、美人……"李白玉贪婪地看着舞池里的人,然后半眯着眼,摇着头,吟哦着,"葡萄美酒夜光杯,人面桃花相映红,举案齐眉不胜醉,红袖添香最销魂。"

"别酸了,学过几句歪诗就来瞎凑。"肖天鹅的脸皱着,像喝了米醋。

"哎,情不自禁,情不自禁啊。我本多情应笑我,早生华发全为君,衣带渐宽终不悔,为伊消得人憔悴。"

"得了得了,又来了。说你胖你就喘。你该不是学中文的吧?"

"怎么不是?就是啊,古诗词专业。"

"难怪呢,受不了。"

"我叫李白玉,就是李白加贾宝玉。"

"酸加色。"

"不色不行啊,能怪我吗?处处充满着诱惑。那么多的美人在眼前晃荡,穿得那么暴露,又香气袭人,哪能自制?不信你问问大家,是不是这样?"

34

"唉,好色是人的本性,不色还能叫人吗?我就是太喜欢美色,才搞时装这一行的。你看,我天天接触到的都是年少美貌的,想不色都难呐。我哪适合结婚?婚姻和家庭太压抑人性。我现在这样最好。我一遇到美人就有激情,一有激情就有灵感。就像毕加索,每一段美好的爱情都给了他无数的灵感。艺术需要灵感,灵感需要激情,激情需要爱情,这是一切艺术的源头。"

"我赞成,爱情是社会前进的动力,人为色死,鸟为食亡。"李白玉说。

尚小宁说:"我发现这里的男的都留胡须,长发,穿裙子,男模除外,没胡子,剪短发,穿裤子,都化了妆。女的都短发,穿裤子,衣着随便,不化妆。

"这不是很正常吗?"

"正常?"尚小宁转过头来看着肖天鹅,像不认识她似的,"你说正常?这怎么正常?比如像你,我,白菊花,我们女的这样打扮才正常。"

"你酒喝多了吧?我们现在这样打扮才另类呢。你看看哪个女的像我们?我就是以这样打扮另类,才引起人们注意的。人们都说我变态狂,说我整过容,漂白过皮肤,不该化妆,说我男性化。"

尚小宁如坠入云里雾里,她皱着眉头,看看肖天鹅,看看李白玉,又看看白菊花,再看看舞池里的男男女女,再回过头来看这几个女人。

"白菊花,你说说这是怎么回事?我们是不是在做梦?"

"我……我也不知道,我怎么觉得怎么到处都奇奇怪怪的,是不是风俗习惯不一样?也许这里是少数民族?我这几天也在想这样的问题。"

尚小宁又转向了肖天鹅,"那你说,什么是男人,什么是女人?"

"你连这个问题都搞不清啦？我看你多半也是疯了。"肖天鹅笑道。

"要不就是她们是受了太大的刺激，比如掉到海里，失去家人，失去记忆……"李白玉说。

"怎么会？我就是再傻，傻到不会吃饭，男人、女人我还是分得清的。"

"那你说什么是男人，什么是女人？"肖天鹅反问。

"不就是男人长着喉结、胡子，梳着短发？个子高一点，力气大一点，讲话粗一点，皮肤黑一点，动作硬一点，火气大一点，相貌丑一点，比较好色一点……"白菊花抢着说。

"女人梳着长发，有胸部，胆子比较小……"尚小宁补充道。

35

"你们只说对了一部分,你们说的是男人的第二性征。第二性征就是除了下身之外,第二个能表现性别特征的东西,男的有喉结、胡子、嗓子粗没错;女人也一样,有胸部、嗓子细;但是,其他都说反了。女人才个子高一点,力气大一点,讲话粗一点,皮肤黑一点,动作硬一点,火气大一点,相貌丑一点,比较好色一点。"

"怎么会!"尚小宁非要抬杠,辩个是非黑白。

"倒是发型和服装,这里有个审美和习惯的问题。因为女人要干活,干事业,长发不方便,就一直短发;至于服装,也有个约定俗成的问题。男人是处于一种被审美的状态,男为悦己者容嘛,所以就穿裙子啊,化妆啊,穿高跟鞋啊,要取悦于女人。我们这就是个女性社会,当然是要以女人的眼光来看待男人的。"

"你正好讲反了,女人才穿裙子,化妆,穿高跟鞋。"尚小宁说。

"不不不,是你讲反了。正因为男为悦己者容,所以他们的特征,包括第二性征和美色,就是个很好的借题发挥的东西。比如齐胸的长须,齐肩的长发,乌黑亮丽,就很有男人味;喉结,最能反映男人的曲线美,若隐若现的喉结,就非常具有视觉冲击力,给人一种震撼。现在你知道了我为什么要用透明的纱巾围住了喉结吧?这在一般人看来,简直翻了天。哼,我什么时候还要去掉纱巾呢,彻底露点。既然大家都喜欢看,就让她们看个够。"

"喉结有什么不能露的呢?我看小青年留着长胡子更难看,又不是古时候。"

"你看看,你比我还激进,还大胆。你简直就跟我想的一样嘛,还要抬杠什么呢？所以我这次的模特表演，就没有穿裙子和高跟鞋，全是短发，胡子也剃了，以冷峻、柔中带刚、靠近中性为基调。"

"本来就应该这样嘛，女人要打扮还差不多。"

"所以我自己就穿了裙装，打扮了。就因为女人们都是短发，我留了长发，李白玉也留了长发，就被人看不惯。我们这些搞艺术的就喜欢留长发。"

"女人不搞艺术也要留长发，你看我、李白玉和白菊花就都是长发，女人短发不成个样子。"

"可能你们这儿有点不一样。总的来说，我们这个社会就是个男性社会，一切一切的根源就在于此，为什么女的就非要胸大？就非要漂亮？就非要温柔、贤惠，相夫教子？就非要做家务？就非要从一而终？男的就可以三妻四妾，拈花惹草？"白菊花想起自己的遭遇就气愤难平。

"你那讲的是以前，现在哪有三妻四妾？"尚小宁忙纠正她。

36

"实质还不是一样？现在更坏。她们都在暗处算计我们，我们遭人暗算还不知道，最后财产和人都转移走了，我们落得个人财两空。"白菊花说。

"对的，就是以前也还有个大老婆，她还掌管着家里的大权，小老婆还得伺候她；大老婆得不到丈夫，还落得个舒服。"尚小宁说。

"现在有人说年轻女人资源过剩，应该给她们出路，允许她们做成功人士的小老婆和妾，这总比她们在街上做妓女好，有利于社会的安定。一个茶壶要配许多茶杯，没有一个茶杯配许多茶壶的道理。反正这些成功人士也养得活她们，优秀的男人就应该拥有多个女人。不成功的男人找不到老婆活该。"白菊花说。

"那你到底愿意不愿意做人家小老婆呢？"尚小宁问。

"我才不愿意呢。我不喜欢和别人共享男人，特别是过几天他又看上谁了，最后把家里的保姆、佣人都弄上了。还不如离了婚，得些财产，再找一个。"白菊花说。

"怎么样？跟我的想法一样，我不就离了吗？"

白菊花说："就是嘛，我做小老婆，谁能保证我是最后一个？除非他明天就死，我今天就嫁给他。不过说实话，我不喜欢老的，我喜欢和我年龄差不多的。真要和那些可以做我爸爸、爷爷、太爷爷的老头子在一起，我情愿死。不怪蓝花花天天咒老头子死，她要偷跑出去会情人。这些老头子就不想想，谁会爱上他们？那么老，那么难看，还不是钱好？但是我要是有钱，也绝对不要这些小的，危险，定时炸弹，说不定哪天就引爆了，谋财害命。我还不如花钱在外面玩玩，完事走人。"

"但是蓝花花那样做也不对，把人家彩礼收了，钱收了，东西骗到手了，就把人家一脚蹬了，跟人跑了。如果不愿干，开始就别答应。"尚小宁说。

"可能家里穷，逼的。"白菊花说。

"逼的？那后来能跑，一开始就不能跑？" 尚小宁说。

"一开始就跑了，怎么搞得到钱？这不跟现在骗婚放鸽子一样？先把女人卖给人家做老婆，陪他睡几天；有的还不陪睡呢，把新郎用酒放倒，半夜跑了；有的新娘还是男人装的。"

"哈哈哈哈……"

这两个人自顾自地说着，把旁边的两个人晾在那里。

"你们说的这些怎么正好把性别说反了呢？现在是说，一个女人可以拥有多个男人，这样男人就不会去做男妓了，也不会去破坏别人家庭了……等一等……为什么你们说的情况都刚好和我们完全相反呢……啊啊啊……我知道了，你们是从外国来的。"

"什么外国？我们不都是中国人吗？"尚小宁说。

37

"中国人?中国人才是外国人。"

"我看你是酒喝多了,你不也是中国人吗?如果我们是外国人,你们是哪国人?"

"我们是女儿国人啊。"

"女儿国?别胡扯,我听都没听说过。"尚小宁说。

"啊,我知道,母系社会,走婚,泸沽湖畔的摩梭人。我看过一本书,是一个女的叫杨二车娜姆写的。她就是摩梭人,后来跑了出来,成了歌星。现在嫁给了一个老外,外交官。"白菊花十分兴奋。

"你瞎说什么呀。什么摩梭人?我们根本就不是少数民族,是正儿八经的国家,和世界上所有其他国家一样,有自己的主权。"

"刚才看你们在抬杠,我就猜你们不是我们国家的人。你们不是从海里被救上来吗?"李白玉说。

"哎呀,现在就清楚了。难怪我们总说不拢。原来不是一个国家的人。"肖天鹅说。

"那你们既然不是中国人,怎么讲话、生活习惯,还有文字,都跟中国一样?还跟我们的城市一样,我还以为我没出这个城市呢。"尚小宁说。

"不对,我学过地理。世界上根本就没有这样一个国家。"白菊花说着伸过手来掐了一下尚小宁,又掐了一下李白玉和肖天鹅,最后又掐了一下自己。四个人都哎哟地叫了出来。

"干吗,有病啊?"尚小宁问。

"我看我是不是在做梦。"

"不是梦,绝对不是梦。"肖天鹅说,"我也听小温说,他老婆说过,外国和我们国家不一样。她老婆经常出海。所以我才想起你们可能是外国人。"

"是的,我也听我妈妈说过这样的话,我也考虑这样的问题。那现在问题就清楚了,我们不是一个国家的人,那就不要抬杠了,不同的国家,风俗、习惯都不同。"

"不对,世界上和中国类似的国家只有新加坡一个,语言、文字、生活都一样,绝没有第二个国家。"白菊花仍要坚持。

"具体的什么情况我就不清楚了,我也不是学这个的。你们也别管那么多。既然你们是外国来的,我们就要尽地主之谊,好好招待了。也好让你们看看我们这个女儿国的风采。我们先去跳舞吧,别尽在这儿讨论这些大是大非的问题,浪费了光阴,辜负了美人。"

刚好一曲开始,李白玉早就忍耐不住了,抓起白菊花的手,就拖着她冲向男模扎堆的地方。她邀请了一个最漂亮的男模做舞伴,然后推着呆若木鸡的白菊花。

38

"你邀请啊,怎么站着不动,跟个傻瓜一样?"又转向男模们,"弟弟们,你们愿意不愿意跟这位帅姐跳舞啊?"

"愿意,愿意……"男模们乱叫着。

还没等白菊花做出反应,一个长得跟胡兵一样的小伙子站起来说:"我来吧,我来邀请她。"

"噢——"男模们起着哄。

白菊花登时脸羞得通红。她以为她是过来人,可以对这些青年漫不经心,没想到她现在就像真的见了大明星一样,心里扑通扑通地跳个不停,人也就羞答答地、机械地跟着这个小伙子走进了舞池。

不过他们的双手和舞步没法协调,两个人像是打太极拳。这是怎么回事?白菊花正奇怪着,忽然头脑一激灵,想起这个国家是反过来的,那就是说,小伙子跳的是女步,那她就应该跳男步,幸亏她有学过,遇到舞场里没男人时,她就跳男步。果然当她跳男步时,问题就迎刃而解了。

"大姐你这是第一次到这里来跳舞吗?"小伙子温柔地问。

"哎哎。"白菊花有点慌乱。

"我叫黄花彩。"

"黄花菜?"白菊花扑哧一下笑了出来,也忘了紧张,"不过我的名字好不到哪儿去,我叫白菊花。"

"就是我们喝的菊花茶的那个白菊花?"

"对,一个字都不差。"

"不过我不是黄花菜,是黄花彩,彩色的'彩',前面两字和黄花菜一样。"

"嗨嗨,有意思。两朵花,一个是菜,一个是茶。"

两人在舞池里转着,根本不在跳舞,像走大路一样,或者说像在散步一样。

"我比较喜欢腼腆的女人。"

"是吗?"

"腼腆的女人有味道,特别有魅力。"

"嗯。"

"腼腆的人,一般内心的情感体验特别深,特别细,这也是他们温柔、具有爱别人的能力的一种具体体现,所以就特别让人有股冲动,要爱他们。"

"你怎么这么博学啊?还有一点,当女人在她所爱的人的面前时,她就羞涩和腼腆。"

"这句话加得好。也只有少数女人是这样的,多数女人都大大咧咧的。"

"我是个腼腆的女人吗?"

"是啊,不然我为什么要说这番话呢?"

39

　　白菊花的心跳又加剧了起来,她的腿有些发软,头有些晕。就好像真的是大明星胡兵正在对她说这样的话一样。但是她还没有失去理智,应该说这时她的大脑的思维速度和反应速度都达到了前所未有的巅峰。再笨的人,这时都最聪明,都是天才。她要再次确定这男人的话的意义,这话的真实性,以排除有任何其他的歧义的可能性。

　　"还是我刚才的话,有些女人在她所爱的人的面前,才会羞涩和腼腆。"

　　"这我知道。知道我为什么要说这番话吗?你一来,我就爱上了你。"

　　"真的吗?我也是。"

　　"这就叫一见钟情吧?我从来没有过这种感觉,我要牢牢地抓住它,不让它溜掉。"黄花彩说着握紧了白菊花的手,头也靠在了她的肩上。不过他比白菊花高出半个头,所以头要侧着低下一点,才能碰到白菊花的肩膀。

　　白菊花的心快要蹦出来了,她感到呼吸困难,喘不过气来,脸上在发着烧。她轻轻地闭上了眼睛,深吸了一口气,把头也靠在了黄花彩的头上,同时抱紧了他。

　　这边肖天鹅非要拉尚小宁跳舞。

　　"我不会呀。"尚小宁死活不肯站起来。

　　"不行,我今天非要教你,由不得你。"肖天鹅半拉半拽地拖着尚小宁离开了座位。

　　"这倒有什么难的呢?不就跟走路一样?你连路都不会走啦?站好,我俩脚尖对脚尖,当我退的时候你就进;当我进的时候你就退。"

　　"就这么简单?"

　　"就这么简单。"

"我不是看人家跳得直旋,还翻着花样?"

"那是舞蹈家跳的,一般的人就走走路。"

"那我怎么知道什么时候要前进,什么时候要后退,什么时候要转弯?"

"我指挥你啊,我右手在你背后推你,你就前进,我左手托着你的右手,推你的手,你就后退;我带着你转弯,你就转弯。"

"哦,就这么容易?"

"就这么容易。你就是不肯试。"

两人下了舞池,尚小宁低着头,盯着脚,就这样还经常踩到肖天鹅的脚上。

一曲过后,两人回到了座位上。尚小宁累得不行,她太紧张了,手心都是汗。到音乐又响起时,肖天鹅又拉着尚小宁跳。几支曲子下来,尚小宁竟有点入门了,她放松了许多,也就越发随和起来,真的就可以像走大路一样,不动脑子了。

到又一曲结束的时候,两人坐了下来,喝了点茶,歇一口气。这时一个男人走了过来。

"我可以在这里坐一下吗?"男人问道。

40

肖天鹅一抬头，立刻用一种讥讽的语调说："哟，这不是著名的男权运动家，男联顾问，大名鼎鼎的焦亮焦记者吗？你怎么会到这个乌七八糟的地方来？难道你的私生活也像这样乌七八糟？"

"正因为我的私生活光明磊落得如同孩童一般纯洁，我才具有免疫力，这就叫出淤泥而不染。"

"高见高见。那就怎么见得我不是出淤泥而不染，我就没有免疫力呢？"

"你不需要免疫力，你如鱼得水。"

"说得不错，我干吗要免疫力？我亲和还来不及。"

"好了，我们也别打嘴仗了，我来不是找你的，我是来找这位女士的。"

"你找她？你认识她？"肖天鹅指着尚小宁问。

"是的，我俩刚才看演出的时候正好坐一块，还聊了很久。我俩很投缘。"

"哦？难得难得。我还以为你是死硬派，硬撑到底不近女色呢。终于有改变的时候啦？那你现在的那种极端的男权主义的观点也会要改改罗？"

"我干吗要改？决不！我将誓死捍卫我的观点。"

"好，勇敢，佩服。"肖天鹅鼓起了掌。

就在他们讲话的时候，尚小宁仔细地打量着这个男人。他很有一种阳刚之气，和这里男人们都不一样。尚小宁还拿他和女船长的老公温碧玉相比较，那真是一个在天上，一个在地下。女船长的老公什么都好，就是太娘娘腔，软得让人受不了。唉，在这女儿国，真难得见到像焦记者这样的男人。

"所以你就剪短了头发和胡子，穿着随便，不施粉脂，不修边幅，一切向女人看齐，你以为这就是男权吗？"

"这只是表象，表明我有这个决心，有这个胆量，来破除这个魔戒，向世人宣布我的不屈服。我要争取的当然是平等的权利。什么时候女男真正平等了，我的男权也就自动消除了。"

"你会武功？"尚小宁忍不住插嘴问道。

"什么武功？"

"你不是说男拳吗？我只知道有南拳、北拳，还有南腿、北腿。呵呵，我也不太懂，都是在武打片里看到的。"

"哦，你是说那种？打来打去的？哈哈，有意思。可以这么理解，我是个斗士，就得有武功。男拳，这个词好。就是要给她们重重的一击！不过我们刚才说的那个男权，不是这个男拳，是男人的权利，男权。"

"噢——这个男权啊。男人还要争取权利？哦，对了，你们这里男人是要争取权利，就像我们那里妇女要争取权利一样。"

41

"你说什么？"

"我们的大记者遇到新的难题了吧？这位女士是外国人，不是我们这里的，你别弄错了。"

"什么？外国人？"焦亮盯着尚小宁，仔细地把她从头到脚看了个遍，"难怪我说，这位女士怎么思想蛮传统的，穿着打扮却和嬉皮士一样？还好我没有放弃。"

"你就不怕这种女人会大女子主义？"

"她才不会像你们那样过着醉生梦死的腐朽生活。她的这种本分是一种正直和善良。这在哪个性别里都很重要。只有这样，女男才能平等。"

"对对对，我主张男女平等，大男子主义也不好，大女子主义也不好。"尚小宁赶紧说。

"我就知道你是这种人。我的眼光不会错，四十而不惑。如果到了像我这种年纪还看不准人的话，那我就白活了，一辈子也成熟不了，因为过了生长期。"

音乐响起了，焦亮站了起来，左手背后，右手向前，对尚小宁鞠着躬，问："我可以请你跳舞吗？"

尚小宁正要答话，肖天鹅却说："嗨哟，连跳舞这种事都要主动邀请呐？"

尚小宁赶紧站起，她巴不得有这样的机会。既然这个男人这样欣赏她，她也对他有好感，为什么不去跳跳，接触接触呢？尚小宁的心又活了，不再排斥男人了，相反她认为这是个很好的机会。

"慢，你还没征得我的同意呢。"肖天鹅说。

尚小宁和焦亮都诧异地望着肖天鹅。

"这是我的舞伴,和我跳得很好,你凭什么横刀夺爱呀?"

"怎么,你霸占了那么多异性,玩弄了多少人,恐怕你自己都数不过来吧?"

"啪!"肖天鹅猛地拍着桌子,站了起来,"我对你一忍再忍,你也太放肆了。你这个没人要的丑货,世间少有的丑八怪,守着你的贞节牌坊,过一辈子老处男的生活吧!看到我整天和美男在一起嫉妒是不是?我还就有这个本事,你还就没有。怎么,现在见到绝色美人,你也动心啦?你不是高调唱得好,要誓死独身吗,那不过是没人要你,你假装要独身,现在这个帅姐对你客气了,你就昏了头了。你以为她会对你有兴趣?做你的大头梦去吧!人家不过是礼貌而已!"

"算了算了,不要为我吵架。"尚小宁挡在两人中间说着,想想又转向焦亮,把他往外推,焦亮回过头来还在大声地说着:"请你摸着良心好好想想。要是你的弟弟、儿子被人家玩弄了,你作何感想?"

42

"我没有弟弟,也没有儿子,我才不会想!"

"算了算了。"尚小宁使劲地把他推走。他说道,"给我打电话。"说着掏出名片给她,才依依不舍地走了。尚小宁赶紧把名片塞进口袋。

尚小宁推走了他,又回到了座位上,"你干吗这么气啊?你不是都不在乎的吗?"

"他怎么说我我不在乎,但是想动你就不行!"

"哎呀,就你把我看成个宝,人家不一定把我当回事。"

"不,你是不知道你的价值的,这人对你有意思。"

"那就随他有意思好了。"

"不行,他那么丑的个老处男,心理已经不正常了。哼,癞蛤蟆想吃天鹅肉,也不撒泡尿照照自己,没门!要是像小温那样我还倒没话说。"

"好了好了,别气了,我们再去跳舞。"这次是尚小宁拉着肖天鹅下的舞池。

她们一曲又一曲地跳着,肖天鹅后来渐渐地也不气了,看尚小宁舞步已趋娴熟,开始教她各种花样。尚小宁也越跳越高兴,心里却老想着那个记者。

到她们再也跳不动的时候,天已经快亮了。她俩趴在桌子上,像两只癞皮狗。

"哎哟,我的脚都肿了。"尚小宁说。

"你的脚肿了?我还穿着高跟鞋呢,幸亏我早就把它脱了,光着脚在跳,不然就要骨折了。好在裙子长,遮住脚,没人看见。"

"那两个死鬼死到哪里去了?自从跳舞以来,就没见她们回来过。"

尚小宁向舞厅的各个角落张望着,男模都走得差不多了。工作人员小张已经趴在桌子上睡着了。

"我们开个房间去睡一下吧?走不动了,不回去了,把小张也喊上。"

尚小宁歪歪倒倒地走到小张面前,摇晃着她,"起来,起来,我们到房间去睡。"

"啊?"小张睁开血红的眼睛,傻傻地看着她。

"我们开个房间,到床上去睡。天亮了。"

"哦,好好。"小张站了起来,东倒西歪地走了过来。然后她们三人互相架着,叫服务员带她们到房间去。一进房间,她们就都栽倒在床上,睡了过去。

43

到了下午,尚小宁第一个醒过来,在确定了她是在什么地方和什么人在一起后,不由得想起了这个异常的国家。世界上真的有这个国家吗?怎么没听人说过?为什么白菊花那样不相信?她是大学生,很有学问,应该知道这方面的事,她说世界上没有这个国家,也许就没有。但是没有这样的一个国家,那么现在这个地方又是什么地方?尚小宁想不明白,而且这里男男女女古怪的样子,叫她实在受不了。

呀,不得了,尚小宁一下从床上跳了起来。她答应打电话给记者的,他一定等得急了。尚小宁又看看床上的两个人,还都睡得很香呢。可能为了举办这个时装表演多少天都没好好地睡了。睡着了正好,尚小宁想起肖天鹅那样地讨厌这个记者,如果她知道她要打电话给他,说不定会不让她打呢。

尚小宁希望她俩不要很快就醒来,这样她也好独自处理自己的事情。打从掉到海里以来,她还没有一个人独处过。她又想到了白菊花,这个死鬼不知又窜到哪去了。

要不是她非要吵着出海,她们哪会来到这个地方?不过来了也好,尚小宁变成了美人了,这也值得。吃得苦中苦,方为人上人。

尚小宁轻轻地要往外走,但又一想,自己身上一分钱没有,怎么打电话给记者?哎呀,这是外国,用的是什么钱?她就是口袋里有钱也用不掉啊。管它呢,就拿她们的钱吧,不管什么钱都能用得掉。尚小宁偷偷笑了一下,又轻轻地走了回来,看看她们的包在哪里。她记得昨天晚上三个人都没带包,就来睡了,那哪有钱啊?不对,既然没钱,人家又怎么会让她们睡呢?

尚小宁来到她们身边,左看看右看看,就是没发现包或钱包一类的东西。

钱包会不会在她们的口袋里？但肖天鹅还是昨天晚上的皇后装，根本就没换下来，这种衣服是不可能有口袋的。小张的衣服口袋倒多，上、下有十来个，但哪个口袋才有钱或钱包？尚小宁考虑了半天，决定还是不去掏人家口袋，万一人家醒了，怎么说呢？即使她不介意，尚小宁也还是要说出打电话的事，这事是不能说的。

尚小宁站在那里，再开动脑筋，也想不出办法。还是先出去吧，出去再说。她们醒了，被发现了，就没有出去的机会了。想到这里，尚小宁赶紧转过身来，蹑手蹑脚地向外走，生怕她们突然醒来。她走到门口轻轻拧开门，又回头看了一下，然后再轻轻带上门。

来到门外后，尚小宁朝走廊两边一看，看到一边有个出口，就朝这出口走去。在经过了出口处的一个服务台时，尚小宁想了想又走了回来，朝服务台里的一个姑娘问道：

"请问这附近有没有公用电话？"尚小宁想好了，如果她回答说有，那么尚小宁就说自己的钱包丢了，想打个电话回家，但又没有钱，她能不能借点钱给她？哪怕尚小宁打个借条给她，以后再来还。

44

姑娘正低着头在看书,听到问话,头一抬,有长长的胡须。是小伙子。

小伙子也显然在用疑惑的眼神看着她,在判断她是男人还是女人。如果他是男人,怎么没胡子,脖子还半露在外面,被领子遮着,嗓音又那么脆?如果是女人,怎么又留着长发,穿得这么讲究?

见小伙子盯着自己,尚小宁又说起了设计好的第二句话。可她刚说起了钱包丢了没钱打电话时,小伙子开口了:

"大堂里就有公用电话,在那边,住店的客人免费。"小伙子指着大堂的服务台。

就这么简单?也太出尚小宁的意料了。尚小宁还准备了各种哀求,打算好好表演一番,结果全白费。不过这样更好,马上就可以打电话了,不需要求人了,骗点电话费还真不容易。尚小宁立刻向电话奔去,拨通了记者的电话。果然记者一直在等她,以为她出了什么事;要不就忘了。尚小宁解释了原因后,动情地说:

"怎么会忘呢?"

"我怕那个变态狂把你关起来了。"

"不会的,她人很好,对我也很好。"

"我们什么时候见个面,见了面再聊。"

"这个?我不知道……不晓得肖天鹅会有什么安排。"

"别听她安排了,立刻离开她!"

"离开她?我到哪里去?又没钱,回不了家。"

"你现在在哪里?"

"还不就是昨天跳舞的那个酒店吗?我在705号房间。你到大门口等我。"

尚小宁满心欢喜地挂了电话,又向客房那边看了看,没有人影。她们还没起来呢?尚小宁又犹豫了一下,觉得这样不太好,人家对她那么好,像发现了宝贝一样,她说背叛就背叛,扔下这么好的人,去投靠一个不认识的男人。

就先到大门口去吧,到时候再说,她是不会背叛肖天鹅的,再说,也不会随便就跟一个不认得的男人走。尚小宁还是往大门口走去。

45

到了门外,尚小宁就有机会来看看这个国家了。她到今天都还没来得及仔细地看一看。不过,在这之前,她又怎么知道这是另一个国家呢?

酒店似乎是在市中心,外面很热闹,车水马龙,和中国的没两样。街上那些时髦的女孩,不,男孩,也都一拨一拨的。他们打扮得花枝招展,穿着高跟鞋,一边走着,一边吃着零食,一边嘻嘻哈哈地笑着,很快乐、很无忧无虑的样子。尚小宁不由得想到中国的姑娘们,她们不也这样?自己以前不也这样?人生最美好的年华啊!到什么时候,自己就失去了这些呢?就变成了妇女了呢?再往后就是老太婆了。

这些姑娘,不,这些小伙子,有的穿着超短裙,有的穿着牛仔裤,有的光脚穿着拖鞋式的凉鞋,趾甲上还涂着指甲油。要不是他们的胡子和喉结,尚小宁一定觉得就在中国自己的家乡,看到了一群姑娘。

胡子的样式那可就多了,有的烫了,像卷毛狗,这一般是年纪稍微大一点的人,三十多岁的人;有的就垂直飘着,齐胸,这一般是二十多岁的,比较稳重的那种;有的染成了黄色,还削得七长八短的,就和中国现在流行的碎发差不多吧;有的梳成了小辫子,有正中一条辫子的,有分开梳两条辫子的,有梳无数根辫子的,也有的用蝴蝶结一把扎着的,相当于中国的"马尾巴",不过这个"尾巴"是在前面啊,应该叫"山羊胡",也有的分两边扎着;有的是用夹子夹着,夹子也五颜六色的,造型各异;还有的和头发在耳朵边扎在了一起,弄了个造型,这个尚小宁就归类不出来了。

这些都是嘴唇下面的胡子,嘴唇上面的胡子,年轻人就把它分开在嘴两边,用摩丝定型,再垂下来;也有的用夹子夹着,蝴蝶结绑着,梳着小辫;年纪大的人就齐着上嘴唇把胡子剪平了,就像鲁迅嘴上面的胡子。上面的胡子是要这样处理,不然不好吃饭的。下面的也就无所谓了。呵呵呵呵,尚小宁想到这里,笑出了声。

极少数的小伙子胡子寸来长,但他们依然浓妆艳抹,耳环叮当,还是完全像个女人。年纪大的都是胡子有半尺长,但都不弄什么花样,不过有许多人都把胡子染黑了,和他们的头发一样。尚小宁之所以判断他们是染了,就因为也有许多人的头发和胡子的根部是花白或全白的。

不过太小的少年,胡子还没长,就很难区分他们是男孩还是女孩了。嗨呀,你怎么这么傻?这不是全反过来的吗?看到女孩,那就是男孩;看到男孩,那就是女孩。尚小宁虽然早就知道要这样想,但有时还是情不自禁地用中国的思维方式。

46

　　他们的衣服也是很好玩的,背可以露在外面,但脖子却是用围脖包着的。时髦的人,衣服是半透明的,也有许多人上衣短小,肚脐眼露在外面,裤子挂在屁股上,一弯腰露出十分之一的屁股。有一半的人穿裙子。

　　要不是尚小宁时时提醒自己这是在女儿国,她就要以为那些男人脖子受伤了,就像喉咙得癌的人,开过刀后,脖子上都围着个纱布。哦,难怪呢。他们的喉结是不能露出来的,就像我们女人的胸部吧?但是他们又非常想露,就戴围脖,或者穿有弹力的高领衣服,相当于我们女人穿紧身衣吧?肖天鹅就说过,喉结就是曲线美。

　　尚小宁又笑了起来。尚小宁发现,人们走路都竭力要挺着脖子,以让人远远就看见那突起的喉结。有的人喉结特别大,尚小宁都以为那是长了包,像乡下人以前得的大脖子病。

　　哎,这倒哪点好看?该不会是假的吧?尚小宁想到了整容,又想到了自己,不由得脸一红。她不是也在做假,去搞了什么整容?现在看起来,真是好笑,不和这些人一样?

　　也不时有行人向尚小宁投来奇异的目光,并上下打量她,尚小宁就坦然地让他们看,反正她的穿着打扮正常,她也就心安理得。也许他们看她,就像她看他们一样地觉得奇怪吧?如果在中国大街上看到一个男人穿着花衣服、裙子、高跟鞋、戴着耳环、围着围脖,露出大半个喉结,人们也会怪异的。

　　这样一想,尚小宁不禁摸摸自己的脖子,她的喉结部位全是暴露的。这就是一般的衣服嘛,不就这样?她穿的还是衬衫,有个半高的领子,只是第一个扣子没扣。不过即使扣了,喉结部位也还有一半在外面,还是"怪异"，让人不能容忍！相当于中国的姑娘内衣外穿，并且走光！男人光着膀子上街。哈哈哈哈……尚小宁又笑了。

一群姑娘，不，一群小伙子，在尚小宁面前走过，进了旁边的一个店。尚小宁的眼光追着他们，却看到那店的侧面的招牌，是"佳人美须店"。什么是美须店？尚小宁有点好奇，就跟了过去。

在店的门口，尚小宁看到橱窗上贴着各种男人的照片，一个个都美如天仙，他们的胡子被做成了各种款式，广告语有：

"吹、剪、烫、梳、焗油、粘贴须、种植须、纹须，贵宾的服务，大众的价格。"

"111生须水，用完1周见效，无效退款。"

对联有："新事业从胡做起，旧现象尚须留情"

47

  这胡子还有假的、种植的和纹的？尚小宁又看那些照片，果然有一组图片，是几个男人用完"111"后，由嘴上光秃秃的没胡子，到长出齐刷刷的胡子，到齐胸飘逸的胡子的对比照片。另一组图片是各种各样的假胡子。

  嘿嘿，尚小宁觉得很好笑，难怪街上的男人多数都有胡子，而且都还很浓密，原来是这么回事！尚小宁没敢进去，她没有胡子。她就在橱窗外面往里看，想看看那些人在干什么？没想，不一会儿就有个姑娘，不，小伙子出来了，朝她媚笑着，娇滴滴地用粗哑的嗓子问道，

  "小姐，您需要什么？"

  尚小宁冷不丁被他吓了一跳，她的本能地撒腿就跑，要是在过去她就以为碰上了人妖，现在她时时都要提醒自己这是在女儿国。尚小宁稍微定下心来，说，

  "我不需要什么。"

  "我们这里可以挑的。"

  "挑什么？"

  "就是这些照片上的人啊。"

  "挑他们干吗？我又没胡子。"

  "不是的，"小伙子见她是个外行，忍住了笑，"是特殊服务，是……是陪你的。"

  "陪我干吗？我又不认得他们。他们肯定不是学雷锋，陪我逛商店，陪我吃饭，都是要收费的，对不对？"

  "不是的啦，是可以开房的……"小伙子的脸上稚气未脱，还没胡子，仅仅是毛茸茸的，还不能称他为小伙子，应该叫少年更恰当。他的衣服高

领比较低,也是半透明的,可以清楚地看到里面的围脖。他应该比自己的儿子也大不了几岁吧?唉,这么小就出来工作,也真是的。尚小宁又想到了自己的儿子。不知他过得怎样了,没有妈妈在身边,那个后娘肯定对他不好,说不定他现在也不上学,去打工去了。

小伙子见尚小宁半天不作声,又加了句,"就是可以出台的,带回家也行,在这里也行。"

"什么?"尚小宁还是没反应过来,但是"出台"和"带回家"这样的字眼刺激了她,她突然想到了什么,张大了嘴,呆住了。她的丈夫就是带着发廊妹出台,回家,被她撞个正着的。

她那天感冒很严重,头很痛,丈夫又去进货去了。她就叫隔壁的老板娘帮她照看一下小店,她回家去拿药。进了家,推开卧室的门,正好看见丈夫和发廊妹在床上。她狂怒之下,冲进去,扇了发廊妹几个耳光,接着又扇了丈夫的耳光,然后一把揪住发廊妹的头发,使劲在她脸上抓。

这个发廊妹她是认识的,就在她家不远的小发廊里,还给她洗过头,吹过头。丈夫护着发廊妹,硬把她拉开。这更让她生气,她就抓东西砸他们,抓到什么是什么,两人躲在角落里发抖。然后她就开始砸自家的东西,拿起椅子砸电视、把桌子上所有的东西全都扔到地上,一边扔,一边号叫着,哭着。

48

"不过了,不过了,跟你们同归于尽,放把火烧了你们这对狗男女,让你们到阴间去做夫妻去。我要到阎王那里去告你们,让阎王把你们下油锅炸,用锯子锯,用磨子磨,上刀山,下火海……"

到她蹦累了,骂哑了,泪流干了,东西也砸完了,她瘫坐在地上,觉得要昏厥过去了。丈夫忙来掐她人中,她醒了,一见是丈夫,又想扇他耳光,但她已经没有力气了,扇不动了。丈夫把她抱到床上,和发廊妹两个跪在床边,求她原谅。

"不行,坚决离婚!这种东西,叫我以后还怎么跟你过?一想到这些,我就要吐!"尚小宁费力地用哑着的嗓子叫道。然后尚小宁努力挣扎着坐了起来,丈夫不知她要做什么,赶忙来扶她,尚小宁挣脱了他的手,"别碰我,我嫌你脏!"

"你要干吗?"

"我还会睡在这个脏床上?我就是马上死,都不睡!"

尚小宁摇摇晃晃地走出了家门,任丈夫怎么在后面喊,都不答应。后来尚小宁就一直住在店里,店也不开门了。丈夫多次来找她,她就是不开门。再后来东西都盘掉了,店也卖了。离婚时她得到了房子和部分的钱。她故意不要儿子,就是不想让丈夫太自在。不论丈夫以后和谁结婚,拖个油瓶总没那么顺心,哪个后娘的日子也不好过。儿子只会恨他们,不会给他们好脸色看。要让他们活着比死还难过,让儿子替她出气。

尚小宁和丈夫一离婚,丈夫就买了房子,和那个发廊妹结了婚。尚小宁这时又好后悔,干吗这样成全他们?这下好了,本来他们是偷偷摸摸地,现在是正大光明地,还扬扬得意,一道进,一道出,是她自己把自己这块绊脚石给他们搬了，替他们去掉了眼中钉，肉中刺。不然发廊妹一辈子也别想转正，只配做个地下工作者，最多也就老二。亏啊，亏。

但是要叫尚小宁再和丈夫和好，那也是绝对不可能的。破镜不可能重圆，事实上怎么圆都有裂痕。因为夫妻就是男女的事，在这个事上背叛了，尚小宁就不能容忍。

"要是童男子的话，价格贵5倍。"小伙子误解了尚小宁的沉默，进一步说道。

"你啰唆什么？"尚小宁从往事回到了现实，怒火还在胸中燃烧，"真不要脸！你把我看成了什么人？"尚小宁的脸因为气愤和痛苦而扭曲得变了形。

小伙子惊恐地看着她，不明白说错了什么。这时尚小宁又觉得有点不忍心，毕竟这孩子没有对不起她，他又和她儿子差不多大。真造孽啊，这么小就出来做这种事。尚小宁摇着头，闭了下眼睛，叹了口气，离开了美须店。

49

美须店的隔壁是家"高美围脖店"。尚小宁的气还没平息下来,没有心情看这些东西,但这些东西确实又吸引了她,不看不行。尚小宁一步跨了进去,她没喉结,看看还不行吗?

店老板奇怪地看着尚小宁,尚小宁不理他,只是自顾自地看。乖乖,这家店的围脖真多。尚小宁还没仔细看过这些东西,现在终于有机会了。只见围脖做工精巧,都镶着花边,有的都成了艺术品了,当然价格也不便宜。一些是双层布料做的,一些里面垫了泡沫。

啊,这就对了,难怪街上看到有的人喉结那么大,原来是假的。呵呵,尚小宁又笑了,她已经忘了悲愤,变得非常开心了。这一点也不奇怪,尚小宁想到了中国的胸罩店,一回事!

尚小宁看到漂亮的围脖,忍不住用手去摸摸。这样精美的工艺品,放在哪儿都会惹人喜爱的,她的赞美和喜爱之情溢于言表。她的这一举动吓坏了旁边的几个少年,他们赶紧逃到一旁,像看怪物似的看尚小宁,一边小声议论着:

"哎哎,她该不会是变态狂吧?"

"我看差不多,不是说有些女人就喜欢收集男人的内裤和围脖吗?"

"对对,有的人还去偷。"

"就是,有的人去偷大明星的内裤和围脖嘛。"

"小心点,别被她盯上了。"

"报纸上说,现在经常有女人跟踪少年入室劫财、劫色。"

"还有的绑架少年,把他那个了后,再弄死他。"

尚小宁听了这些话真是哭笑不得,当她把目光转向这些少年时,他们全都吓得低下了头，有的佯装在看围脖，却在用眼角的余光偷看她。唉，尚小宁只有苦笑。

老板的眼睛一直没有离开过尚小宁，他上下打量着她，揣摩着她的意图，观察着她的行动。这些少年的话也给他提了个醒，他警惕了起来，但是他又不愿意放弃一笔好的生意。他从尚小宁的神情上看，她是很喜爱这些东西的，那么这里面一定就有很大的商机。

老板笑嘻嘻地走了过来，对尚小宁柔声地说道："这位女士看中了哪种款式？是送给男朋友的吧？"说完暧昧地一笑，好像他很了解这种女人，也很解风情，"这一款里面的垫子是可以取出来的，"老板拿下了挂在架子上的一个围脖，然后从它的夹层里取出一团东西，"夏天热了，就可以拿掉；脏了洗的时候，也可以把它拿出来。这个垫子是高科技产品，吸汗，不伤皮肤，还可以起到保健作用。长期用了，还有增大喉部的效果。这也比那种泡沫的方便多了。"

50

"哈哈,确实很漂亮。我本来倒没想买,给你这一讲,就真想买了。"尚小宁忽然想要给儿子买一个,这是个多么好玩的东西?

"我就知道这位女士有眼光。到我这店来的都不是一般的人。像你这样穿着打扮的人,一定是很新潮,长得又这么帅,肯定有很多男孩子爱的。买点这个做礼物,真是最好的东西……咯咯。"老板就像皮条客和老鸨,讨好地笑着,同时自己也在卖弄着风情,希望这位女士会突然心血来潮,看上了他,来啃他这个老草。

但是尚小宁一摸口袋,想起了自己没钱。不但想起了自己没钱,还想起了因为没钱打电话给记者,才到大堂打电话,然后约好在宾馆大门口等记者的事。

"不得了,不得了,差点忘得一干二净。"尚小宁自言自语道,拔腿就往外冲。

"你东西还没买呢?"老板在后面叫道。

"以后有空再来买。我现在有急事,我也没带钱。以后肯定来买。"尚小宁边跑边回答着老板,她实在是很想买。

尚小宁跑回到宾馆大门口,什么人也没有。她又到处望望,看看是不是记者也到附近逛去了,没看到人。他该不是来了,看她不在又走了吧?尚小宁很后悔,不该去看那些店的,有什么意思?耽误了这边的大事,也许还就是终身大事呢。尚小宁一时变得很焦躁,心绪不宁,在宾馆门口来回走着。

也许他有什么事临时不来了吧?或者路上堵车?要不就遇到了什么熟人,聊住了走不开。尚小宁把所有可能的情况都一一加以排除。啊,是不是他突然对她不感兴趣了，就不来了？这是尚小宁最不愿意想到的。是啊，她凭什么就相信了他？她对他完全不了解。男人是个靠得住的东西吗？她本来就不该又去相信男人的。尚小宁又懊丧起来，恨自己没用。人家的几句甜言蜜语就又把她俘虏了，而且还没说多少呢，远没她丈夫当年说得多。

"女士，要不要服务？"一个男人的声音把尚小宁从沉思中惊醒。尚小宁抬头一看，一个小伙子正朝她媚笑着，"我一直看你在这边走来走去的，心情好像很不好，要不要我陪你玩玩？"

尚小宁一下就懂得他什么意思了。宾馆门口有三三两两的浓妆艳抹的小伙子在晃荡，尚小宁本来没注意，现在一看就知道他们是干什么的了。尚小宁朝他狠狠地瞪了一眼，转身就走。

尚小宁朝酒店走去，因为她还漏掉了一种可能，就是记者找不到她，就直接冲到她住的房间去了。

51

果然，当尚小宁来到房间门口时，就听到里面有激烈的争吵声，有男人的声音和女人的声音。男人的声音就是记者的声音。记者不会不来的，尚小宁没有看错人。尚小宁一激动，就推开房门，进去了。

"你这个疯子、变态狂，我倒要找你要人！尚小宁明明睡在这里的，现在没人了。肯定是你把她绑架了，故意来演这一出，好像跟你没关系。告诉你，我没那么傻！"

"你才是疯子、变态狂、色魔。今天你不把尚小宁交出来，我跟你没完。"

"真是奇怪，尚小宁是你什么人？你有什么权力要她？皮真厚！"

"别吵了，别吵了。赶快找人要紧，别真出了什么事。"小张说。

"对，报警！"肖天鹅说。

"报警！"焦亮说。

"喂，011。"焦亮已经打开了手机，按了号，冲着手机叫道。

"不要报警，我在这里。"尚小宁急忙喊道。

"哎呀，你可回来啦！"

房间里的三个人都同时喊出了这句话。

"你到哪里去了？也不打个招呼？"肖天鹅搂着尚小宁埋怨着。

"你还好吧？"焦亮握着尚小宁的手，暗暗使了一下劲。

尚小宁知道他的意思，就边说给她听，也是说给大家听，但内容稍稍有些改动，省去了和记者相约的这一段："我醒了就睡不着了，看你们睡得那么香就没叫醒你们。我就到门口逛逛，看看商店。可惜没带钱，不然就会买许多东西了。"

"哎呀，我怎么没想到这一点？"肖天鹅拍着自己的脑袋，"你是从海里救上来的,身上肯定什么都没有。我应该给你一点钱的;还有手机。你人生地不熟的,万一走丢了都找不到。小张,把你口袋里的钱都掏给她,我以后还你;还有你的手机也先给她,我明天再给你买一个。你那手机上也有我的号码,方便。"

小张掏着自己的口袋,把手机、钱都掏了出来,正准备给尚小宁,焦亮说道:"把我的给你,还有我的钱包。"说着就掏口袋。

"别要他的东西,他不怀好意。说不定他手机里还有窃听器呢,然后听到什么消息就拿到报纸上去爆料。他们是什么消息都能拿去卖钱,不惜出卖亲情、友情、法律、道德。"

"你还讲道德?你要讲道德就不该把尚小宁软禁了。"

52

"我把尚小宁软禁了?"肖天鹅冲过去要揍焦亮,但一跑,被她的拖地的皇后裙给一绊,差点跌倒。这更让她恼羞成怒,她索性把裙子提起来,把下摆分成两个角,把它们当绳子,在屁股的部位扎了起来,这样就利索了。

"怎么?想打架?告诉你,我从小就是个野孩子,我可不是娇滴滴的大男孩。许多女孩子都被我打得哭。你也想来试试?那就来吧?我当年就是想当警察的,我会武功。还有许多老板想请我当女保镖呢。"

焦亮把手从口袋里拿了出来,也不掏手机和钱包了,蹲起了马步,双手竖在胸前,拉开了架势。

肖天鹅说:"呵呵?我倒真要见见,我这一辈子还没打过架、发过威呢。我从小就是好学生,乖宝宝,人家都喊我奶油小女,说我爹爹腔,没女人味。我今天就要做一回真正的女人,也让你知道知道我的厉害。"

眼见这两个人要扑到一起去了,尚小宁赶紧夹在其中。

"又吵啦?又打啦?你们能不能不要这样?有什么话就不能坐下来好好谈吗?"

"那是不可能的。"肖天鹅挺着胸说。

"那也是不可能的。"焦亮也学着她的样子说。

肖天鹅又要冲上来揍他,尚小宁张开两手拦着她,"哎呀,你们两个是怎么搞的?"

"我决不罢休!"肖天鹅挥动着拳头说。

"我也是!"焦亮也挥着拳头。

"哎呀,你们两个真是烦死人了。你给我走!"尚小宁假装生气地推着焦亮往门外走,边轻轻地说,"我有空打电话给你。"把他推到门外后,尚小宁把门砰地关上了。

　　焦亮又嘭嘭地捶着门，叫道，"我不会善罢甘休的，我会再来的。"

　　"去死吧，你！"肖天鹅也对着门叫着。

　　"好了好了，别生气了。"尚小宁安慰她道。

　　"本来不是好好的嘛，我们昨天晚上玩得那么高兴，今天又睡得很好，我的心情很好的。等下还有活动，给他这么一弄，真的没心情了。"

　　"别气了，别气了，什么活动？"

　　"去了就知道了，暂时保密。小张，对吧？"肖天鹅一提到活动，又露出笑容，还有些得意。

　　"有什么大不了的？还不是什么没穿内裤的表演？你那最大胆的我都看过了，我还怕什么？我都有抵抗力了。"

　　"哈哈哈哈，你真是……"肖天鹅爱怜地在尚小宁头上摸了一把，"我就说你大胆、新潮嘛，我都远远不及你。"

　　"我觉得我一点也不新潮，老土得很。"

　　"你要老土，这全世界就没有新潮的人了。"

53

尚小宁坐到床上，甩着两腿晃悠着，心里乐滋滋的。她很喜欢肖天鹅夸她，而且肖天鹅不是说假话，是真的喜欢她，从心里喜欢出来。要叫她抛弃肖天鹅，去跟记者走，她还真有些舍不得呢。她一辈子也没碰到过这么喜欢她的人。所以她刚才只能把记者推走。

"小张，去把我的衣服讨来。我穿够了这种裙子，真不知道男人穿着它是怎么过的。刚才还差点跌倒，出洋相。你没看到吧？我还一直光着脚呢。"

"我看到啦。你光着脚，裙子扎在屁股上，滑稽得不得了。"

"对了，你又提醒了我。这是个好创意。"肖天鹅拍了一下手，"就我这种造型，上了舞台，一定会引起轰动吧？"

"肯定会。哈哈哈哈……"

"哎，你总是让我充满了激情，灵感不断。你真是世间少有的奇女子啊。"肖天鹅抱着胳膊，摇着头，对尚小宁赞叹着。

"你说我好就好啰，世界上只有你一个人喜欢我。其实我什么本事都没有。"尚小宁噘起嘴，撒着娇。

她从来不知道有这种感受，她也不会撒娇。从小她就是自卑的，顺从的。不会哄人，不会骗人，不会乖巧，不会耍手段，在不断的埋怨和责骂声中修正自己的行为。什么事她都是一忍再忍，到忍不住的时候，顶撞两下，家里人就受不了了，说她犟，脾气古怪。

她只知道本本分分地做人，到了结婚后，还是这样，直到她发现了发廊妹，她从小到大一直不曾发出来的火，终于以最大的限度喷发了出来。在那一刻，她变成了恶魔和母夜叉，她恨不得用刀砍了他们，用火烧了他们！她还曾想过各种折磨人的、让人极度痛苦的酷刑，来教训他们。

现在尚小宁知道了，在有人疼爱的时候，人就会自然而然地自信、顽皮、活泼、聪明、伶俐，当然也会撒娇。这种感觉真的很好。原来不是她不会这些，而是没有人让她有这样的机会。这就是天性啊，不要人教的。尚小宁现在正在充分享受被宠爱的喜悦，电视剧上的刁蛮公主，哪个不是被宠坏的？叫她去做童养媳，遇个恶婆婆试试。那就也会变得呆头呆脑，脾气古怪，惹人讨厌的人。

尚小宁想到这里，歪着头，不禁扑哧一笑。

"你看你这个样子，不知道有多可爱。"肖天鹅在她身边坐了下来，"说真的，我从来没有像喜欢你一样喜欢一个女人。我也同时想到了我的侄子。他是我最疼爱的孩子。这真是件很奇怪的事。"

"是吗？我也很喜欢你呀。因为你天天夸我。"

"瞧你，尽跟我调皮。"肖天鹅用手指点了一下尚小宁的头。

54

两人这样亲密地聊着天，一会小张回来了，提了一个大包，这是演出时带去的。里面有衣服、鞋子、袜子和手提包。然后三个人都洗好、弄好，出了门。

"我们也不用开车了，就步行吧，反正就在市中心。"

"也好，我也顺带看看风景。"

三人边走边聊边看着，因为尚小宁刚才在酒店门口看够了，吃惊够了，现在也就见怪不怪了，能和她们一样平静了。但是满街挂的巨大的广告牌还是吸引了尚小宁的注意。基本上都是男人的广告，很少有女人的，要有，也是什么名牌的衣服、名牌的车、名牌的电脑。女人很潇洒、傲慢、故作深沉地，或者懒洋洋地摆着架子。多是些中年妇女，一副成功人士的模样。

而那些大多数的男人广告都是些年轻、美丽的男子，做些围脖、内衣、床上用品、厨房用品、美容用品、盥洗用品等等的广告。他们在做围脖广告时，身上是三段式的，围脖、胸衣、内裤，连透明的外衣都不遮一下。也难怪肖天鹅索性把他们身上的这三样东西都去掉，来个透视装。这种外面剥光了只穿内衣，还不如里面剥光了只穿外衣。现在尚小宁就完全接受了肖天鹅的想法，实际上就是这么回事！既然想脱就干脆脱光，那才叫大胆。人们能接受这些广告，却不能接受肖天鹅的无内衣透视装，真是怪事。

路过一家店，只见招牌上写着"芙蓉美体部"，再看橱窗，上面贴着"无痛增大喉结，一抹见效。""祖传秘方，绿色植物，天然精华。"

尚小宁忍不住笑了，说："我可不可以抹点这个？让我的喉结也肿起来？"

"那你就成了人妖了，立刻出名。"肖天鹅说。

"这么可怕？那我还是不抹了。"

尚小宁经过一根电线杆，见上面贴着许多小广告，就凑到跟前看，只见上面写着：

"专治男科各种炎症、感染。"

"专治妇科各种性病，一针见效。"

"你准备去看性病啊？"肖天鹅见状，不怀好意地问。

尚小宁有点不好意思，"我只是想看看那上面写的什么，我哪有病？"

三个人来到了市中心的一个广场。广场中间搭着个台，台上挂着巨大的横幅标语"原生态行为艺术展"。这里已经被围得水泄不通了。

"还不算晚，反正它是要弄一下午的。我们就直接到台上去看。"肖天鹅说。

三人走到台后面，上了台阶，登上了台。那些艺术家见了肖天鹅，也都和她打着招呼。这些艺术家都是女人，她们头发蓬乱，衣冠不整，手上都握着画板和笔，在一个个小伙子的身上画着。小伙子们都只穿了内裤，坐着或躺着让她们画。

55

  当然喉结是全裸的。但这些喉结都被巧妙地画成了花、眼睛、火山等等。有两个艺术家还更绝，合伙抱着一个小伙子。他是戴了围脖，穿了胸衣和内裤的，用他的长发和胡子当画笔，把他的头塞进一个个桶里，沾满了墨汁和各色颜料，在台上地板上铺着的一块大布上画着。

  "就这个？我见过，电视上看到过，叫人体彩绘。"

  尚小宁的这个话让肖天鹅有点失望，"这个我是专门带你来看稀奇的，原来你见过，那就没意思了。"

  正说着，台下有一个观众小伙子爬上台来，立刻脱掉衣服，脱到只剩里面的三段内衣后就没再脱了。

  "这在干吗？他们也参加进来画，思想这么开通？"尚小宁问。

  "你看嘛，看看就知道了。"

  只见一个年轻的男主持人在对着台下叫道："你们看，这位弟弟就很勇敢，他就敢于当着大家的面脱衣服。他的身材是如此漂亮、动人，曲线这么优美。现在他穿上'高美保健紧身内衣'了，这套价值1000元的内衣就归他了。我们为他鼓掌！"

  男主持人自己握着话筒鼓起掌来，单调的掌声被扩音器放大了无数倍，在广场上飘荡，很像空洞的雷声。

  台下又有几个小伙子在往台上爬。

  "啊，我们欢迎，又有几个漂亮的弟弟上来了，他们对自己的身材就很自信，敢于脱衣服，这套内衣就都归他们了。我们为他们鼓掌。"

  尚小宁撇了撇嘴，"就这个啊？我也在电视上见过。"她所没说的只是，她在电视上见到的是大姑娘做这些事，这里只不过换成了小伙子。

"唉，没劲，你这么新潮，什么都见过。干脆我们去吃饭，我们起来到现在，还没吃什么东西呢。我带你们去吃一个最有特色的餐馆。昨天那顿饭不算，等于工作餐，今天这个才算正餐。"

"好啊。"尚小宁现在真觉得饿了，很想吃东西。

三个人又从台上走了下去。

肖天鹅领着她们，穿过几条街，来到一个气势恢宏的饭店。她们一进门，立刻就有一排穿着旗袍的迎宾小弟向她们鞠躬，说："下午好。"他们的胡子在下巴上扎成了个髻，用黑色的网兜套着，网兜上有个非常漂亮的红色蝴蝶结，与他们的红色旗袍相对应。当然头发在脑后也都弄成了这样。

56

尚小宁有些习惯看这些服务员了,觉得他们这样打扮也很漂亮,不过有些人应该年龄不大,还没长胡子吧?但是胡子不是可以贴假的吗?尚小宁又想到自己的整容手术,不禁脸一红。

立刻有个领班模样的小伙子,过来问道:

"几位?想到哪里用餐?楼上有包间。"

"那就上楼吧。"肖天鹅说。

领班在前面引着路,把她们带到了一间叫"牡丹"的包间里。三人坐下后,有小伙子送来了茶,她们喝着茶,领班拿起菜单,要她们点菜。

"哎,你们这里的特色菜现在还有没有了?"肖天鹅问。

"有啊,这是我们的招牌菜。"

"什么招牌菜?"尚小宁问。

"就是有补的功能的,女士吃最好。"领班说。

"哦,那是活血的?我就经常腰疼。"尚小宁说。

"嗨嗨,那就更要补啰,阴虚。你可能劳累过度。这里的菜都是壮阴的。"肖天鹅阴阴地笑着。

尚小宁看肖天鹅的笑不是一般的笑,那个意思……尚小宁懂了,这就好比中国的男人喜欢吃壮阳的东西。

"我没你那么坏,我是个好人。"尚小宁忸怩地打了肖天鹅一下。

"还不好意思啊,好人坏人,要到以后来证明哦。"肖天鹅瞅着尚小宁,咯咯地笑着,然后对领班说:"就这样,来个牛阴炖甘蔗、羊阴荔枝煲、青蛾汤、清蒸皇帝鱼、雪蛤炖木瓜、红烧鲍鱼。再来三瓶啤酒,我们一人一瓶。"

"哎哟,不要点这么贵的东西,鲍鱼贵得很。"

"鲍鱼最壮阴，尤其你阴虚。"肖天鹅又坏笑着。

不一会菜上来了。

肖天鹅边用勺子在汤里搅着，边给尚小宁舀到碗里，边问："哪有这么多牛阴、羊阴？一头牛、一只羊身上不就一个吗？"肖天鹅笑着说。

"什么牛眼、羊眼？这里面有牛眼、羊眼？哎哟，我不敢吃，好怕人，再补我也不敢吃。"尚小宁侧着身子，远远地躲着碗，很害怕地望着碗里的东西。

"哈哈，这是牛阴、羊阴，懂了吧？母牛、母羊身上的，就好比牛鞭、羊鞭，那是公牛、公羊身上的。"

"啊？是这东西啊？那有多脏啊，怎么吃？"尚小宁还是躲着那个碗。

"说你新潮吧，你有的时候又老土得很，怎么这么不统一呢？这个东西好啊。你看我，身体多棒？就是天天有18岁的小伙子陪我，我也吃得消。就是这东西补的。"

57

"我不需要这东西,我不是那种人。"

"哎,怎么能这样说呢?食色性也。一个女人不喜欢吃女阴,不喜欢男人,她还算是个女人吗?"

"那我就不是女人了?"

"是啊,所以你这方面要好好补补课,跟我学学。"

"我不学。"

"没关系,和我在一起时间长了,你就会放开了。这就是人的本性,干吗要抑制它呢?来,吃,吃了你就会有不一样的感觉。"

但是尚小宁还是无法吃这些东西,"这个我以后慢慢适应,我先吃鱼,我喜欢吃鱼,一天都离不掉鱼。"尚小宁用筷子夹了一块皇帝鱼的白嫩的肉,沾了点汤,送到了嘴里,说:"你说这鱼怎么家里就做不来?在家里也是清蒸,就是没这个嫩,没这个鲜。"

"这个时间不能太长,刚好熟。还有配料也有讲究,料酒是一定要放的,去腥。"

小弟过来给她们倒酒。他嘴上毛绒绒的,胡须还没长出来。肖天鹅笑眯眯地问小弟:"你多大啦?"

"17。"

"这么小就出来工作?"

"嗯,家里还有个妹妹要读书。"

"你叫什么名字?"

"唐招妹。"

"哦,肯定你家有许多男孩,你妈妈想要女孩,对不对?"

"嗯。"

尚小宁看着肖天鹅满心欢喜地看着唐招妹的样子，知道她不仅仅是关心他，就说："这些孩子这么小就出来工作，不容易。我儿子在家还娇生惯养的。真应该让他来好好学学怎样自立。"

肖天鹅还是看着唐招妹，没把尚小宁的话放在心上。唐招妹虽然对肖天鹅浅笑盈盈，但边回答边忙他自己的，但眼神中分明有种期待。

"吃啊，吃你的女宝。"尚小宁招呼着肖天鹅，肖天鹅这才回过神来，开始吃菜、喝酒，和她们聊天。

小张很少说话，只顾吃菜、喝酒。

酒饱菜足后，三人起身离开座位，向外走去。

肖天鹅边走边依依不舍地看着唐招妹，唐招妹也含情脉脉地送着她们走出包间，"慢走，欢迎光临。"他的眼神中的那种期待更加明显。

走出包间老远后，肖天鹅还回头看看唐招妹，然后意犹未尽地说："这个小弟真好。"

58

"真好给你做儿子。"尚小宁说。

"嘿嘿,做表弟,我的表弟很多的。"

"我能猜得出来。"

"不过我有个侄子是真的好,不仅人帅气,对我也好。我把他当儿子。他都26岁了,还没结婚。所以,结婚,生孩子有什么用,有个侄子就够了。"

出了饭店,肖天鹅停住了脚步,"现在还早,我们到哪儿去呢?"

"回家,我太累了,就想靠在床上看看电视,看看书。昨天舞跳得浑身都疼。"尚小宁说着,然后又突然想起了什么,"哟,我把那几本杂志丢在剧院里了。我看人都往后台跑,不知发生了什么事,也跟着跑,书忘了拿。"

"没关系,我也不要了。你要看的话,我车里还有几本,等会拿给你。"

"好的。"

尚小宁说:"先到酒店取车吧,然后回家。"

三人往酒店的方向走。当她们穿过一条小巷,经过一座楼时,忽然楼上扔下了一个纸团,正砸在肖天鹅的头上。

"什么东西?"

肖天鹅往地上一看,就发现了这个纸团。她立刻把它捡起来,打开一看,上面写着"救我"。纸是从小学生的本子上撕下来的,字是用铅笔写的,写得歪歪斜斜,很仓促。

"有人被绑架了,还是个小学生。"

肖天鹅往这座楼房看去,这是座7层楼的楼房,纸团到底从哪儿扔出来的?肖天鹅注意到只有2层和7层的窗子开着,有灯光。其他的都关着。

"人在二楼,我们去救人!"

"你怎么知道在二楼?"

"从7楼往下扔东西不会这么准,别的窗子都关着,没人。"

"赶快报警。"尚小宁掏出小张给她的手机,问:"号码多少?"

"011。"小张答道。

"别,就我们去。"肖天鹅一把夺过手机,把手机关了,然后又还给了尚小宁。

"哎哟,我不敢,万一歹徒有枪怎么办?"

"那怕什么?你瞧我的。"肖天鹅带头朝楼房走去,小张立刻跟着她,尚小宁也只好跟在后面了。但是尚小宁突然有了个主意,她故意慢走了一步,转过身去,悄悄地打开手机打电话给记者,电话号码她早已背熟了。她觉得没个男人在身边壮胆,就三个女人,她太怕了。

电话通了,尚小宁用手捂着嘴,轻轻地、急促地对着手机说:"你赶快来,我们在解救人质。"

"人质?你们现在在哪里?"焦亮焦急地问。

59

尚小宁退后几步,退到楼外,看到门牌号码,念道:"天心街54号,二单元、二楼。我关机了,你赶快来。"

打完了电话,尚小宁觉得心里镇定了不少,这才小跑着追赶着前面的两个人。

三人来到二楼,到了那个与扔纸团窗口相对应的房门前,肖天鹅示意她俩闪开,叫她们贴着门旁边的墙壁上,又指指门上的猫眼。她俩就明白了,马上蹑手蹑脚地照做。

肖天鹅轻轻地敲门,敲完,立刻摆出一副狐媚的姿态,一手软软地叉着腰,一手把一缕长发弄到嘴里咬着,脸则侧过来,双眼风骚地对着猫眼看着。

果然过了一会,门里传出一个粗声粗气的女人的声音:"你找谁?"想是她从猫眼里看到了肖天鹅。

"哎呀,你真是的,我都不认得啦?我是小弟呀。"肖天鹅学着男人的声音,发嗲地说,边说还边扭着。尚小宁在一旁看了差点笑出声来。

"你有什么事?"

"我就是想你嘛,好久都不见了,你死到哪里去了?我今天买彩票发了点小财,我,我就来找你了……我今天倒贴还不行吗?"

门里面的人显然犹豫了一会,问:"就你一个人?"

"哎呀,我还会带谁来?带来了也不方便啊。"

过了一会,门打开了,说时迟那时快,只见肖天鹅一脚将门踢开,边用手对贴在墙边的两个女人一挥,说了声:"上!"边冲进房间,大声喝道:"我是警察,不许动!"肖天鹅说着伸直双臂,两手合掌,对握着,两个食指向前伸着，很像警察双手握枪的姿势。

趁房里的女人一愣的时候，尚小宁和小张冲进了里面的房间，床上果然有个男孩被绑起来了，嘴上还蒙着胶布。尚小宁赶紧把孩子嘴上的胶布撕开，孩子哇的一声哭了。

"别哭，别哭，现在没事了。坏蛋已经被我们抓住了。"尚小宁把孩子抱在怀里，轻轻拍着他。小张则手脚麻利地给孩子解身上的绳子。没错，正是这房间里的窗子对着小巷子。"你很聪明，救了你自己。我们是看了纸团才上来救你的。"

小张则在仔细地检查着孩子身上的衣服，"她没对你怎样吧？"

孩子摇摇头，用手擦干了眼泪，"我是乘她去拿绳子的时候，赶紧写了纸条扔下去的。她刚把我绑起来，你们就来了。"

"这个女人是什么意思？干吗要抓个女孩？是想搞钱吧？"尚小宁说。

"我是男孩。"

60

尚小宁又昏了头了,穿花衣服的才是男孩啊。

"她是不是想拐卖儿童?"

"拐卖儿童,怎么会拐卖男孩?男孩没人要,要拐也是拐卖女孩。那一般还都是四五岁以下的。这么大的男孩就更没人要了。"小张说。

尚小宁正要跟她抬杠,说哪有男孩没人要的?女孩才没人要。又想起,这里的一切都是反的,才忍住了话。

"那这孩子一定家里很有钱。"

"你看他穿得像有钱的样子吗?"

"那她把他弄来干吗?"

"这都不懂?这女人肯定是个光棍,变态,色魔,她要侵犯这个孩子。"

尚小宁努力把这话反过来想,不然思想就互相打架了,听不懂这些话了。中国不也是有这样的男人吗?把小姑娘绑架了做坏事,做完了还杀人灭口。这样一想尚小宁就觉得顺多了,可以理解了。

"还好我们来得及时。肖天鹅说得对,来不及报警了,只能我们自己来救。我还怕呢,不敢来。要是没来,这孩子就完了。有时什么事就几分钟的工夫。唉,万幸。"

尚小宁又搂着孩子。

外屋传来乒乒乓乓的打斗声,小张跑了出去。肖天鹅正和那女人在相持不下。那女人见肖天鹅手里并没有枪,胆子也大了起来,还朝她扔东西砸她。肖天鹅也朝她扔东西,但就是靠近不了她身。到底肖天鹅没学过这个,怎么也制服不了这个女人。

小张冲过去就要抱住这个女人,但这个女人朝小张的胸口踢了一脚,小张倒到地上。肖天鹅一看气坏了,扑过去就要捉她。这时小张也忍着痛,爬起来向她逼去,两人把她逼到了墙角,眼看着没地方跑了,她突然一翻身,跃过了窗子,朝楼下跳去。

"抓坏蛋啊——"肖天鹅对着楼下叫道,小张也跟着叫了起来。然后两人又转身朝往门外冲去,这时外面响起了警笛的呜呜声,警车嘎的一声停在了窗下。然后楼梯上响起了急促、纷乱的脚步声,一群警察冲了进来。

"快去抓坏蛋,坏蛋跑了。"尚小宁朝警察喊道。

"已经有人去抓了,孩子怎样?"一个留着半截胡子的男警察朝孩子走来,其他的警察在房间里散开,查找着有用的线索。通过这些警察的说话声和胡须,尚小宁判断她们都是女人,只有这一个是男人。

焦亮这时也急匆匆地跑了进来,"孩子没事吧?我们没来迟吧?"说完从尚小宁的怀里拉过孩子,很疼爱地抱在怀里,然后又从怀里拉开孩子,看看他,理了理他的头发,说:"没吓坏吧?你很勇敢。"说完又搂着他。

61

这时有几个医生抬着担架进来了,"孩子在哪里?赶快。"

医生、护士都戴着帽子、口罩,尚小宁看不到他们有没有胡子;他们穿的白大褂又很宽大,看不出女人的特征。尚小宁无法判断他们的性别,现在只能根据声音。尚小宁已经养成了坏习惯,遇到人,就非要辨别他是男还是女。听到她们讲话了,才知道全是女的。

孩子望着医生,有点害怕地说:"我没有受伤,没有生病。"

"那也要去检查一下。"

"我不去。"孩子紧紧地抱着焦亮。

"孩子,我陪你去,没关系的,不要怕,不会打针的。我们在医院里等你的家里人来。"

"我的哥哥在这里打工。"

"他在哪里上班?叫什么名字?"

"我不知道他在哪里上班,他叫唐招妹。"

"唐招妹?是不是我们今天在酒店吃饭遇到的那个?"

"他是说他在酒店里上班。"

"那就对了,就是他。"

"什么酒店?我来打电话。"焦亮掏出了手机。

"好像叫什么……我只记得我们吃饭的那个包间叫牡丹,反正在中心广场附近。"尚小宁说。

"我知道了,金艳饭店。"焦亮打通了电话,对唐招妹诉说着发生的事,说完,对孩子说:"我们走吧,你哥哥在医院等我们。"孩子这才愿意躺到担架上,焦亮握着孩子的手,随担架一起往外走去,尚小宁也跟着他们一起走了出去。

房子外面的警戒线外挤满了人,一群记者见他们出来,立刻围了上来,闪光灯"咔嚓咔嚓"地亮着,话筒也全都塞了过来,夹杂着记者的各种问话:

"请问孩子有没有受到伤害?"

"歹徒抓到了吗?"

"你们是几个人与歹徒搏斗的?"

"……"

这么多人七嘴八舌地问话,尚小宁不知道回答谁的好,她此刻也没有心情。她只想尽快地陪孩子到医院,等孩子见到了哥哥,安定下来,再打听孩子为什么会落到这个女人的手里。

那个男警察简短地回答道:"歹徒还没有抓到,孩子没有受伤,其他的无可奉告。"尚小宁、小张及警察跟着担架一起上了救护车。

到了医院的急诊室,医生、护士忙了好一阵,唐招妹也赶来了。唐招妹一来就抱着孩子哭,又把他身上到处摸摸,然后问医生:

"他没事吧?"

"没事,很健康,只是受到了惊吓。"

男警察也抄下了医生记录的病历,开始做着笔录,先从当事人问起。通过孩子断断续续的描述,加上哥哥唐招妹在一旁的不断补充,大家才知道了整个事件的始末。

62

孩子叫唐来妹，在家里排行老三。老大就是唐招妹，餐馆里的服务员；老二也是男孩，已经离家出走了。因为妈妈在生完了老三唐来妹后，就真的生了个女孩，家里人都认为这个妹妹是他带来的，所以就连带着他也比较受器重，允许他一直念书，并答应他，只要他念得好，可以一直念到上大学。

可是今年爸爸突然得了重病，住院开刀花了许多钱，还找别人借了债，家里就没法再让两个孩子念书了，于是决定让他辍学，在家种地，出去做小工，以保证妹妹读书。这让他受不了，他的成绩很好，又是班长，他本来一心要上大学的，这下他的梦想破灭了。

他在家又哭又闹，结果被妈妈痛打，他爸爸劝了几句，也被妈妈痛打。爸爸要去寻死，被亲戚拦住了，他趁着乱，就背上书包，偷偷跑了出来，混进了长途汽车里，来到了这里找大哥。他想着大哥已经上班了，有钱让他念书。

但是下了车他才发现，他不知道怎样才能找到大哥，他不知道大哥的地址。天也快黑了，他很怕，急得要哭了。就在这个时候，一个女人，就是那个坏蛋，问他怎么一个人在这里。他说他从乡下来，要找大哥。那个女人说，正好我认识你大哥，我带你去。

这样他就跟着这个女人来到了她的家。他一进家门就问大哥在哪里，这时那个女人把门一关，一脸凶相，说谁认识你大哥。他就哭着吵着要走。这时那女人说，你再哭我就杀了你，杀完你再杀你的大哥，然后再杀你的全家。他就吓得不敢哭了。

那女人说，我叫你做什么你就做什么，我就不杀你。但是她想想还不放心，就说，我得找条绳子来把你捆起来，不然你会乱动。说着就到厨房去找绳子。唐来妹想从窗子里爬出去，但是窗子外面正对着小巷子，没地方落脚，他又不敢跳下去。

他正着急，就看到有3个人走了过来，他就轻轻地喊着"救命"，但是她们没听见。他急中生智，想到了扔纸团。他曾听老师讲过一个故事，就是一个人被绑架后，扔了纸团才活了命。

这时他飞快地打开书包，拿出一本本子，从本子上撕下一张纸，快速地写了两个字，就把纸搓成了团，对准中间的那个高个子扔去，正好砸中了她。他就赶紧缩回来，把本子和笔收好，这时刚好那个女人找到了绳子回来了。

63

女人见他神色慌张，问他在干什么，他说没干什么。女人也没多想，就把他的嘴用胶布贴了，又把他手脚绑了起来，正在这时，有人敲门。原来是街上的那三个人来救他了。

听完了他的讲述，大家都为他捏了一把汗，同时又夸他聪明。如果他没有想到用这一招来让别人救他，他就完了。

那个男警察把笔录记好后，让尚小宁过了一下目，签了字，就走了。

尚小宁打电话给焦亮和肖天鹅，说他们在医院。肖天鹅刚才下去抓坏蛋了，这时气喘吁吁地赶来了，"哎，坏蛋抓到了。她跑得好快，我怎么追都追不上，要不是后来警察赶来了，开枪把她腿打伤了，还真抓不住她。喔，我的腿都快跑断了。"

肖天鹅的衣服都汗湿了，满脸的疲惫，但她还是过来先看看孩子，笑着问："还好吧，没事吧？我们没来迟吧？"

唐来妹摇了摇头。

肖天鹅的脸上立刻荡漾开了得意和自豪的神情，"怎么样？我说我们去救吧？等警察来就迟了。是不是，小弟弟？"

"嗯。"唐来妹点了点头。

肖天鹅在唐来妹的脸上摸了摸，"这孩子真可爱。叫什么名字？"

"唐来妹。"

"唐来妹？不是有个唐招妹？"

"这就是他的弟弟。"尚小宁说。

"真的？这么巧？那我们也算是有缘了。"

"大姐，我在这里，谢谢你啊。"唐招妹走到了肖天鹅的面前，眼里充满着爱慕和敬畏，同时又很羞涩。

"哦，呵呵呵，你们这兄弟俩都这么可爱。我也算是英雄救美了，哈哈哈哈，小弟弟，是不是？"

这时焦亮来了。又来了几个人，后面跟着些记者和台风电视台的人。焦亮一见到他们，立刻迎了上去：

"余主任，你来啦？你怎么知道的？"

"有记者打电话给我，基本的情况我都知道了。"

焦亮向小兄弟俩介绍着："这是男联的余主任，他是专门管男童的，男童有什么困难都可以找他解决。"又对着余主任说，"这就是那孩子，这是他哥哥。"

余主任过来和唐招妹握了握手，又摸摸唐来妹的头，问道：

"小弟弟，现在你安全了。以后有什么事，有什么困难，找我，好吗？我们男联就是你最坚强的后盾！"

唐来妹似懂非懂地点了点头。

摄像机一直在跟着余主任拍，记者也都围着他拍照片。余主任对后面跟着的几个人伸出了手，接过了他们手里的水果和补品，递给了唐来妹，又从口袋里掏出一个红色的信封，对唐来妹说：

"这是给你的补助款，1000元，先解决你的目前的生活困难，以后我们再解决你的具体问题。"

64

然后余主任就和唐来妹并排站着,一手搭在他的肩膀上,一手拿着红包,对着摄像机的镜头。唐来妹吃力地拿着手里的东西。等拍完了,唐招妹才接过弟弟手上的东西,替他拿着。

"那我明天就可以上学了?"

"是啊。如果你妈妈、爸爸不让你上学,你就再找我们,打电话给我们。"

"我还要回去?不,我不回去。回去了就要被妈妈打死了。"

"你妈妈经常打你?"

"嗯。"

"打得严重不严重?"

"严重。"

"还打别人吗?"

"打,经常打爸爸,有一次把爸爸的腿都打断了。"

"你有没有被打伤过?"

"没有,她一打我,我就跑。"

"我就是被她打得跑出来打工的。"唐招妹在旁边说,眼睛红红的。

"唉,家庭暴力。"余主任摇着头。

摄像机又单独对准了余主任,余主任双手在肚子前握着,开始了演讲:

"贫困地区的男童失学依然是一个严峻的问题,虽然经过我们的努力,已经有所好转,但对每一个个体来说,都是需要立刻解决的,读书成了他们最大的愿望。知识改变命运,奋斗成就未来。我们不能让孩子输在起跑线上。虽然这与经济落后有关,但传统的重女轻男思想也在起着重要的作用。在同样困难的情况下,总是男童失去读书的机会。所以我们除了要在政策、法规上下功夫，还要大力宣传女男平等思想，提高男人的社会地位，让男童失学不再发生。也希望有能力的人能给予他们资助，让他们享受和女童同等的受教育的机会。

"家庭暴力问题在落后地区时有发生，虽然还是与贫困有关，但大女子主义思想是最主要的因素；文化程度低也是一个原因，这使得她们不能很好地与家人沟通；而家庭暴力的受害者往往不知道救助，认为被女人打是应该的，丈夫和孩子是属于妻子的，要打要骂是她的权利。这也是家务事，外人管不着。

"现在我就要告诉男同胞们，你们应该挺起腰杆做人，女人是人，男人也是人，你们也有同等的地位，她们不让你们上学，打你们，是违法的，你们可以去告她们。男联就是你们的娘家，这里有你们的亲人，当你们遇到委屈、遭受家庭暴力时，就要来诉苦，我们会帮你解决问题的。我们的热线电话是 12345678。谢谢大家。"

65

接着是对台风电视台记者金瓶梅的拍摄。他在对整个事件作了介绍后,呼吁大家给予失学男童更多关注:

"我们已经开通了资助电话,如果有人捐款,或要给予帮助,可以拨打电话87654321。另外,我们的这位焦亮记者,他不光是位资深的高级记者,报道过许多重大的社会问题,负责报纸专栏的写作,还是个热心男权的人,他是男联的高级顾问。以后大家有什么困难,也可以找他联系。他的电话是13912345678。"

摄像机的镜头这时又对准了焦亮,焦亮对着镜头摆了摆手:

"大家好,我是一个斗士,永远为女男平等而奋斗!有事找我。"

这时余主任又问医生:

"他的身体还好吧?需不需要住院?"

"不需要,现在就可以回家了。"

余主任又问唐来妹:

"那今天晚上,你住在哪里?"

"我就住在哥哥那里。"

"你有地方住?"余主任转过来问唐招妹。

"我住集体宿舍。"

"那也不是个长久之计。你今天先带他回去休息,以后我们再来想办法。"

"我还要上班,把他一个人丢在宿舍里我不放心,万一又被哪个坏人拐跑了……"

"那,要不先住到我家去?"余主任说。

"住到我家，我家条件好，我也养得起他。"肖天鹅抢着说。

"不行，绝对不行，别才出虎口，又入狼窝。"焦亮一步跨出来，挡在唐来妹的前面，好像肖天鹅要把他抢走似的。

肖天鹅的脸色骤然变了，她气愤得挥舞着拳头，朝焦亮冲过去，"我就知道你欠揍，你这个缺乏女人爱的东西，只有尝尝女人的拳头，才能让你清醒！"

人们都拉着肖天鹅，余主任不太高兴地说：

"刚才还在说大女子主义，家庭暴力，现在就出现了。"

"我不是个崇尚暴力的人，我也有文化，有修养，但是当好心被曲解的时候，谁都会愤怒。他这样的人就是欠揍！"

"你才欠揍！"焦亮说，然后把唐来妹揽在怀里，对他说，"就住到我家，好不好？"

唐来妹看了看哥哥，又看了看尚小宁，再看看余主任，最后看了一眼肖天鹅，说，"我还是住在男人家比较好。"说完抱着焦亮，并把头靠在他胸前。

66

"呵呵,小鬼,精得很,吃过一回亏,学乖了。那就这样吧,尊重他的意见,暂时住焦亮家。"余主任又转向唐来妹,"以后你就在这里上学。上学的事,我来想办法帮你解决。"

这一行人要走了,大家都和他们握手告别。他们走后,焦亮就带着唐来妹走了。临走前,他深深地看了尚小宁一眼。尚小宁心里一热,她好想和他聊聊,就是一直没捞到机会。但是机会总会有的,何况现在尚小宁有了手机。尚小宁暗暗地朝他点了点头,这个动作别人几乎都看不出来,但焦亮看出来了,他也朝她暗暗地点了点头,她也看到了。

因为唐招妹还要上班去,就和焦亮、弟弟一道走了出去。当焦亮转过身后,肖天鹅在他的背后又挥舞了一阵拳头,等他走后,骂道:

"这个又老、又丑、又粗、又高的家伙,老是自以为是,绝对心理变态。一般人们说老童男子都会变得脾气古怪。一个人过嘛,有什么劲,当然要变态。"

"你、我不是也一个人过?我们也没变态。"尚小宁反驳她道。

"嘿嘿,我这打击面太大了点。我是说,他老是这样孤独地一个人过,精神迟早要出毛病。我们虽然一个人,但是很快乐啊。"

"你怎么知道他不快乐?"

"是啊,也许他快乐。不过他老是表现出愤青的样子,真让人受不了。哎,不谈他了。我们也回去吧,我实在是太累了。小张,我们坐你的车,我也开不动车了。"

"我到哪里去?"尚小宁问。

"当然是到我家了,这还用问?你还没到我家去过呢。"

三人走出了医院，打的到了前一天睡觉的酒店，小张取了车，她们坐了进去。

"哎，好累，好想睡，但又兴奋得睡不着。"肖天鹅靠在座位上说。

"我也是。"

"我就想泡泡澡。"

"我只想冲个澡，然后躺在床上看电视。"

"那还不容易？等会你先洗，洗完了我慢慢泡。"

"行。"

车子到了肖天鹅的家门口后，肖天鹅和尚小宁走了出来。

"哎，还有杂志。"小张在驾驶室里的地板上抓起一把杂志，从车窗里递给了尚小宁，然后开着车子走了。

"小张真是个不错的人，还记得别人。别看她不讲话，但靠得住。"尚小宁看着远去的车子，不禁对肖天鹅说。

67

"是啊,不然我俩性格这么不同怎么能搞到一起?就是因为她诚实可靠。你别看那些人跟我热乎,嘴甜得很,也许背后骂我八代祖宗呢。到了利益相关的时候,出手比谁都狠。这个我见多了。"

两人说着进了小洋楼。这座小洋楼虽然外表看和女船长家的差不多,但进去了,才知道,这里完全是艺术家的作风,浪漫、豪华、随意。尚小宁没见过这种阵势,被镇住了。她一路走,一路看,眼睛都不够用了。

楼下客厅里,垂着巨大的吊灯,吊灯全是用闪着奇异光彩的玻璃串成的。客厅中央的地上有华贵的地毯,墙上有油画,客厅一角有钢琴,一边有壁炉,壁炉前有摇椅,窗前有名贵的花和绿色植物。她们上楼时,连楼道上的墙上都挂了油画。

肖天鹅带尚小宁看了卧室,卧室也是皇宫一般,垂着黄色缎子的帏幛,巨大的床在帏幛下面。窗帘也是金黄色的鹅绒的,挂着流苏和花边。卧室里的梳妆台和衣橱也是古色古香的,墙上贴着花的墙纸,挂着裸体的男人油画。尚小宁乍看这些不穿衣服的男人还不太习惯。这个房间里唯一现代化的东西就是电视机。

肖天鹅从衣橱里拿出了一件淡绿色的丝绸睡衣,扔给尚小宁,"你先去冲,然后我泡。"

"内衣有没有?我也是一身臭汗,不换不行了。"

"要什么内衣?在家里有什么关系?"

"有的话还是给我吧,我不习惯不穿内衣。"

"你呀,有的时候又保守得要死。"肖天鹅翻出了两件,扔给了她,"我带你到浴室去。"

浴室就在隔壁，尚小宁一看，乖乖，那个豪华。尚小宁以前装修时买浴缸时见过，好像要1万多块，里面有按摩、水柱翻花等等的功能，可以两个人在里面洗，是正方形的。这个不知要比那个高级多少倍。浴缸好像是玉做的，半透明的，放在浴室的正中央。尚小宁忍不住用手摸摸，确实是玉的。尚小宁有个玉手镯，所以她对玉有一点了解。不过玉手镯这次也在海里落水时丢了。

"好了，你洗吧。"肖天鹅丢下尚小宁，带上门走了。

尚小宁在这样的浴缸里也想泡泡了，但是她已经说冲冲澡的，就不好临时再改了，肖天鹅还等着泡呢。要泡以后再泡，机会有的是。这在她家还不多住些日子？

尚小宁匆匆冲过澡后，就来到了卧室。

肖天鹅正在上电脑："这么快就好了？"

"好了。你也喜欢玩电脑？"

这应该是这个房间里第二个现代化的东西。尚小宁想。

68

"这是个好东西啊,谁不迷?"

"我儿子就天天在电脑上下不来。"

"你不玩?"

尚小宁摇了摇头,"兴趣不是很大。天天在店里,哪有时间?再说儿子整天搞电脑,也没我的份。"

"以后在我这里,一定要把这一课补上,让你也成为电脑迷。"

"网络不是个好东西,我们那里还专门请了专家来,讲怎么戒网瘾呢。"

"怪事!这种高科技的还要戒?那就都拿着锄头去种地好了。不过,锄头在当时也是高科技,也要戒的,哈哈哈哈……"肖天鹅拿着衣服到浴室去了。

尚小宁躺靠在床上,打开了电视,电视上正在播广告。

一个胡子齐胸的小伙子夹着双腿,说,"要是没有问题呢,就用清水洗。"

另一个年纪稍大一些的,留着半长的胡子说,"那要是有问题怎么办?"

又一个更老一些的男人,烫着胡子,出来说:

"20。"

"30。"

"40。"

这三个男人分先后说着,最后齐声说道,"都用洗必净。哈哈哈哈……"

另一侧广告,一个小伙子昂首挺着脖子,突出了他那硕大无比的喉结,虽然喉结外面围了围脖,但围脖只遮住下面的一半,上面的一半完全裸露。小伙子无比自豪、醉心地边用手抚摸着自己的喉结,说道:

"做男人,还有什么比这个更重要的呢?"

这时画面转了，这个小伙子出现在街头，他的围脖外很随意地围了条透明的纱巾。立刻有许多男人投来羡慕和惊讶的目光；许多女人看他都看得魂不守舍，有个女人还一头撞在了电线杆上。

然后画面又一转，小伙子得意地出现在一个餐馆里，当他经过一个餐桌时，一个女的对着他一直贪婪地看着。可那个小伙子忽然一回头，原来就是她的丈夫，现在他的喉结也硕大无比了。两人开心地哈哈大笑。这时电视上出现了一个医院的画面，画外音介绍道：

"丽脖美容院，世界一流的水平，打造无与伦比的、坚挺的颈部曲线美。"

原先的那个小伙子又穿了制服，双手叉腰，挺着喉结，做着媚态，"有了这样的颈部，我更自信。"

69

接下来的广告是做褪毛剂的,一个小伙子在街上慌忙地蹲下来,捂住自己的双腿,又缩着双肩。另外一个小伙子走过来问:"为什么不用'光溜溜'褪毛霜?"

然后特写,一条猴子似的毛乎乎的腿,被涂了点乳白色的药膏后,再用手一抹,毛全没了。小伙子跳着、张着双臂,露出白花花的腋窝和白嫩嫩的腿。

尚小宁换了个台,这个台的广告更稀奇,看得尚小宁目瞪口呆。

一个小伙子穿着紧身内裤,挺着下身,下身肿得像得了小肠气。如果在中国的电视广告上看到这样的人,尚小宁一定以为是医院在做下身肿瘤手术的广告。

小伙子说:"穿这样的内裤,我的臀围一下就增加了10厘米。"说完对自己的下身满意地看着,立刻围过来两个同样穿着紧身内裤,但下身肿得不太厉害的小伙子,羡慕地看着他的下身,"哇,你用的是什么方法?"

小伙子得意地说:"我用的是南瓜保健内裤,它具有促进血液循环,按摩重要穴位,把外太空信息转换成人体必须能量的功效,从而使下身饱满、挺立。穿上即可见效,久穿可持久增大。"

电视上出现了电脑制作的画面效果,下身真的在内裤内迅速膨胀,立刻变成了小南瓜。"看,这就是它的效果。"画外音强调着。

小伙子正挺着个如小南瓜般肿胀的下身,一个中年女人走了过来,从背后一把搂住小伙子,亲昵地把脸贴在他的脸上,小伙子满脸幸福地说:"我还能给老婆什么呢?这就是幸福的源泉。"

尚小宁又换了个台,这次真的是医院广告了,但又出现了一个穿内裤的巨大的下身，比刚才的小南瓜还要大一点。这肯定是医院做肿瘤手术的广告了。尚小宁有点幸灾乐祸地看着广告，自己跟自己打赌。

画外音："冬瓜美容医院，采取最新高科技增大法，不开刀、不吃药、不流血、不痛苦，10分钟搞好，会让你有个无比傲人的下身。"

尚小宁又换了个台，这次终于有女人做广告了，一个中年女人举了一盒药，说："女宝女宝，必不可少。"一个小伙走来贴在她的胸前，忸怩作态地说："女宝女宝，她好，我也好。"

尚小宁又换了个台，她不相信电视上全是这些东西，她非要找个一般的电视来。结果这个台是在搞选美。一排高挑的小伙子只穿着三段式服装，脖围外已经没有任何遮拦，还都露出一小半喉结在外面；几乎等于没穿的内裤，当然是紧身的，把下身勾勒得无比"曲线"，内裤上挂着牌子，表明自己的代号；他们已经很高了，但仍穿着起码有半尺高的高跟鞋，把全身的重量压在5个脚趾头和这"一指禅"的鞋跟上。

70

他们瘦得皮包骨,像集中营里刚放出来的,可以清楚地看到一根根的肋骨,但他们没有任何衰竭的样子,还充满活力地在台上走着,扭着。到底年轻,可以撑一阵,尚小宁要这样,怕也爬不起来了。

旁边有主持人介绍着每个小伙子的4围:

"9号,身高1米80,体重55,脖围50,胸围80,腰围60,臀围70。"

小伙子们一会穿着晚礼服出来,一会穿着自己设计的服装出来,一会穿着婚纱出来,反正折腾够了,又开始智力竞赛。

"请问,《本草纲目》的作者是谁?"

一个小伙子翻着贴了假睫毛的巨大的眼睛,想了很久,说:"金庸。"

"错,是李时珍。请问,水的分子结构是什么?"

"是冰、水蒸气。"这回小伙子答得很快,也很肯定。

"错,是两个氢一个氧。"

尚小宁打了个哈欠,又换了个台,这回是电视剧了,尚小宁来了精神。

这是古装戏,只见一个老女人被一群小伙子围着。小伙子个个浓妆艳抹,轻纱薄裳,手捏香帕,与老女人调笑着。老女人也乐得色眯眯地左拥右抱地享受着这来自四面八方的"美人"的包围。尚小宁根据自己在中国看的电视剧的经验,猜这应该是在妓院里。

果然,一会,一个老一点的男人浪笑着出场了。他的骚劲一点不亚于这群小伙子,他同样打扮得花枝招展,但年岁的风霜已经让他的媚态变成了丑态,他还一点没察觉到,硬搔首弄姿地往上凑。这应该就是妓女院,不,妓男院的院长,老鸨了。

"哎哟,什么风把姐姐您给吹来啦?春红,上茶。"

老女人嘿嘿地笑着:"不来我想啊,这么多美人,我怎么舍得不来呢?"

老鸨用手绢往前空打了一下,身子往左侧扭了90度:"想我这醉香楼全国鼎鼎有名,皇上都要光顾这里,哪个女人不想来哟?"说完用手帕捂着嘴,吃吃地笑。

"你那头牌还在吗?"

"哟,姐姐,今儿个秋香可是要等贵人,不接客的。"

"那贵人可就是我?"

"那就要看姐姐您是不是贵人出手了,如果你比贵人出手大方,不要说一个秋香,就是十个秋香也愿意伺候您啊。"

71

"哈哈哈哈……"老女人用手点着老鸨,开怀地笑着,接着从怀里掏出一包银子往桌上一放,说:"这总够了吧?"

老鸨一见银子,立刻面露喜色,一把抓住它就往怀里揣,一边朝楼上喊道:"秋香,还不快来伺候姐姐。"

楼上一个小伙子答应着,用一把宫扇半遮着脸,飘然而下。

尚小宁又换了个台,这次是现代戏,一对情侣在幽静的夜晚散着步,还没走出多远,突然,姑娘猛搂小伙子,对着他的嘴就啃,边啃还边喘着粗气,边解开他的衣服。接着是小伙子脖子的侧面的特写。姑娘解开了他的围脖,喉结的1/4暴露了出来。姑娘的手也顺势摸了上去。紧接着,画面上衣服一件件地被抛了出来,然后是小伙子裸露的整个背部,姑娘紧抱着小伙子,滚到了地上。

尚小宁准备关电视,但无意中碰到了另一个按钮,电视自动换了台。一个老太太在侃侃而谈:

"我就主张女男同厕。女人不是喜欢偷窥吗?那是因为她好奇心太强了。如果女男同厕,就会消除她的好奇心,她也就不会去偷窥了。开放、打破男人的神秘感,是治疗偷窥的最佳良药。没吃过肉的人,总想吃肉。让她吃,天天吃,她吃够了,就不再想吃了。"

画外音介绍着:"这就是我国著名的国学大师,祝希瘦,她虽然已年高86,但治学精神仍然不减,每天孜孜不倦地学习着,尤其对历史、人文、社会有着独到的见解。"

画面上出现了一个记者,他有着很漂亮的齐胸长须,上唇的胡须用摩丝定在了嘴角上方的两边,脖子上的围脖连着下面的衣服,他的长发是用漂亮的夹子夹在脑后的,这样,脖子的后面,连着背,一直到腰就一览无余了。尚小宁记得这裸露的后背,上次在肖天鹅的记者招待会上,她见过,因为上次她看的是他的背面,不知道他的脸像什么样。上次记得他也是叫什么"梅"的,是什么电视台的记者。

"我是金瓶梅,台风电视台的记者。今天,我们有幸采访到著名的国学大师祝希瘦,我们不仅可以聆听到国学大师的精彩理论,还可以一睹她的超凡风采,了解她的日常生活。现在,祝老师已经走进了这家美容馆,让我们一起进去看看。"

电视上出现了一个年轻美貌的小伙子在给祝希瘦按摩面部的画面。祝希瘦闭目躺在那里。金瓶梅问那小伙子:

"请问,您经常给这位姐姐做美容吗?"

"呃,是的,她经常来。"

"请问祝老师,您是不是特别钟爱美容?"

"我是来治病的。也不经常来。不过有一条,我要年轻漂亮的小伙子给我做按摩。这就是一种享受,不然我是不会来的。"

72

接着,电视画面一转,祝希瘦脸上涂了厚厚的面模,眼睛上贴了两片黄瓜,已经鼾声大作。"她每次来都会睡觉。"小伙子在旁边偷偷地笑着说。

金瓶梅接下来又采访了几个知名人士,也都是半老的女人,要她们谈谈对祝希瘦的看法。

"她爱男人,一看到年轻漂亮的小伙子就眼睛发亮。这说明她还有爱的能力,她在爱情面前永远不老……"

尚小宁关了电视,躺在床上,呆了半天,又顺手拿起刚才小张留给她的几本杂志。这几本杂志的封面全是小伙子的脸部特写,个个都青春靓丽,神采飞扬。尚小宁打开了一本,读了下去:

"深夜,荷塘的水面上漂浮着一具裸体男尸,一个少年散步至此,吓得尖叫了起来。

"事情还得从2年前说起。一个小伙子名叫宫绿竹,是海湾大学的高才生。他有着高挑的身材,丰满的喉部,挺拔的下身,白皙的皮肤和姣好的面容。在学校,他是人人追逐的对象。一个偶然的机会,他认识了富家小姐王成才,并成了她的男友。

"他们的第一次,王成才永远都记得。那是一个月黑风高的夜晚,王成才把宫绿竹带到了他家的一个无人居住的别墅,一阵激情热吻之后,王成才解开了他的衣扣,露出了他那绣花的围脖,一阵沁人肺腑的香味袭来,令王成才心旌摇荡,她不顾一切地撕开宫绿竹的围脖,一个雪白硬挺的喉结跃然而出,王成才惊呆了,她忍不住扑了过去……

尚小宁没兴趣看下去,又翻了翻杂志的后面,也翻了其他几本杂志,内容不外是"少夫偷情记""大学生、二爷、命案""少年情迷网吧""80

岁教授迎娶 20 岁小伙"。

  尚小宁扔了这些杂志,出了口气,最后实在无聊,一眼瞥到电脑还开着,就情不自禁地走了过去。也许肖天鹅说得对,高科技的东西就是好,应该着迷,而不是禁止。还好,尚小宁以前被儿子拖着上过几次网,大致知道怎么点开文章,怎么看。

73

电脑的画面停在一个网站的首页,尚小宁看了一下这些文章的标题:"偷窥弟弟裙下 10 招""著名影星祖脖露巨喉""著名体育男星奔跑走光""男名模露点照""世界十大男明星美喉欣赏"……

现在尚小宁看到"男人的喉结"的字样就烦,她希望看到一点不一样的东西。在一篇篇标题逐一筛查后,尚小宁发现了一篇《一个男人的内心独白》。也许这才是一个男人内心真正的东西吧?尚小宁点开了这篇文章。

首先映入尚小宁眼帘的是两幅照片,一个模样普通的小伙子没穿衣服,剪着短胡子,只是脖子上草草地围着围巾,基本没有露出喉结。围巾拖在胸前,遮住了胸前两点。他的双手捂住了下身。另一张照片是躺在沙发上,张开着双腿,虽然穿着薄如蝉翼的连衣裙,也穿着三角内裤,但这个姿势实在不雅,像在妇产科的产床上。

下面是他的文章:

"我要对这女男不平等的社会强烈控诉,凭什么女人就可以大谈情欲,而男人就不能?凭什么女人就可以在文学作品中大量地描写性,而男人就不能?凭什么是她们玩弄我们,我们就不能玩弄她们?在我跟了无数女人上床后,我厌倦了……"

文章底下有许多回复,基本上都是女的回的,有的骂,说现在简直没有了体统,网上怎么可以发这样的文章和照片?……

尚小宁赶紧关了这篇文章。刚想喘口气,又见一个似乎熟悉的名字,唐带妹。这个……哎呀,是不是唐招妹的弟弟,唐来妹的哥哥?尚小宁记得他家是三兄弟的。既然小弟弟的二哥也在这里,为什么他不来找他?尚小宁接下去就明白了。

这个标题是"唐带妹人体艺术写真"。尚小宁虽然知道大概是什么，但还是忍不住好奇，想看看他艺术到什么程度。因为这个人似乎和她有着某种关系。

一幅幅的照片，是一个骨瘦如柴的少年，有坐着、躺着、站着的，姿势都挺艺术的。也就是姿势美些，关键部位遮着，当然喉结全是裸露的。尚小宁现在看一个男人，也看他的喉结了，尽管她很不情愿，但自然而然地就看了过去。

74

尚小宁无心再看这些艺术照了,她要看看介绍这个少年的文章。果然,少年很早就从家里逃出,学了舞蹈,又做了裸体模特儿。这让在乡下的家里觉得很丢脸,家里人也就和他脱离了关系,不认他了。现在他更是要为艺术献身,把自己美好的身体展示给大家了。文章结尾说,他很想念他的哥哥和弟弟,也很想回家,但是他知道,他一旦走了这一步,就再也回不了头了。

这一定就是他了,三兄弟中的老二,看着脸也有些像,年龄也符合。

尚小宁正看着,想着这个家庭的问题,肖天鹅洗好了澡出来了。

"在看什么呢?"肖天鹅轻柔地说着,走了过来。

"哎,随便看看。你看,这是不是你救的那个小孩的哥哥?看这名字。"

肖天鹅扒在尚小宁的肩膀上看着,一股浓烈的香味向尚小宁袭来。尚小宁又用力闻了闻,确实好闻,沁人肺腑。

"哎哟,是他?这个我知道啊,在网上都好久了。对呀,我怎么没把他和那个小孩联系起来?对,是他,肯定是他,没错。"

"还有那一篇……"

尚小宁正准备把她刚才看到的《一个男人的内心独白》找给肖天鹅看,可肖天鹅却伸手拿过鼠标把这些都关了,最后电脑也关了。尚小宁觉得自己有点难为情,她怎么会对这些感兴趣呢?她又不是一个下流的人,也不是一个好色的人。别看肖天鹅花,她在这方面还挺正派的呢。尚小宁不由得又对肖天鹅尊敬起来。这才叫好色的人比想象中的正派,正派的人比想象中的好色。

肖天鹅关了电脑,顺势搂着尚小宁的脖子,脸贴着她的脸说:"现在是我们的'两人世界',其他什么都不存在。"

肖天鹅把广告词学得这样像,用得也是地方。尚小宁笑了,但她还是觉得被一个女人这样搂着,这样皮挨着皮地亲近很不习惯。她站了起来,想挣脱肖天鹅。

"哈哈,还有天知,地知呢。"尚小宁想到了丈夫在外面的偷情行为,当时他大概也是这么想的吧?哼哼。尚小宁下意识地回了这句话。

趁肖天鹅手一松的时候,尚小宁离开了肖天鹅的怀抱。尚小宁刚想喘口气,一看肖天鹅的衣服,又吓得要闭上眼睛。

"你,你怎么穿这样的衣服?"

"这衣服怎么啦?好看得很。"肖天鹅张开着双臂,低头看了看自己的衣服。

75

"也太透明了。"尚小宁的眼睛不敢朝肖天鹅身上看。

"哈哈哈哈……你呀,我能让男人穿全透视的衣服我就不能穿?这是在我的卧室啊,又没在大街上。"

"那……总归有外人在场,又不是你一个人。"

"外人?你是外人?我就是要穿给你看的,我可没把你当外人。"

"这个……"尚小宁一时语塞,"起码要穿个内衣内裤。"

"那多不方便?也太不浪漫,太不刺激了,这样才能激起人的无限美好的感觉。"

"哎哟,两个女人在一起,用得着吗?你要是和一个男人在一起还差不多。"尚小宁说这话的时候,脸都有点红了。

肖天鹅坐到尚小宁旁边,握着她的手,真诚地说:"你有没有经常听我提到我的侄子?他真是一个好人,长得又漂亮。是我从小一手带大的。那比亲儿子还亲。自从我第一眼看到你,就喜欢上了你,也替我侄子喜欢上了你。你看我最近一直很忙,都没工夫让你俩见个面,他和小温的性格有点像。我相信你俩肯定会一见钟情的。

尚小宁一听,连忙摆手说:"不行不行,他才26岁,比我小许多。我还有个孩子,拖油瓶。"

肖天鹅说:"在真爱面前,什么都不是问题。你还没和他相处,怎么知道不行。"

"小温的性格我不是顶喜欢,并不是好男人就值得我爱。"

"看你说的,我怎么会害你?我也不会害我的侄子呀。"

76

  肖天鹅说:"你俩在一起才会是真正的恋爱,这个恋爱是蜜拌的黄连,又甜又苦,不吃会发疯。"
  "我一直把你当姐姐,你的侄子就是我的侄子,怎么爱得起来?"
  "两人相爱年龄不是问题,你看船长,那么大,找个小丈夫,那么好,多么幸福的家庭。"
  "可是小温不是也和你好。"
  "我们那只是玩玩,不是刻骨铭心的爱。"
  "你怎么就见得我和你侄子有刻骨铭心的爱?"
  "这是我的感觉,不会有错。"
  "但是我没有这样的感觉。"
  "那是因为你没有见到他。"
  此刻,尚小宁心里只有记者焦亮,再也容纳不了别人。如果是焦亮这样说,她会愉快地答应的。老天真是和她开了一个莫大的玩笑,把这感人的话由一个当姐姐的人说了。她有种哭笑不得的感觉。
  没想到,肖天鹅一下子变了脸,说:"我看好的事不会有错的。你和我侄子的事,成也得成,不成也得成,我做主了。"
  正在这时,响起了猛烈的敲门声,尚小宁像看到救星似的冲向门口,打开了门,门外站着的人令她又惊又喜,正想着他,他就来了,真是天意啊。来的人就是记者焦亮,旁边还站着那个小孩——唐来妹。
  尚小宁赶紧跑出了门,躲在焦亮的身后,说:"她硬要把侄子介绍给我。"
  "我就知道是这事。她到处宣扬她的侄子,把他说成了一朵花。其实她的侄子嗜赌成性,是个赌徒。我们走。"

焦亮拖着尚小宁就跑,一边手还不忘了拉唐来妹。三人咚咚咚地冲下了楼

等肖天鹅醒悟过来的时候已经迟了,肖天鹅发了疯一般地冲向楼梯,声嘶力竭地喊道:"焦亮——你不是人!我跟你没完。"

77

　　肖天鹅正准备冲下楼，低头一看自己穿的全透视睡衣，懊恼地又冲回卧室，打开橱子，脱掉了睡衣，在里面胡乱地找了件衣服套上，又找条裤子穿上，这才冲下楼，冲到门外，但这三个人早已无影无踪了。肖天鹅气得直跺脚，又冲回卧室去找车钥匙，她不相信他们会插翅膀飞了。他们就是跑到天边，她也要把他们找到。

　　眼看着肖天鹅的车子走远了，这三个人从花丛里钻了出来，尚小宁惊魂未定，唐来妹却拍手笑道："哈哈，还是我的主意好，她肯定要追的。"

　　"幸亏我把车子停得远，她看不到。"

　　"哎，你们是怎么找到这里的？"尚小宁问。

　　"嘿，你要看我是干什么的。记者嘛，说得难听点，就是包打听，什么事都瞒不过我。像她这样的名人，我找媒体一打听就知道了。她上过电视，上过杂志封面。"

　　"那怎么刚好这时候来？"

　　"心灵感应。我们回去睡下后，我就想你和肖天鹅的事，越想越不放心。她的侄子非常有名，她肯定要拉郎配，强迫你和他好，让他嫁给你。她是不会放过你的，你一定在她家。我就立刻起来打电话，打听她的地址。我本来是要一个人来的，但让小弟弟一个人在家怕又出什么事，就把他喊起来一道来。就在我们下车时，我突然又有了预感，已经出事了。我就拉着他飞快地跑进去，果然有事。

　　"哎，幸亏你们及时赶到，不然我真不知道怎样对付那个局面。"

　　"我们上车吧。"焦亮说。

　　尚小宁跟他们来到车前，刚要上车，但是又犹豫了，她就这样跟着一个她不熟悉、不太了解的人走吗？而且去他家，住那里？万一有了别的什么问题，那又该谁来救她呢？船长？一想到船长，尚小宁的脑子就一亮，她立刻有了个冠冕堂皇的理由。

78

"我们还是到船长家吧,肖天鹅肯定不会放过我的,一定到处找我,她不会想到我在船长家。"尚小宁很高兴在关键时刻能想出好主意。现在的她不是刚来的她了,什么事都留个心眼。

"这……"焦亮一时也没了主意,只得问:"船长家在哪里?"

"就在隔壁。我们还是先进去再说吧,别等下肖天鹅追不到我们,回来又看到我们。"

尚小宁也不等他俩是否同意,拖着两人就往船长家跑。

开门的是船长的丈夫温碧玉。他见了尚小宁有点不高兴的样子,说:"我还以为你失踪了,被绑架呢,正要去报警。"

"嗨,也差不多?"尚小宁随口应着。

"哼,不回来吃饭睡觉也要招呼一声,害得我们好等,还以为你出事了呢?"温碧玉噘着嘴说。

"哎,一言难尽。我们进去说。"

尚小宁不等温碧玉邀请,就急忙往里走。温碧玉看了一眼焦亮,脸上露出很复杂的表情。他也不邀请焦亮。焦亮只得硬着头皮往里走。温碧玉在后面默默地关了门。

"谁呀?"船长在里面问。

"我。"尚小宁高声答应着,人已经走了进去。

"嗨呀,你这个人,怎么能跟那种人走?我一回家就听说了。我就觉得大事不好,马上到她家去找你,谁知道你们都不在家。到哪儿去混了?"

"唉,还是船长英明,眼睛毒。我就觉得她是好人嘛,不过就是漂亮一点,时髦一点,又喜欢我,哪知道她……"尚小宁对周围看了看,问,"孩子们都睡了吧?"

"都睡了,有什么话就说吧。"

尚小宁向船长价绍着两位来者:"这位就是救了我的记者焦亮,这位是被我们救的小朋友唐来妹。来来,都坐。"尚小宁自己先在沙发上坐下了。

船长一脸的迷惑:"什么啊?谁救了谁?遇到什么事啦?没那么惊险吧?哎哟,你还穿着睡衣。"船长这才注意到尚小宁的衣着,看来真的发生了什么事。

尚小宁低头看了一下自己的睡衣,不由得苦笑了起来:"唉,也不能说她是坏人,只是我们不对路,她是一厢情愿。"

"什么?什么一厢情愿?"

温碧玉这时拿了个托盘,端了4杯茶来,不冷不热地放在了每个人的面前,然后安静地坐在一旁。

尚小宁喝了一口茶,喘了一口气,定了定神,这才一五一十地把她所遭遇的事一股脑地说了出来。最后说:"她非要把她的侄子介绍给我,拉郎配。我不同意,她就不放我走。这不是一厢情愿吗?"

79

船长听得目瞪口呆,听到最后,连连说:"这怎么可能,怎么可能?她这样的人,侄子也好不到哪儿去。听说她侄子很有名。"

听到最后,温碧玉的表情变了,说:"她怎么是这样的人呢?一直都以为她是个好人。"

尚小宁飞快地瞥了他一眼,他的脸一红,但是很快,他的脸上又恢复了往日的神情,不再冷淡了。

尚小宁说:"想想她也怪可怜的,孤苦伶仃的一个人,在家里连个说话的人都没有。她只是替侄子着想,并没有错。"

"又心软了,又心软了。"船长不满地翻着眼睛,"我看你八成也是同情她,对她侄子抱有幻想。"

"唉,我哪是喜欢她?我拿她当好朋友,好姐妹。平心而论,她不是个坏人,也很有才华,为人也不错……只是我对她的侄子没有感觉,虽然我没有见过他,但我可以猜出,她的侄子一定像她一样可怜。她那么爱她的侄子,我的拒绝一定让她痛苦。"

"又来了,又来了。非要她把你杀了,吃了你的肉,你才肯回头。到时候就迟了。"

众人都笑了。

"没那么严重吧?"尚小宁笑着说。

唐来妹已经在沙发上睡着了。一开始讲的是他知道的事,他亲历的事,他还有兴趣,到后来,听他们说什么花不花的,他就没兴趣了,加上最近一直劳累,疲于奔命,所以眼睛再也睁不开了,就睡了过去。

"哎哟,这孩子睡着了。"温碧玉最先发现。

"我看这孩子就住在这里吧。他跟着你,你要上班,还要带他,万一有什么事,跑起来也不方便。"尚小宁对焦亮说。

"对对,就住在这里,正好可以和我的孩子作伴。"温碧玉急忙表态。

"当然住在这里,不然还能住到哪里?"船长说。

"那……"焦亮还想说什么,温碧玉已经走了过来,抱着唐来妹往卧室走去。

"今天我和他睡了。"然后边走边说,"这孩子好可爱呀。"

船长说:"今天晚上我跟你睡。"

80

稍过了一会儿,船长问尚小宁,"现在你有什么打算?是先在这里旅游呢,还是找份工作定居下来?这样闲逛下去也不是个事。"

"定居下来?这个我从来没想过。我还是要回去的。"

"那好,我就先陪你玩玩。"

"玩是好……我就怕碰上肖天鹅……"

"怕她干什么?有我在,她敢动!看我不拧断她的脖子!你刚才还说她好,怎么现在又怕她啦?"

"不是,我是怕惹麻烦……其实我也不怕她,要打架我也打得过她,我只是不想太伤她的心,毕竟人家没有恶意……"

"又开始替她讲话了!以后我们不要提她!你跟着我,包你没事。"

尚小宁觉得踏实了,像是真的回到了自己的家,不由得松懈了下来,打了个哈欠。

"我该走了,你们休息。"焦亮说,然后又对尚小宁说,"我们再联系。"

"好的,我来送送你。" 尚小宁站了起来。

"有空过来玩。"船长也站了起来。

尚小宁和焦亮走到了门口,焦亮转过身来,深情地对尚小宁说:"记得给我打电话……其实,你住我那里更好……"

尚小宁的脸红了,她忙避开话题,说:"你也需要好好休息了,就让船长陪陪我。我会给你打电话的。"

焦亮拉起了尚小宁的手,用力握了一下,才依依不舍地走了。走了几步又回过头来看看尚小宁。尚小宁不好意思地低下了头,等他走了,才关了门。

船长也打了个哈欠,说:"我们也去睡吧,明天我还要给你安排活动。"

尚小宁和船长洗了澡,来到了客房,但上床后,两人的瞌睡似乎又没了,又聊了好久才睡。

第二天早上,尚小宁和船长都按时起了床。温碧玉早已做好了早饭,孩子们也已洗漱好了。

吃早饭时,温碧玉说:"小弟弟,你今天就在我家玩,等会我送完他们到幼儿园后,就回来陪你。我要带你好好玩玩。以后你就住在我家上学,好不好?"

"嗯。"唐来妹使劲地点着头,很香甜地吃着饭菜。

温碧玉爱怜地看着他,"来,多吃点饭,你有点营养不良,要多补补。"这边船长的儿子和女儿噘起了嘴。

81

"爸爸是不是以后就喜欢这个哥哥了，不喜欢我们了？"女儿说。

"他又不是妈妈生的，你干吗这么喜欢他？"儿子又说。

"嗳，不能这样没礼貌。这位哥哥家里很穷，没钱上学，暂时住在咱们家里。他也有自己的爸爸妈妈，他的爸爸妈妈也很喜欢他，很想念他。他们还不愿意把儿子给我们呢。他现在在咱们家是客人，我们是不是要好好地招待客人？"

"是的——"两个孩子齐声应道。

"我们今天出去玩，还是把他带着吧，他也没见过世面，和我一样。"尚小宁说。

"你看呢？"温碧玉问唐来妹，然后又用眼神征求船长的意见。

"好吧，我们也带他玩玩。"船长表了态，这事就这么定了。

玩了好几天，尚小宁也没捞到独处的机会。当着大家的面，她也不好意思打电话给焦亮。只是焦亮有时晚上打电话来问候时，她才和他说说游玩的事。

这天晚上，孩子都睡了，焦亮又打电话来了。尚小宁简短地和他说了几句就挂了电话。

船长说："大大方方的，谈恋爱不联系怎么行？"

尚小宁的脸红了，"没有的事，谁和他谈恋爱？"

"你就不要遮掩了，从他一来，我就知道你俩的关系了。这也很正常嘛。他没结婚，你离了婚，刚好。"

"我也看出来了，他对你很好，你也对他很好。"温碧玉有点酸溜溜地说。

"这样吧，你约他一下，看他什么时候有空，我放你假，你跟他玩玩。"

谈恋爱是要玩的。"船长说着,望着温碧玉,眨了眨眼,说,"是不是?老婆?"

温碧玉脸一红,忸怩地说,"谁和你谈恋爱啦?是你硬追人家的。"

"哈哈哈哈哈哈……还不好意思呢,都老夫老妻了……"

尚小宁拿着手机,当着大家的面,不太好意思马上打电话给焦亮;而且,他刚打了电话来,她立刻打过去,也显得太性急了些,但她又确实想和焦亮约个时间。她突然有了主意,拨通了焦亮的手机。

82

"喂，焦亮，是我……我想让你帮我打听一下白菊花的下落。自从我们那次跳舞后，她就不见了，我也联系不上她……啊？哪个白菊花……哦，我还没对你讲过。她就是和我一道出海，然后掉到海里，又被救到这里的一个姑娘……对对对，我们那天在舞场，一开始和我在一起的就是她……我们在吃自助餐时，你就看到她了？对对，当时我们是又哭又叫，都以为对方死了……啊……哦……我还忘了说，她也被一个船长救起，现在住她家……船长的女儿叫李白玉，在什么大学上学……哦，对了，上次记者招待会上，她还提过问题的……你有印象……对对，吃饭和跳舞都和她在一起，后来她们就不见了……啊，好好，再见啊，就这个事。"

尚小宁很为自己的这个借口满意。不过她也确实牵挂白菊花，这人真是的，怎么也不和她联系！不过白菊花怎么能跟她联系得上呢？她不是也联系不上白菊花吗？想到这里，尚小宁笑了。这下好了，交给焦亮就肯定没问题了。

83

不久,焦亮打来了电话,他有了白菊花的消息,"真的?那我明天去找她。"尚小宁脱口而出,立刻又补上一句话,"明天你带我去,不然我找不到她。"这一句明显是多余的,因为船长也能带她去。她说完脸孔有点发烧,然后偷偷看了看船长,船长好像根本就没在意这事,尚小宁的心定了些。

还没一会,尚小宁的手机就响了。尚小宁一接,是白菊花的。尚小宁高兴得跳了起来,"你这死鬼,疯到哪里去了?到现在也不和我联系……啊?哦,我也是和你联系不上……明天一定要到你那去?好好,我就是打算明天到你那去的,叫那个记者带我去。对,就是打电话找你的那个男的……唉,一言难尽,见面再说。我也有好多话要对你说……好好好,你忙你忙,我们明天见。"

"嘿嘿,她谈恋爱了。真想不到她有这么大的本事,一来就谈到一个。"尚小宁说。

"人之常情嘛。哪个女人能离得开男人?你的问题也该考虑考虑了。我看那个记者还不错,就是他了。"船长说。

尚小宁不好意思了,难道她也是个离不掉男人的女人?船长说得也太直了。

"这有什么不好意思的?你又不是头一回,不是结过婚吗?还这么放不开。"

"哎哎,也还不一定,还没问人家意见呢?另外也要多相处,以后才能决定……"

"对,慎重一点也好。"

船长打开了电视,不断地换着频道,想看看新闻。这几天晚上,她都等孩子睡了才开电视的。

一个镜头一晃而过,尚小宁突然指着那个画面,叫道,

"停停,刚才那个台……对对,就是这个。这个男的我见过,他怎么死了?"

画面上正在介绍一具男尸,旁边是他的照片。播音员正在说着:"……死者生前系台风电视台,是一名记者,叫金瓶梅。他被发现死在局长家里的床上,身上没有任何衣物,至于他为什么会裸死在局长家里,警方正在做进一步的调查……"

"他怎么会死?我前几天还见过他……"尚小宁喃喃地说着。

"你怎么会见过他?在哪里见的?"船长问。

"就是在一个记者招待会上;后来我在电视上也看到过他。唉,好可惜,那么年轻、漂亮。"

"就是年轻漂亮才坏事,又是公众人物。我儿子将来才不会要他去做这种事,那是害了他。"船长说。

他们又就这个话题讲了好久,才去睡觉。

第二天,尚小宁早早就起床了。孩子们都还没起来,温碧玉已经起来了。

84

"你干吗也起这么早？今天周末，你早上不睡睡？"尚小宁问。

"给你做早饭，你总不能空着肚子去约会。"

"哪里是约会？只不过和他一道出去就是了。"尚小宁嘴上还不承认。

"我早上也习惯了，早点起来做好饭，他们起来就有的吃。"

"你真是个贤……贤……我们国家叫'贤妻良母'。"

"我们这儿叫'贤夫良父'。"

尚小宁愣了一会，然后又笑了起来，"哈哈，对对，应该这样说。哈哈，真有趣。"

这时外面响起了汽车喇叭声，尚小宁奔到窗口一看，只见焦亮在对她招手。尚小宁也对他招了招手，立刻就要走。

温碧玉拦住了她，"你饭还没吃呢。你喊他进来一道吃，吃完再走。"

"不吃了，我要跟他上街吃小吃去，我要他请客。"尚小宁说完就换下睡衣，穿上衬衫和牛仔裤跑了出去。

温碧玉在后面撇了撇嘴，一脸的无奈。

上了车，尚小宁问焦亮，"你怎么来这么早？"

"有没有把你吵醒？我几乎一夜没睡。"

"什么事？"

"激动的。一想到要和你单独相处，我就非常激动，哪睡得着啊？"

"没那么夸张吧？"尚小宁有点不好意思。

车子开动了。焦亮又问，"你怎么起这么早？是不是也失眠了？"

"没有，怎么会？我平常都起得很早。不过因为你要来，怕你来早了要等，就早点起来做好准备，你一来就走。"

焦亮笑了，"起码你不讨厌我，也希望早点见到我，对不对？"

"哎呀，你这个人真是的。"

"好好好，不说这个，说点别的……"

当尚小宁提出要他请她吃小吃时，焦亮非常高兴，立刻把车开到一家最高档的酒店。尚小宁坚决不肯，一定要吃街头的小吃。焦亮只好依了她。找到一个宁静的小街，坐在一个摊子前，两人一起吃起了锅边糊、海蛎饼、鱼丸。锅边糊就是锅里煮点水，然后用泡过的米磨成的浆，用小碗舀了，顺着锅边浇下去，等这熟了的锅边糊铲到锅里，锅里的汤里放了芹菜、花蛤、鱿鱼须，再盛到两个碗里。海蛎饼是用一个浅勺，倒上点面糊，加海蛎和包菜，上面再浇点面糊，放到锅里炸，等成型，再倒到油锅里炸到金黄。鱼丸是包心鱼丸，外面的皮是鱼浆和上地瓜粉，里面是猪肉馅。焦亮也没吃早饭。他们这一顿饭吃得很愉快。

85

还不到 7 点呢，焦亮正准备带尚小宁到处转转时，尚小宁的手机响了。是白菊花。

"你起来了没有？我已经起来了，你过来吧。"

"这么早？没打扰你吧？"尚小宁说。

"哎呀，打扰什么？快来快来，来了再说。"

"好好好，这就来，我早就起来了。"

当车子来到白菊花的住处，也就是李白玉的家时，白菊花早就等在门口了。

"快进去，我还没吃饭。我们边吃边聊。"

白菊花显得很急切，但同时不忘对焦亮打量一番。从她的表情来看，她还是满意的。她和尚小宁交换了一下眼神，暗暗点了点头。尚小宁笑着，假装糊涂。他们跟着白菊花走进李白玉的家，她家其他人还没起床呢。

"你快吃饭吧，什么事这么急？玩也不要这么赶嘛。"尚小宁说着自己坐到餐桌前，也招呼焦亮坐下。

白菊花舀了一碗瘦肉皮蛋粥，和他们边吃边聊。

"可不是嘛，我昨天晚上正在忙，没来得及跟你说清楚。"

"忙什么？忙着谈恋爱吧？"

"嘻嘻。"

"谁追的谁？"

"是他追的我。"

"你也喜欢他，然后就在一起了？"

"对，就是这样。"

"他是干什么的？"

"模特。就是那天我见到你时，我跟他在舞场遇到的，他是第一个和我跳舞的人。"

"你不了解他，就在一起了？"

"当然要了解了。一边相处，一边了解。不相处，怎么了解呢？"

"了解的结果怎样？"

"当然还不错了。"

"那我很快就要吃喜糖了？"

"嘿嘿，还没那么快。"

"你不是有什么急事吗？"焦亮看她们聊起来没完，在一旁提醒着。

86

"哦哦,赶快讲正事。我一到这个国家来,就对这个国家产生了浓厚的兴趣,它的一切我都想知道。哎,我这个人也不是只想着谈恋爱,也会考虑生死存亡、国计民生的重大问题。我就想,既然它不是梦,是真实地存在,而地图上又没有,这里面一定有什么秘密。一想到这些,我就激动得浑身发抖。

"我就向李白玉打听,但是她在这方面知道得很少,几乎讲不出所以然。我又到图书馆里找,里面什么资料都没有。我只好叫李白玉帮我找有关的人来问,结果她找到了一个记者,这个记者又找人,终于找到了一个著名的国学大师。你们知道国学是干什么的吧,就是专门研究这个国家的历史、人文、民俗等等的学问。这不正是我所需要的吗?

"我高兴得要死。马上就想去找这个国学大师。可是,李白玉说,这个国学大师一般的人不见,尤其是长得丑的异性。我说我长得还可以啊,他应该喜欢吧?李白玉说,你瞎说什么啊?她是女的,她只见年轻漂亮的小伙子。

"我说,那可怎么办啊?临时到哪儿去抓啊?"

"就叫你男朋友去嘛,他肯定年轻漂亮。"尚小宁说。

"啊,不行,我还不放心呢。再有,他去了,有什么借口呢?如果记者去,可以说是采访她啊。我们找到了这个记者,想叫他再想想办法。结果记者自己就很年轻、漂亮。"

"你没有又看上他了吧?"尚小宁笑着说。

"嗨,我也没那么轻浮吧?我这人是从一而终的,除非人家不要我。这一点和你一样。我就说,那就你带我们去得了。记者说,他也没见过她,还得和她联系一下，征求一下她的意见。

"联系时，国学大师首先就问，你漂亮吗？记者说，应该还可以吧？我周围的人都没说过我丑，也有很多女孩子追我。国学大师问，你自己的评价呢？记者说，我到目前为止，还没发现哪个小伙子比我漂亮。国学大师立刻同意了。两人说好了今天早上8点见面，带上我。我当然肯定要带上你，你也应该知道一下这个国家的事情。我正想托李白玉的妈妈找你。李白玉的妈妈也是船长，也许认得你那个船长。"

"这个记者叫什么？也许我认得？"焦亮说。

"对对，你也是记者，应该认得他的。他叫金瓶梅。"

"什么？"尚小宁跳了起来，"是电视台的那个金瓶梅？"

"怎么啦？你认识？"

"他死了，在某人的床上……"

"啊？"白菊花吃惊得张大着嘴，半天都合不拢；手上的碗也掉到了桌子上，"他昨天还和我们在一起，我们就是昨天才和那个国学大师联系的……"

"那他不能联系后不久就死了吧？"尚小宁说。

"听说他是突发哮喘而去世的。"焦亮说。

"那怎么不死在家里？"白菊花问。

87

"他们正在谈工作吧。他们是上下级关系。"焦亮认真地说。

"谈工作谈到床上去啦?"尚小宁对他白了一眼。

"领导整天辛苦,回家还要和部下谈工作,当然累啦。"

"现在不是领导在床上,而是下级在床上。"尚小宁说。

"这很好解释。领导也体谅下级的辛苦。下了班了,还要往领导家跑,汇报工作。领导就喊他一起到床上躺着。"

"那怎么又没穿衣服呢?"尚小宁紧追不放。

"肯定是领导发现他哮喘病发了,给他做急救。那就必须要做心脏按摩,只有脱光了才有效果。还要嘴对嘴做人工呼吸。最后抢救无效死亡。"

白菊花突然忍不住,扑哧笑了出来,"宁姐,你不要听他,他在讲笑话,你还在跟他认真。没想到他还这么幽默……"

"啊?他在讲笑话?"

"没有啊,是领导这么对医生和警察说的。"焦亮仍然不笑。

"那也许是这样的吧?领导也是好心。"尚小宁说。

"哎呀,宁姐。即使是领导真的这样说了,也不一定就是实情。不然他怎么说呢?总得有个说法啊。"

"哦,我还以为是真的。"

"那你们不是见不成国学大师了?"焦亮问。

"哎呀,对啊。那可怎么办啊?好不容易联系到她……"白菊花懊恼地说。

"那还不就算了?你还有什么办法?"尚小宁说。

白菊花皱着眉头想了一会,眼睛一亮,说,

"有啦。喏，首先，这个国学大师没见过这个记者；如果见过了，听到他的名字就不会问他漂亮不漂亮了。这样的美男子谁会忘记？尤其是她那样的人。这样的话，即使她看了新闻，也不知道找她的这个人就是死者。"

"那你总要他去吧？你又不能叫死人带你去。"

"嗨，那是下下策，那叫国学大师马上见阎王还差不多。我这是叫记者'不死'。"

"你还有什么借尸还魂法啊？"尚小宁说。

"我现在不说，留个悬念。好，我把这饭吃完，我们就走。"

"到哪去啊？去局长家搬尸体？"尚小宁问。

"还搬尸体？那不早就送到太平间去了，还用得着我们？再说我也没那个胆子。我可不敢看尸体，多吓人啊。"

"那你要到哪儿去？"

"等下就知道了。"

88

白菊花准备端起饭碗,一看桌子上的饭碗早就翻倒了,刚才从她手上掉下来的,她都没在意。

"哎,不吃了,我们走。"

还是坐焦亮的车,白菊花指挥方向,"朝这边,朝这边……向右拐……对,绕过去……"

"你都变成活地图了,还要指挥人家本地人。"尚小宁说。

"本地人!本地人有我这几天走过的路多?我都烂熟了。你以为我光是谈恋爱,什么都不问?我一边谈,一边了解这个地方,一边考察。这里的每一寸土地都留下了我的足迹和汗水。"

"够辛苦的,所以人家说,谈恋爱的人都是疯子。"尚小宁说。

"这话你可不要说早了,我能看到你的。到时候你比我还疯狂。"白菊花用手指点着尚小宁。

车子在白菊花的指挥下,来到了一座小洋楼前。一行人下了车。白菊花又对着门牌号码仔细看了看,说,

"没错,就是这里。香榭里舍大街518号。"

"你怎么记得这么清楚?"尚小宁问。

"这还不好记?'想谢你啥?'我要发。哈哈哈哈……"

"这个地段很贵。最有钱的人才住这里。"焦亮说。

"今天我就要带你们去看看最有钱的人。"

尚小宁觉得白菊花变了好多。人漂亮了,洋气了,皮肤好了,还聪明、活泼了。完全不像原来的样子。唉,爱情的滋润啊。尚小宁不知道自己将来会不会也变成她那样。这都要看焦亮的啦。尚小宁不禁对焦亮望了一眼。

白菊花按响了门铃，一个年轻漂亮的男佣来到院子门口，问：

"你们找谁？"

"啊，我们和祝希瘦先生约好了，她叫我们8点来的。我们是来采访她的。"白菊花伸手看了看手表，"现在刚好8点。"

尚小宁没见过这个手表，再说，白菊花现在有手机，也用不着手表，手表肯定是男朋友送的。尚小宁很羡慕她，她自己什么时候才能得到这样的礼物呢？

"哦，我听先生讲过的。她要我在这等你们。你们进来吧。"男佣打开了院门，让他们进来，然后关好了门，带他们走进屋子。他把他们带到一个客厅，这里古色古香，放的全是仿古的红木家具，墙上挂着字画，角落里放着几盆兰花。

"我去通知先生。她在楼上工作。"

"她这么早就工作？今天是周末。"白菊花说。

"她天天早上5点就起床，然后读书，写字，画画，不分周末的。"男佣说。

89

男佣走了后，尚小宁说，"就祝希瘦？这个人我知道，在电视上看过。"

"印象怎么样？"白菊花问。

尚小宁撇了撇嘴，"不怎么样。都七老八十了，还那么花心。"

"有那么老？那她一定懂得很多。到现在她还那么用功。"白菊花说。

"再有学问我都不喜欢。"尚小宁说。

"现在不是喜欢不喜欢的问题，而是来获取我们需要的东西的。"

听到楼梯咚咚咚的声音，他们停止了讲话。祝希瘦人还没进门，就先响起了热烈的招呼声：

"啊，我们最美丽的小伙子来啦。我的心跳都加速啦。"

祝希瘦走了进来。白菊花迎了上去和她握手。祝希瘦却用眼光在找着大美人。当她看到唯一的男性——焦亮时，一把甩开了白菊花的手，毫不客气地说，

"就你？还没有人超过你？你到街上看看，哪个不比你强？是没有人超过你丑吧？"

白菊花赶紧解释，"老先生，是这样的。大美人马上就到，那绝对是绝色美人，我的好朋友嘛，我还不知道？他刚才打电话给我，说路上车子抛锚了，叫我们先来。因为他知道我特别崇拜您，特别想听您的教诲。我是您的超级'粉丝'。能见到您是我三生有幸，我有好多好多不懂的东西要请教您。"

祝希瘦的脸色缓和了下来，"一般的人我是不见的，我哪有工夫教小朋友？你们要想学知识，可以到图书馆，到学校去学嘛。"

"图书馆我都去了，但查不到我所要的东西。这东西只有您这儿有。

全都在您的肚子里呢。"

"哦？那是什么？"祝希瘦来了兴趣。

"关于女儿国的来历，以及它的一切。"

"你们是什么人？为什么对这个感兴趣？"祝希瘦警觉起来。

"我们是外国人。但我非常热爱这里，我喜欢这里的一切。以后我要定居在这里，所以我很想知道这是个什么样的国家，我对这非常有兴趣。"

"唉，"祝希瘦叹了口气，眨了眨眼睛，像是要哭的样子。

"老先生，有什么难处吗？"白菊花紧张地问。

祝希瘦摇了摇头，声音哽咽地说，"我高兴……高兴。来来，快坐。"

90

大家都有点莫名其妙,互相看看,也都坐下了。这时男佣端来了茶,放在每个人面前。祝希瘦端起茶,喝了几口,放下后,说:

"今天我真的很激动,真的。从来没有人对这个国家的历史感兴趣,也没人想研究。我自己的孩子都这样,孙子也是这样。我又能活几年?我一肚子学问就要带到棺材里去了。"

"把它写成书,不就可以保留下来了?"白菊花说。

"写给谁看啊?学校都没有历史课。我们这里只研究世界史、人类史,就不研究自己的历史。一说就说五千年文明,和中国一样。我的研究成果只能发表在学术刊物上。但这种刊物也没人看,根本卖不掉。所以我发表了文章,不但得不到稿费,刊物还要我出400块。他们卖不掉杂志,没有收入,要等着我们这些作者的钱发工资呢。天理何在啊?"

"那谁还写文章啊?"

"不写不行,评职称要论文。有了职称既有钱,又有地位。所以人们愿意花钱。有的人连写都不写,直接找刊物的编辑,要他们代写、代发,给钱就是了,也是400块。"

"啊?怎么会这样?那你就写书嘛。"

"写书!没人愿出我的书,出版社都不愿意出,说卖不掉,要我自己花钱出。我印了一千册,领回来了,到现在还堆在地窖里呢。"

"你给我,我要。"白菊花兴奋地说。

"行,都给你都行,只要你喜欢。"祝希瘦又眨了眨眼睛,"我连招研究生都招不到,现在也取消了资格。"

"我来当你的研究生,我有兴趣,你要不要?"白菊花赶紧说。

"真的？你说真的？"祝希瘦睁着孩子般天真的眼睛。

"真的，就是不知道能不能考得上。不知道需要考哪些课？"

"什么都不要考，就这样还没人来报名。既然我研究的是国学，就按旧式的礼仪收，带徒弟。只要拜师就行。"

"真的？"白菊花惊喜地大叫起来，立刻从椅子上跳了起来，倒身便拜，嘴里说着："请受徒儿一拜。"

祝希瘦慌忙起身，扶起白菊花："徒儿请起身。"

两人都坐下后，祝希瘦颇感欣慰地说：

"没想到我这把年纪了，还能收到学生，真是老天有眼啊。这下我后继有人了，死也瞑目了。"

然后老人就慷慨激昂地说出了这个国家的来龙去脉。

三百年前，中国福建沿海的几十个女人夜里偷偷了家里的船，一起出海。她们要到蓬莱仙岛上去，求仙成道。她们都是自梳女。

91

那时,海边的男人都要出海打鱼,女人在家种田、带孩子、伺候公婆。女人一个人在婆家是很难过的。婆婆、姑子,哪个都不好伺候。而且,出海也很危险,丈夫随时都有可能回不来。有时要伺候到老,变成终身的奴隶;有的会被婆家卖掉。

许多姑娘一提到嫁人就怕,也根本不想嫁人。与其一辈子守寡,伺候没有血缘关系的人,还不如守在娘家,伺候父母,落得个有人疼。所以许多姑娘到了嫁人年龄,就自己把头发梳成已婚妇女的样式,表示决不嫁人。这就叫自梳女。

这些自梳女因不堪忍受兄嫂、弟妹,甚至父母的闲言碎语,都想离家出走。可是,人海茫茫,到哪里安家?又以何为生?而且女子在外,多有不便。有个姑娘叫毛安慧,就提议到蓬莱仙岛上去。这个提议一经提出,就得到了大家的一致赞同。于是,在男人们都出海回来了后,某个夜里,她们集体上了几条船,趁着涨潮的时候,船被水托起,就出发了。

可是,谁也没有出过海,也不知道在海里怎么走。只是隐约听家里男人说过开船的事,也不知道蓬莱仙岛在什么地方。不过既然是仙岛,那肯定是人们没有去过的,一定很远。她们就朝和海岸相反的地方驶去。她们相信总有一天会到的。

然而,不知走了多远,也不知走了多少天,直到船上的东西都吃完了,也没看到蓬莱仙岛的影子,四周一片茫茫大海。这时她们才慌了。许多人哭了起来,她们不想死,她们还年轻。

有人在船上找到了渔具,但她们不会撒网,也不会收网。毛安慧说,她会钓鱼。于是大家立刻看到了希望。以后,她就教她们钓鱼吃。一开始还可以煮熟吃，到了最后，只有吃生的了。

就在她们几乎绝望，人也快都不行的时候，又来了场风暴，差点把船掀翻。在风暴过去后，她们以为可以平安时，一个更可怕的事发生了。船在一刹那，突然解体了，变成一片片木头。她们纷纷落入水中。好在她们都在海边长大，很小就会游泳，所以，没游两下，就都趴到了木板上。

这下，她们彻底绝望了，认为自己都要死在海上了。有的开始痛哭，有的后悔出海。但求生的欲望促使她们不能放弃。到她们再也坚持不住，就要滑进海里的时候，前方出现了陆地。

"啊，到了，蓬莱仙岛到了。"毛安慧先看到了，尖叫了起来，并指着远方。

这一声叫喊，让大家都活了过来。大家一齐朝前看，果然看到了陆地。然后姑娘们就又哭，又叫，又笑，又喊，乱成一团。

92

"大家赶紧向那边划去,快呀。"毛安慧说。

这句话提醒了大家,大家都边扶着木板,边用力用手划,边用脚蹬。正好海流也朝那边流。最后她们都上了岸,然后在海边躺了好久。毛安慧带着几个身强力壮的最先起来找东西吃。她们采来了许多野果,又在石头缝里捡了许多贝壳、螺,还在水坑里捉了活的鱼、虾、蟹。

大家吃过后,又休息了好久,才在毛安慧的带领下,来到一个高一点的地方,躺下继续睡。

不知睡了几天几夜,有的自己醒了,就到海边找点吃的,然后再带点回来。

到大家体力都恢复后,她们开始向更远的地方走,希望能找到神仙。

功夫不负有心人,她们果然看到了"神仙"。那是远处的一座房子。她们叫着、跳着,奔向那座房子。可是,令她们非常失望的是,这座房子不仅破旧、简陋,而且里面出来的四个人也不像仙女。她们穿得破破烂烂,个个面黄肌瘦。

她们看到来的人都非常吃惊,然后又都大叫着,哭着迎了过来。到了跟前时,只听她们说:"这下有救了,我们可以回家了。"

大家顿时冷了下来,难道这些人也是海里落难的人?一问,果然是。大家急着问神仙在哪里。她们说哪有神仙?她们已经把这里走遍了。这里是一个岛,很大,没有一个人,周围也没有一块陆地。

大家都惊呆了,原来这是座荒岛!根本不是什么蓬莱仙岛。大家再一次失去了希望,顿时都没有了力气,也没有了主意,软软地坐在了地上。四个"神仙"在知道了她们的情况后,悲伤地哭了起来:

"哦，我们命好苦啊，好不容易等来了人，还是回不去……"

原来她们是台湾人，那时还是孩子。有一天，看一条船上没人，一个大一点的男孩就把她们偷偷带到船上。他们一起玩起了起锚的游戏，不想涨潮了，船漂走了。他们再哭再喊也没用，船越走越远。最后他们也是钓鱼吃，那个男孩很能干。不知过了多久，也是遇到了风暴，就来到了这里。

一开始他们以为可以找到人家，再后来找不到后，男孩就盖了这座房子，把船上的东西都运了下来。但没多久男孩就肚子疼，死了。她们一直相依为命，活到现在。整整20年了。

"你们的船没有散掉？"毛安慧问。

"没有啊，上面的有些东西我们到现在都还在用。不过衣服早就没了，你看我们身上的衣服已经很破了。"

"那你们这20年吃什么？"

93

"还能吃什么？吃点野果，吃点海边捡的东西。"

"那船现在还在不在？"

"早就没了，不知漂到哪里去了。"

毛安慧沉思了一会，对大家说：

"我们既来之，则安之。其实在这里也蛮好的，虽然做不了神仙，但我们可以做自由的人，难道不是我们所希望的吗？"

大家听她这么一说，又都高兴起来。毛安慧带着大家进了屋子。屋子很小，挤不下，一些人就待在外面。

毛安慧身材魁梧。因为家里只有一个男孩，又体弱多病，家里就把她当男孩养。父亲是造船的，常把她带在身边，她也就像模像样地跟着父亲学。所以她的手很巧，会用各种工具。她在检查了屋里的工具后，高兴地说："不错，有斧子、锯子、刀、锤子、打火石、钉子、罗盘。"

钉子裹在油布里，没怎么锈。工具一直都在用，不用的也都涂上了油，也没锈。毛安慧立刻招呼大家搭简易的房子，先安顿下来，其他的事以后再说。

此后，毛安慧就成了头领。她带领大家栽培野果，大量收集吃的，晒干，以防天气不好的时候可以不用出去。房子后来也盖成了正规的。她甚至还用漂来的船板片拼凑成了一只小船，可以坐两个人出海，钓许多鱼回来。以后她们找到了麻，她又做了织布机，再到后来，她带着大家造了一条真正的船。

她说，必须摸索出去的路。既然有船可以完好无损地进来，就可以完好无损地出去。必须和外面的人做生意，不然日子过不好。这里缺少好多东西，日子没法过。

她派了几个聪明、能干的、水性好的人，把身上都拴上木头，坐小船出去找。万一船散了，还可以游回来。她驾着大船沿着岛的周围不很远的地方巡逻，一有落水者，就去把她们救上来，并听她们的讲述，把地点刻在木片上。

她慢慢地学会了用罗盘定方向，这是向四个"神仙"学的，她们也是跟男孩学的。她用自己做的香当钟，这香也就是锯末屑和树胶和好后晒干的。这样，船从哪里走，走了多久，遇到什么事，她就能很准确地定位了。

经过几年的摸索，她们终于得到了一个非常奇怪的行走路线，像是在迷宫里走。只有在这样的线路里走，船才不会散。毛安慧又派过不少次小船出去做试验，如果按这条路线走，都百分之百地不会出事。

终于有一天，毛安慧驾驶着大船，全都男人打扮，带上自己做的干货，走出了这片海域。然而出了海域，她还是不知道往哪边走。她就每走一段，记录下来。到食物快吃完了，就回来。

94

就这样，经过多次摸索，有一天，她们终于碰到了商船，还是中国的船。毛安慧非常高兴，不仅和他们做成了生意，还确定了这条道上经常有商船来往。另外也学到了很多航海的知识，了解了一些国家的位置、特产等等。

从此，毛安慧就给这个岛起名叫女儿国。在这里，女人最大，不需要打扮，全是男人装束。她也在第二次做生意时，把四个"神仙"送回到了台湾地区。此后，女儿国就没和中国断过联系，一直和中国平行发展。在大家都想把这个国家保留下来时，留下后代就成了她们最强烈的愿望。

毛安慧就不断招些男水手。她招的都是又瘦又小、体弱的；又招些想逃跑的自梳女上船。到了女儿国后，这些男人才知道这船上的都是女人。岛上女人最大，和其他国家是完全相反的。男人都要打扮成女人的模样，做女人的事。男人都叫苦不迭，但没有办法，只好认命。这样，女儿国就有了婚姻和下一代。在达到一定的人数后，就不再进人了。

线路图是船长一代传一代的绝密。任何男人都休想逃出去，不然男人都逃光了。这样，即使男人偷到了船，以后船散了，也要落到海里死掉；要不就被海浪送了回来。

以后，老的死了，男人就不知道外面的世界是什么样了。渐渐地，社会就这样定形了，成了现在这样。女人强大、主外，男人弱小，主内。那时女人是可以三夫四妾的。反正外面的男人怎么做，女儿国的女人就怎么做。

二次世界大战的时候，她们没有做生意，比较苦。中国改革开放后，她们有些东西就要从中国进了，中国的东西便宜。

现在的女儿国，和任何一个国家一样。只是她们出去做生意时，不说自己是女儿国的，怕惹麻烦。虽说外人进不去，但现在科技这么发达，说不定哪天就被平了。现在世界上还有人没去过的地方吗？她们到其他国家就说是中国的，到香港、台湾地区就说是大陆的，到大陆就说是香港、台湾地区的。她们在这些地方都有银行账号，钱可以存进去，然后再买需要的东西。

她们用的也是简化字，是从中国海外版的报纸上知道的。她们也学各种语言，也有各种教育，总之，一个国家应该有的她都有。

"那现在通讯这么发达，男人怎么会不知道外面的世界？现在还有互联网啊，还有电视、书籍。"白菊花说。

"你忘啦？船经过，都散了。"

"这和船散有什么关系？"

"你有没有听过希腊神话？说有个小岛，上面有女人头鸟身的怪物唱动听的歌，他们把这种鸟叫塞壬。怪物唱道，来吧，来吧，留下来吧。听到这歌声的人，立刻就失了魂，就想到这个岛上来留下。可是一靠近这个岛，船上的钉子就都被吸走了，船就散了。"

95

"还真有这回事?这个故事我知道。"

"百慕大三角你知道吧?所有的船只、飞机到这儿仪器都失灵了,然后失踪了。有的船还在,人全没了。人到哪里去?都到女儿国来了。"

"啊?那卫星也看不到你们?"

"当然了,它干扰信号。卫星看到的就是一片汪洋大海。科学家也想来考察,但来不了。你说,我们的通讯怎么和外面联系?"

"那书呢?书总可以吧。"

"书都经过我们处理的。我们买来的书,如果女男等级不明显,就按原来的样子出售;如果很严重,就把性别反过来,出版后再卖。所以他们看到的还是和他们一样的世界。比如,贾宝玉,我们就把他改成女的,林黛玉改成男的。"

"哦——难怪她叫李白玉,是起的'女人'的名字。"

"谁?谁是李白玉?"

"我的一个朋友。我现在就住她家……那孔子也是'女人'了?"

"对,因为他说过,唯女子与小人难养也,近之则不逊,远之则怨。我们改成唯男子与小人难养也,近之则不逊,远之则怨。"

"哦,哈哈,这太有趣了,够我学一辈子的了。"

"其实啊,在自然界,都是雄性的漂亮,为什么呢?因为它要吸引雌性,巴结雌性。那就是说,他们是以雌性为中心的,而且雌性的个头大,力气大。因为它要繁衍后代嘛,必须是能保护幼小动物的。而且自己的身体好,繁衍出的后代也健康,有利于物种进化。

"你看,蜜蜂、蚂蚁,哪个社会性动物不是雌性做老大?它还真长得老大的，大多少倍啊。大象、草原鬣狗，哪个不是母系社会？还有，螳螂，母的就比雄的体格大，老鹰也是。再说卵子和精子，一个是 200 微米，一个是 6 微米，精子加上尾巴才 66 微米。

"就说人吧，一开始也是母系社会。后来因为男性没什么能力，只吃不干，又好打架，头脑简单，想问题都是直的，又不会带孩子和教育孩子，不会照顾人，说句话能噎死人，所以就派他们做些简单的体力活，不做没饭吃。他们只得做了。

"你想，男人比女人少了半根染色体，他怎么能健全呢？尤其是性格和思维，变得常人很难理解。要知道，人要是少了一根染色体就不能活的。他少了半根，结果就少了根筋。你说电脑里的内存是 120 的好，还是 360 的好？那当然是 360 的好。女人有条染色体叫 X 染色体，是叉叉状的；男人少了半根，就成了 Y 状的了，叫 Y 染色体。

96

"不过这样下去后,就又有了个弊病,就是男人天天干些体力活,又都在户外,晒着太阳,呼吸着新鲜空气,身体得到了锻炼,体力得到了增强;而女人做细致活,动脑筋活,教育活,管理活,长期不运动,体力有所下降。在男人终于可以用武力打败女人后,女人的苦难就来临了,过着奴隶一般的生活。以后的世界就是你们所看到的世界。不过现在已经好多了,和古代不能比。"

"哦——原来是这样。"尚小宁不住地点头,然后又佩服地说,"你老人家真有学问,怎么知道得这么多?这些我都从来没听人讲过?"

"谁会跟你讲?男人?我们现在不也不把外面的男人世界告诉这里的男人?道理都是一样的。人类的体格主要是社会选择的结果。外面的世界为什么女人胸大?这是几千年来男人选择的结果。他们都以自己的好恶来规定什么样子的女人是漂亮的女人。女人不能工作,不能学习,要靠丈夫养,当然要巴结他,按他的要求做。

"你看猴子、猩猩,雌性的就没什么胸部,人家照样有奶,孩子照样够吃。我们这个国家也是,女人都平胸,孩子都喂得好好的。相反,我们这里的男人的喉结就比较大,下身也大,但是腰细,皮肤好,性格也温柔。这就是女人社会选择的结果。那些人的那些东西小了,脾气坏了,身材不好了,皮肤不好了,没人要了,就结不了婚,也留不下后代,绝种了。"

"哎,在这里真好,女人真正翻身做主人。"白菊花说。

"我们就是要把颠倒的历史再颠倒过来。男的想参政议政,没门。不过现在也宽容多了,各个部门都规定了要有一定的男人名额,以求女男平等。"

"那你又是怎么知道这些的？既然没书的话？"白菊花问。

"这就是学问了。有书还算什么本事？我是从许多资料中推测的啊，从资料的资料中寻找蛛丝马迹啊，然后以故事的方式讲给你们听。就像翻译甲骨文，翻译密码，考古，都是要自己找路子的。我的资料是全世界各地的。从他们的船只失踪、卫星定位、贸易货单、历史书上的片言只语、传闻、神话，等等的东西里面找，才得出这个结论的。我的书和论文，都是要拿出真凭实据的，不然谁信你呀？连你自己都不相信自己。"

祝希瘦一直滔滔不绝地说着，都忘了漂亮的男记者了。焦亮一直没插嘴，以他男权斗士的作风，他会跳起来和她辩论的。但是，现在祝希瘦越说男人不好，他就越要表现出君子风范；而且尚小宁也在身边，他攻击了女人，就等于攻击了她。他下定决心什么也不说。

97

到了吃午饭的时间，他们都没觉得，时间过得飞快。祝希瘦一定要留他们吃饭，因为她的话还没讲完。吃过饭，她还讲，要把几辈子的话都讲出来。直讲到吃晚饭还没讲完，又在这里吃了晚饭。后来又讲了很久，到很晚他们才回家。祝希瘦说白菊花以后可以住在她家，她家只有她和男佣两人，子女都不住这。这房子以后也给她，反正她就把她当接班人，当孙女了。

然而，就在第二天，出事了。

白菊花的男朋友黄花彩告诉她，有人举报，说记者焦亮是间谍，他正在和人里通外国准备颠覆这个国家。这个来联系的人就是尚小宁。现在国家决定了，如果尚小宁能定居下来就没事，如果她要走，就一定要把她和焦亮按间谍办。

"这又是唱的哪出啊？谁这么缺德？到底是谁举报的？"

"是肖天鹅。"

"这个坏女人。"

昨天晚上在回来的路上，尚小宁就把她跟肖天鹅的事说了，还把白菊花逗得哈哈大笑，可她现在笑不起来了，还咬牙切齿地恨呢。于是她又把尚小宁的这段事讲给了黄花彩听。黄花彩听过后，若有所思。

"咦？你是怎么知道内幕的？"

"我也是听朋友说的，按说这是不能说的，国家机密。因为他跟我太好了，又知道你们是从外国来的，就悄悄地告诉了我，我现在再悄悄地告诉你，你只可以跟当事人讲，千万不能外传。"

十万火急，白菊花立刻把尚小宁约出来密谈，谈过后，又喊来了焦亮，希望他能出些主意。焦亮问尚小宁：

"你是不是愿意留在这里？"

"不愿意。这里虽然一切都好，但是没有我儿子。"

"儿子以后可以再生。"

"但生的不是那一个，是另外一个。"

"这就难了。"焦亮也没了辙。

"要不你们俩都逃走。"白菊花说。

"那你呢？"

"我就在这里了，老死在这里不回去了。在那边我的心还没伤透？"

"那你的家人你不想啊？"

98

"怎么不想？但是可以写信啊，我可以说我在一个什么国家，叫船长把信带到中国邮寄不就行了？或者就到其他国家邮寄也行。还可以带点钱和照片回去。就好比我已经死了，我那次要是自杀了，我的家人不还是见不到我？这里简直就是我的天堂啊，我怎么能回到人间呢？"

"本地的人要生了孩子才让出去，而且一定要回来，不回来就拿船长是问。"焦亮说。

"那还不容易？等我结了婚，生了孩子就可以回去了。"白菊花说。

"男人不许出去，出去了就回不来了。"焦亮说。

"那肯定的了，我要是男人，出去了也不回来。"

"外国人出去前要吃一种药，吃了就会忘掉这里的事。如果忘不掉，就会有杀身之祸。"焦亮又说。

"这么吓人？忘了也好，反正也不想来了。"尚小宁说。

"我俩怎么逃啊？"焦亮问。

"找船长啊，她能带我们来，就能带你们走。"白菊花说。

"不是说这个是机密，不能告诉别人吗？"焦亮又说。

"现在是不说不行了，你们要逃。而且我看船长她人很正义和慎重的样子，应该不会去告密和走漏消息吧？"白菊花说。

"她就是这样的人，跟她讲，没事。"

三人又回到了船长的家，跟船长讨论这事。船长立刻就说："我就说肖天鹅这女人是个坏东西嘛。怎么能这样损人利己？我最恨人诬陷别人。这个忙我算帮定了。我非要把你们送走，气死她。我后天就要开船了。"

"但是怎么走呢？肯定有人查的。"尚小宁担心地说。

"以前都不查,只是我这里把关。要看一份证明,证明可以出去,保证回来。船员出去和回来人数也要求一样,照片和姓名都要对上,交给办公室就没事了。证明也要一道交。证明在公安局开。"

"这也看得蛮严的。"

"这还叫严?我们以前都受过正统培训和洗脑,变得绝对忠诚,人品也绝对可靠,还要考察好久,等结婚了,生孩子了,才能当船长,才能带船出去。要保证这个船长不走私,不偷渡,不贪污受贿,人要能回来,管理起来毫不留情。"

"那你帮了我们不是坏了你的人品?"尚小宁问。

"那这是没办法的事,都有孩子嘛,谁不想家?我当然对任何人也不会说的,这也是保全我自己。我不说,我们就秘密地走,谁知道啊。只是怎么秘密地走呢?船上又有那么多人,而且他们可能要派人来查。这就麻烦了。"

99

他们是躲在尚小宁的卧室里商量的,这时唐来妹却推开门,伸进头来说:"我有办法,但是你们要答应也带我走。带我走的话,我就说。"

"这个小鬼,还在偷听啊。"船长说。

"进来,我看看你有什么好主意。"白菊花说。

唐来妹推开门,走了进来。

"你小小年纪就不要家啦?不要你的妈妈、爸爸?"船长问。

"我这个家不好。我听尚阿姨说,她们那里的男孩子可以上学,可以当科学家,可以当领导,还能当宇航员和总统。说不定我可以当上总统呢。"

小家伙的一番话把大家逗笑了起来。

"那你的妈妈、爸爸舍不得你走呢?"船长说。

"舍得,我一出生时,他们就准备把我扔掉,又想把我弄死,现在他们就好比我死了。"

"哟,这个小家伙讲话不简单,将来也是个做大事的料。"尚小宁赞叹道。

"那你说说有什么好办法?"船长说。

"还有一个,我和你们一道去了,你们一个要做我的妈妈,一个要做我的爸爸。你们答应过的。"

这话把尚小宁和焦亮的脸都说红了。

"你瞎说什么啊。"尚小宁说。

"不是瞎说,是真的。如果我跟你们去了,你们又不要我了,把我扔了,那我还不是和现在一样?"小家伙说着哭了起来。

尚小宁赶紧安慰他:"好好,我答应,保证,发誓。好了不哭了,现在你讲讲你的办法吧。"

唐来妹破涕为笑，他说道："他们查，肯定是查你上船的人，对不对？到你船上搜，搜不到人他们就走了。然后你开船也走了，大家就都没事了。"

"那我们呢，我们在哪儿？"白菊花问道。

"我们在另一条船上。"

"怎么上去？"

"因为他们肯定只查这条船，我们这些人都住在这里，他们肯定都知道了。他们以为我们一定会坐这条船，我们偏偏不坐。"

"那别人的船也要那些证明，我们没有，一查不就暴露目标了？"尚小宁说。

100

"是这样的。船长先打听一下哪个船最近要到最近的一个国家,然后就托她们带上我们,说我有重病,我的妈妈、爸爸要带我去看病,这里治不好,那里有偏方。证明都在你这里。你正好有事要迟一两天开船。你会到那里把我们带回来的,不影响她们什么。"

"嗨哟,这个小家伙真不简单。好,就按你的办。"船长说。

"不过我们走的时候,最好在半夜,不要让人看见。"唐来妹说。

"那当然了,我们又不是傻瓜。"船长说。

一切安排妥当,到了这天入夜,船长开了门,把行李箱子等许多东西都堆在门口,关了灯和门,车子从车库开到自家的门前,正好遮住门。然后打开了车门,又借着微弱的路灯,把后备厢打开,把行李一件件地往里放。

就在她把车开到门前挡住门时,门的下半段被悄悄打开了,原来这里做成了活动门。这也是唐来妹的主意。人们都爬了出来,再爬上车。上了车后都躺在座位底下。焦亮也在这里过夜的。

到船长的行李装完了,船长上了车,开动了车子。直开到自己的船上,放下行李,又往回开,开到一半,拐到了另一个码头,直接上了她联系好的那条船。不过在上船前,船长先停了车,在仔细观察了周围没人后,叫他们都坐到座位上,别像逃跑的样子。孩子也要装出病重的样子,父母也要表现出焦急和伤心。

后来一切都很顺利,那条船上只有船长没睡,大家都睡了,她正在船的入口处等着,然后带他们到了船长室,说:"孩子病重,住我这里,安静,没人打搅。"这个船长也怕人家看见,只有她一个人知道,比较安全。毕竟这事不完全合法,但她也不能硬要人家拿出证明,人家没打算把人交给她，只是让她带着早到一天，治病救人。一切都与她无关。他们即使跑了，也不是她的事。

船长把他们都安排好了，就开车回去了。走到半路，她想想还是又到自己的船上，看看行李。她一看，果然行李都被动过了。难道她还会把人都藏到箱子里？也真够蠢的，还不如一个孩子。

不过现在她也更放心了，有人跟踪到这里，还进去翻了行李，这说明起码后来再没有人跟踪她，她的后来去向无人知道。她假装什么忘记了，把箱子这里弄弄，那里整整，又从怀里掏出什么放进去，把什么又拿出来，放进口袋里，然后才开着车子回了家。

第二天，那艘船就按时起航了，那个船长和这个船长通了话。船长这才一块石头落了地，浑身轻松得不得了。她很悠闲地度过了一天，在和家人作了热烈地告别后，她开车去了码头，把车子停在了码头的车库里，然后只身上了船。

101

船长到了自己的房间，还没来得及休息一下，突然手机响了，把她吓了一跳。这时会有谁来电话？不会是家里人，也不会是那条船上的人。一切都顺利，还要联系什么？一定是什么大事不好。船长的心一下子提到了嗓子眼，手都有些发抖，不敢接电话了。

她干咳了一下，镇定了一下情绪，才打开手机，一看是白菊花的电话。顿时心里定了不少，她会有什么事？还不是问她有没有开船？一般性的关心，当然也和那事有关。

可是她听了内容后，一下子又变得紧张起来。原来白菊花的男朋友黄花彩这几天有点神神秘秘的，经常找不到他。找到他时问他到哪去了，为什么关机，不回话，他又支支吾吾地说不周全。特别是今天早上，他又不见了，也联系不上。白菊花就到他家去，他肯定有相好的了，她准备在床上抓到他们俩。可是，还没到他家，就见他急匆匆地走了出来，白菊花赶忙闪在一边躲着，看他要到哪里？结果他七拐八绕，来到了码头，直接到了船上。他把一个什么证件给保安看了，保安就放他进去了。

难道是他的新欢在船上？白菊花也要上船。但保安拦住了她，她拿出了身份证，她已经办了一个，只有永久居民才能领到身份证。但是保安说不行。白菊花说，那前面那个人怎么进去了？保安说，人家是中央情报局的。她听了大吃一惊。难道她一直在跟一个特工谈恋爱？他怎么装得那么好？天啦。

白菊花一回想起来就对上号了，难怪有人举报焦亮、尚小宁。原来他就是特工。白菊花吓出了一身冷汗，幸亏她没把他们逃跑的计划跟他讲，讲了他们就都得死。想到这里，白菊花心里突突直跳。

但是，眼看着就要开船了，他怎么还不走？要是跟船走，发现了秘密可就不得了，船长一家也要遭殃了。白菊花这才急得赶紧打电话给船长。

船长听了这话，吓得魂不附体，赶紧冲出船长室。问人有没有看见一个男人上来？她们都说没看见。船长说："坏了，他是个恐怖分子，身上有炸弹。你们赶快给我搜，搜到了交给我。船推迟开。"

人们一下散开，到处去找了。不一会，听到有人喊，找到了找到了。船长冲了过去，只见这人身材高挑，人也漂亮，但身手不凡，所有的人都不是他的对手，果然是特工。

见船长来了，这人说："不搜到人我是不会走的，我跟你们出海。"船长这下急了，真恨不得手上有把手枪把他毙了。正在这时，有人捣她的背后，她一回头，是大副。大副对她使了个眼色，意思是大副从背后包抄过去，船长在前面吸引他注意力。船长暗暗点了点头。

102

船长说:"你说的话我听不懂,什么人不人的?你要搜什么人?"

"什么人你自己知道,不用我说。"

"我不知道,我只知道你是个恐怖分子,身上有炸弹。"

"嘿嘿,笑话了,你说我是恐怖分子,证据何在啊?我的身份可是有证据在手哦。"

"你那证件是假的,不然怎么能蒙混过关,混进来?"

"不信我给你看看。"黄花彩说着要掏口袋,并要往前走。说时迟,那时快,只见大副在他背后猛地举起灭火器,朝他头上砸去。黄花彩应声倒下,都没来得及哼一声。

船长全身都软了,大汗淋漓,靠在柱子上。大副走了过来,船长一把抱住她,说:"谢谢你,你救了大家的命。"然后喘了几口气,对大家说:"把他弄下船,我们走。"

几个船员把黄花彩抬下了船,交给了保安,又如此这般说了。保安很吃惊的样子。白菊花还在那,没走,见到黄花彩被人抬下船,脸上血肉模糊,痛哭了起来,她捶着自己的头。来不及喊救护车,她只拦了辆的士,就叫人把他抬了上去,哭着跟着车子走了。

几个船员回来了,问船长:"要不要报警?"

船长无力地说:"他们会报的。我们走吧。"

白菊花一路哭着,一只手搂着黄花彩,到了医院,医生马上展开了抢救。医生问是怎么受伤的?白菊花一愣,说是楼上掉下一块砖头砸的。医生正在给黄花彩做检查,黄花彩醒了,他见到白菊花正在哭,就吃力地问她:

"我这是在哪里,到底发生了什么事了?"

"你都不记得啦?楼上一块砖头掉了下来,砸到了你的头。"

"哦……"黄花彩虚弱地点着头,"我有话要对你说……你把头伸过来。"

"你现在什么也不要说。"白菊花哭着说。

"不,我一定要说……我不能带着谎言到棺材里去……我恐怕不行了……就让我说一次真心话……"黄花彩的嘴动着,听不见声音。白菊花只好把耳朵贴到他的嘴上,"我是特工……008……专门调查海内外人员的出入……那封举报信先转到了我的手里……上级并不知道……我之所以对你说……就是要你通知他们。"

"那你干吗还要去查?"

103

"反正我也要死了……说了也不怕……我是想借这个机会偷渡到外面去……因为你把外面说得太美好了……如果我找到她们……我也会装作没看见……但是我没有找到她们……这就说明她们还在这里……不过我假装非要找到她们,要跟她们出海……你要跟船长讲一声……叫她不要害怕……我不是坏人……"

"难道你就忍心丢下我吗?"

"是不忍心……我也很痛苦……但是我更渴望那人间的天堂……男人解放……若为自由故……二者皆可抛……"

"你就这么狠心,这么看重自由?爱情对你就没有意义吗?"

"有意义……意义重大……现在我后悔了……但是迟了……生命好宝贵……爱情好宝贵……可是我得不到它了……只有失去的东西才是最宝贵的……我死了以后……你不要伤心……再找个好的……好好过一辈子……我要最后说一句……我爱你……我来世还要和你结婚……"

"你会没事的,我等你,下辈子还嫁给你……呜呜……"白菊花哭着喊着。

可是,黄花彩已经什么都听不到了,他闭上了眼睛。心电图机子上的心跳也显示出了一条直线。白菊花放声大哭,怎么摇他他都不动。医生忙推开她,开始抢救。

再说尚小宁那边一切顺利,可是当他们来到船上时,船长却硬要他们吃下那种药,就是可以忘记女儿国的药。尚小宁说:

"我们不会讲的,以我的人格保证。"

"我也保证不会讲的,讲话算话。"唐来妹说。

"叫我讲我都不会讲,丢人。"焦亮说。

"那是你们的事,我的事就是叫每个外国人走的时候都要吃药。这又不费什么事,也不痛苦,又没副作用,为什么要为难我呢?这也是为大家好。你们要记得我们国家干吗呢?还会惹来杀身之祸。来,吃了,必须吃。为了你们,也为了我。"

尚小宁他们只好吃了。

船长在接他们上船时,只是淡淡地对船上人说,这是那个船上的人,下船看病。病没看好,要到这边来看。那个船暂时不到这边来,托我带他们一下,手续都在那边。以后她们再来接他们。船上人都没说什么,大家也没在意这件事,都各忙各的。

吃过药后,尚小宁仍然记得女儿国的事,她想,可能药性还没到,她不敢说没效果;如果说没效果,那不是招来杀身之祸?三人都不作声,静静地趴在栏杆上看海。船长忙去了。

突然,尚小宁叫了起来:

"这就是我来的那条渔船,我认得它,它还在,说明上面的人还活着……哎——"尚小宁大声叫了起来,挥着手向对方摇着。那条船已经很近了,可以看清上面人的面孔。

104

待近一些了,船上的人似乎也看到了尚小宁,认出了她,对她挥着手。尚小宁高兴得跳了起来。船长这时走了过来,问:

"什么事?这么高兴?"

"这就是带我们出海的船,我们从那船上掉下来的。他们还在,船还在,我太高兴了。"

"真的?我也为你们高兴。那这样,既然有人来了,你们就可以坐他们的船回去了,我们就不送了。"

"为什么?"尚小宁诧异地问。

"因为,你现在药性还没到,你还记得我们国家的事,我们和他们一旦见了面,你免不了要介绍一番,会说漏了嘴。你们坐小船过去,这时药就起作用了。他们问你,你只会说,我什么都不记得了,我只记得这条船救了我们。现在我又回来了。"

话说到这份上,尚小宁不好再说什么了。她伤心地落下泪来,一把抱住船长:

"我这辈子该怎么谢你?"

"不用谢,只要你过得好就行。"两人抱了很久,船长猛地退开尚小宁,说:

"永别了。"船长强忍着眼泪,又抱了抱唐来妹,"我会想你的。"最后握了握焦亮的手,"祝你们幸福。"

焦亮眼里也含着泪花,说:"谢谢你的大恩大德。"

"你只要对她好就行了。"

"我会的,你放心。"

"那好，你们走吧。我会想你们的。"船长转身喊着："放小船，送他们过去。"

尚小宁他们上了小船，到了海里后，回过头来和船长挥手告别，却见船长在擦眼泪。

上了中国的船后，尚小宁仍什么都记得。他们站在甲板上，目送着船远去。当女儿国的船开远了之后，唐来妹突然说："这个药是假的。"幸好船上的男女都到驾驶室去了，没听到。

"嘘——"尚小宁用食指挡着嘴唇说，"我们什么都不记得了，只记得那条船救了我们，现在送我们回来了。这样就安全了。"尚小宁又眨了眨眼睛。

"现在药起作用了，我什么都不记得了。"唐来妹做着鬼脸说。

三人都哈哈大笑起来。

一会儿，唐来妹又问："这里的男人可以上船？"

"你不是已经忘记了一切了吗？记住，以后看到的一切都是反过来的，懂吗？不要再大惊小怪的了。"

105

"嗯,知道了。"

船长收到了白菊花的电话,她告诉了她黄花彩的事。船长顿时觉得非常抱歉,怎么打了一个好人?

"那他现在怎么样了?"听白菊花讲话的口气,好像他还活着。要是打死了他,她一辈子都不会原谅自己的。

果然白菊花说:"现在没事了,正在休养。不过还要感谢你这一打。你不打,他就还在干特工,还要偷渡呢。现在他把以前的什么都忘了,已经不能工作了。但是他没有忘记生活,没有忘记爱情。"

"那就好。你不会嫌弃他吧?"

"怎么会呢?爱都来不及。"然后白菊花又压低了声音说,"他是装的。这事只有你知道啊,绝密。"

"哦,那当然了,我是什么人?什么时候喝你们喜酒?"

"快了快了。"

船长的心里充满了快乐,一切都是那么圆满。

The Women's Kingdom

1

Shang Xiaoning was despondent, for her transformation of herself had completely failed.

In a fit of intense anger, she divorced her husband upon discovering his infidelity. Subsequently, she grew increasingly dissatisfied with her own appearance. She couldn't help but think that if she were more beautiful and more adept at being alluring, she might have been able to entice and hold onto her husband. The woman who had seduced her husband must have been incredibly charming, perhaps even a vixen-like figure. Otherwise, how could she possess such irresistible allure that it made her husband abandon their home? Therefore, she resolved to transform herself. She decided to channel her sorrow into strength and embark on a journey of reinventing her own self.

The past was now firmly in the past. She was determined to find someone far superior to her unfaithful husband, someone who would make him seethe with envy. Fueled by her anger, she made the difficult decision to leave her son in the care of his father. At that moment, she couldn't bear the thought of seeing her son, nor her husband, and especially not that "vixen" who had caused so much heartbreak. She yearned to bide her time until she had truly made something of herself, until she was as radiant as the celestial beauty she envisioned. Only then would she go to see her son. And once she had built a happy and fulfilling home of her own, she would reclaim her son and give him the love and life he deserved.

Driven by her determination for a complete transformation, Shang Xiaoning rushed to several of the largest hospitals in the area. She firmly told the doctors that she wanted to undergo a series of plastic surgeries. However, the doctors advised her to consult a psychologist first, insisting that there was actually nothing wrong with her appearance as it was. Shang Xiaoning, though, was convinced that the doctors were simply being lazy. She suspected that they didn't want to perform the surgeries on her because the money she paid would go to the hospital's public funds instead of directly into their own pockets.

 In her unwavering pursuit, she then turned to the most heavily promoted private clinic. There, she splurged a staggering $200,000 on a comprehensive facial makeover. The procedures included getting double eyelids, having a nose job with fillers, undergoing skin rejuvenation treatments, reshaping her jaw to make it more pointed, removing her under-eye bags, getting rid of wrinkles, having eyebrows implanted, and eyelashes planted. All in all, she opted for an eight-item "diamond" cosmetic surgery package.

 The reason why the clinic recommended these eight "King Kong" surgery packages to her was that it was more cost-effective, time-saving, and convenient. By choosing this combination, she could endure the pain just once instead of suffering twice, turning the long-term torment into a short-lived ordeal and getting it all over with at once. It was somewhat like a divorce situation. Instead of enduring daily distress and misery, it was better to bring it to an immediate end. This had always been her consistent principle when it came to handling things

 However, the outcome of the operation was far from what she had hoped for. Instead of achieving the desired transformation, she found herself in a state of great suffering and hardly recognizable as herself. She endured the excruciating pain that followed the surgery, having to change the dressings every day and patiently waiting for the day when the stitches could be removed. But when she finally summoned the courage to look into the mirror, she let out a terrified scream. She simply couldn't believe the person staring back at her. The face in the mirror was so swollen that it was even larger than a pig's head, and her eyes were mere slits. The skin on her face had turned a bright, alarming red. Instead of the smooth, flawless appearance of a peeled egg that she had envisioned, it resembled the skin of a peeled cat, raw and grotesque.

She immediately quarreled with the doctor,the doctor was busy comforting her,saying that this is a normal reaction after the operation,one hundred days of injury,a knife cut on the hand will take seven or eight days to be good,not to mention so many operations together,what also have to have two months,such as swelling away?Shang Xiaoning immediately soft,feel their lack of self-restraint,impatient.You can't eat hot tofu when you're in a hurry,you have to calm down a little bit,put it down,maybe her marriage should be the same?

After the swelling on the face all subsided,Shangxiaoning's image in the mirror is like the earth after the melting of the snow,the beach with the retreating tide,the truth hidden inside is exposed in broad daylight,and it has become a miserable scene.Her eyes are big and small,the bridge of her nose is crooked,and her skin is a glaze,the color of soy sauce.If the husband saw this look,wouldn't he laugh?

2

    Can the house leak by the night rain,but the husband came back at this time, no, should be the ex-husband.Her ex-husband didn't recognize her anymore,thought the house was rented to someone else,and almost turned around and left.Thinking that something had happened to her son,she could not look at her face,so she asked about her son.The ex-husband took a step back and looked at her in horror.In a panic,she said that her face had been burned.The ex-husband then stared carefully at her face,and looked at her dress,this outfit should be familiar to him.When he had finished looking at the outfit,he shifted his eyes to her face again,and looked for a long time,but he was still skeptical.

    "Is everything okay with my son?"Shang Xiaoning shouted loudly.

    "No,no,I just came to pick up some CDS I left at home."The ex-husband seemed to be drunk awake from a nightmare and looked away.Now he was half convinced that it was his ex-wife,whose temper he knew.But he did not go about his business,and after a moment moved his eyes again to her face.Embarrassed and angered by this rare display of concern for her face,she said angrily,"Take what you want!"

    Her ex-husband fled in a panic, clutching the CDs tightly. Before stepping out of the door, he couldn't help but glance back at her face one more time and asked tentatively, "Are you all right?"

She frowned and replied, "I'm fine. And don't tell our son about this."

    After her ex-husband left, she forcefully slammed the door shut. Then, she slumped down onto the sofa and burst into bitter tears. She wept not just because of her disfigured face. It was also because her ex-husband had seen her in such an unsightly state. What's more, she felt that her dream of a future family had crumbled to pieces, and she was afraid that she would never be able to see her son again.

After crying,Shangxiaoning painful,she want to take up the weapons of law to get justice for themselves.Can we at least get some compensation for our son?There's a comfort in that.She grabbed her big straw hat,covered her face,and went out to look for the clinic.However,the clinic had changed,and she could not see anyone she had seen before,and would not know who to ask.It's been converted into a venereal disease clinic.Shang Xiaoning was there crying and making noise,and said his misfortune to everyone,people only looked at her sympathetically.A little nurse was kind and said to her,"It's not like we broke you,it's no use crying here,you might as well go to 315."

A word reminded Shangxiaoning,Shangxiaoning non-stop to find 315,but she can not take any evidence to prove that she is in whose hands to do the operation.315 advised her to file a report,saying that these people might be crooks.Shangxiaoning went to report the case again,the police made a record,asked her the characteristics of those people,Shangxiaoning can only think of a sentence to say.She didn't think to keep a hand.How could she have bothered to look at them?She could only say that it was male,female,old,young,and the others were all blurred,and she could not recognize them even if she met them on the road.

Shang Xiaoning returned home,feel the end of the world.She did not suffer,but mainly felt wronged and played,just like her marriage.If she hadn't been cheated and paid too much,she wouldn't have been as miserable as she is.It was not just the failure of the surgery,but the disappearance of the dream,and she could not start again.Shang Xiaoning took out the white wine at home and drank a very drunk.She doesn't usually drink.She gets drunk.All this wine belonged to the ex-husband,who didn't take it with him in the divorce.

3

    Shang Xiaoning woke up to drink,drink and drunk,until there is no white wine at home.Shang Xiaoning woke up for the last time,lying on the sofa,not knowing what to do in the future.Before and her husband opened a shop,but divorce to divide property,her family has two houses,just a set of one.She sold the store for half the money.Now that the money was half gone,she felt there was no point in remaining in this world.So she began to write a will,giving the rest of the money and the house to her son,no one else can take it.Then,after dark,Shang Xiaoning went out.She had been afraid to leave her house during the day for months,but now she could finally walk the streets openly.After her operation,in addition to changing medicine and removing stitches,she needed to wear a big straw hat to the clinic,and she hid at home,did not cook,and called the shop next door to send food every day.

    Now she could hold her head high and be a free man.However,this is to the death before the freedom and free and easy,Shang Xiaoning can not help but smile miserably.Farewell to this world of devils;Goodbye,horrible people. Shang Xiaoning again think of son,she very reluctant.How much did she want to see her son one last time?But her appearance of not being human and not being a ghost will not frighten her son?Shang Xiaoning cruel,let her son leave a good impression.Shangxiaoning tears while walking,and then the car came to the seaside.

    Shang Xiaoning avoided the busy bay,where many people were swimming. Shang Xiaoning walked away along the beach,into the darkness.As she walked into the lonely darkness,she became afraid again.The roar of the sea and the endless darkness seemed to conceal some great danger,and all the invisible things were transformed into an invisible demon king,who was waiting silently for her arrival with his mouth wide open and his eyes like copper bells.Shang Xiaoning hair all over the body stand up.

The courage to die and the fear of illusion cannot cancel each other out. Fear comes from the instinctive desire to live,and death is the reason to yield to pressure and seek relief.In the battle between instinct and reason,instinct has the absolute advantage.Otherwise,why would a man want a femme fatale rather than a cauliflower?There is only one Zhuge Liang in the world,his wife is very ugly,but there are few men who like the inner beauty of women.

Shang Xiaoning stopped his pace,shrank his shoulders,and suddenly turned around,ready to go back.But when I looked up,the swimmers seemed to have all disappeared,and the darkness ahead was more terrible.That's when she knew she'd gone too far.She looked around,but there was not a little hole to hide in.Instinct needed a little hole to save her,and she was almost frantic.

Suddenly,Shang Xiaoning found that there seemed to be a light on the distant horizon,and the light was the hope she instinctively desired.Instinct drove her to use all her strength,like a strong clockwork,she screamed wildly,desperate to run towards the light.

Gradually,the lights became more and more obvious,as if it were a village. After approaching the village,Shang Xiaoning's heart settled a little,she stopped the pace,gasping for breath,the internal organs were pulled into a ball.After a long rest,she walked towards the nearest light.

When she got to the house,Shang Xiaoning stopped.What was she doing?Ask someone for help?Tell someone about your misfortunes?Would someone feel sorry for her,understand her,put her up,and then she would go home the next day?No,no,no.She's not going back.When the desire to live is satisfied,instinct is relieved and begins to retreat,and reason reasserts itself.

4

    The fear and running all the way made Shang Xiaoning feel funny,and she still had to consider her serious life problems.There was a huge rock not far from the house,and Shang Xiaoning walked up to the end,and then sat down.She looked down at the dark,white,roaring sea and closed her eyes.She began to fear again,the sea was like a hell with its mouth wide open,and in a moment it could chew her to the bone.She hesitated,she grew up so big,suffered so much,walked so much,just for this moment?She was a little reluctant.

    Then came the footsteps behind,the Shang Xiaoning scared a shudder,the desire to survive immediately seized her,she fumbled on the ground with her hand,touched a stone,immediately hold it tightly in her hand.She looked back,see is an old im(old aunt),Shang Xiaoning spit out a breath,tight heart,immediately relaxed down.

    "What are you doing here so late?"Asked old Im.

    Shang Xiaoning said nothing.

    "You won't jump into the sea,will you?"

    Shang Xiaoning still said nothing.

    "People often come here to jump into the sea.I also saved a little sister yesterday,and she is still in my house.My house is just over there."Old Im pointed to the nearest light here,that is,the house that Shang Xiaoning ran toward it desperately.

    Shang Xiaoning looked towards the house,see a figure in the room shaking.So,sitting in that house,you should be able to see here.Shang Xiaoning sighed a sigh,is really people even death have to have someone to interfere.

    "Would you like a cup of tea at my house?"

Shang Xiaoning did not move.

"Why not?Did you fight with your husband?Women don't want to."

"Well,it's much worse than that.We're separated."

"So what?I'm the only one in my house,and that girl.I can't sleep anyway,so you can tell me your story before you die.I'll tell you mine,too.It is easier for me to jump into the sea.The sea is at my door."

Old Imu's last sentence aroused Shang Xiaoning's interest.An old woman living alone must have greater suffering,but why should she not die?Shang Xiaoning ready to go with her,but she suddenly remembered,the old woman should not be a human trafficker?Sell her to a peasant ?This she would rather be the wife of a countryman,in a place where women resources are scarce,a woman is a treasure,will not be choosy,and will never be abandoned.Thought of here,Shang Xiaoning could not help but smile.

"You don't have to go to my house,I'll listen to you here."Tell me,what's the big deal?"Old Im said,sitting next to Shang Xiaoning.

Shang Xiaoning but embarrassed,she concluded that the old Im is not a bad person.Bad guys are always trying to get something done,like her cosmetic surgery.If old Im wanted to sell her,he'd be talking big.Shang Xiaoning stood up and said:"Go,go to your house."

5

Shang Xiaoning also need to find a person to talk about their suffering. She can't say it in front of acquaintances, relatives, and even less in front of parents. Parents will be sad, others will laugh or gloat, what is more despised than a woman's marriage is not secure, abandoned by her husband? If it does not happen to you, no one can experience the taste of the individual, and everyone can say that it is her responsibility, what is not gentle enough, not beautiful enough, will not cultivate love, will not cook to keep her husband's stomach, in fact, nothing.

When she fell in love, she was such a person now, why did her husband chase her so hard? She was worse then than she is now, a pampered girl who did not know how to be considerate, housework, and love her husband, and now she is a better, more perfect woman. At that time, she was very confident that all the men in the world had changed their hearts, her husband would not, and her marriage was ironclad, all because she was a good woman.

However, everything changes, it has nothing to do with her. Men can have aesthetic fatigue for women, but why don't women have aesthetic fatigue for men? This is just a man's excuse for his womanizing. You give him an 18-year-old girl today, and another one tomorrow, and he's just as tired of today's girl. This is precisely, the man married began to flower heart, women married began to feel at ease; When a man marries, he goes from slave to general; when a woman marries, she goes from princess to slave. General, of course, the woman behind is Han Xin, the more the better.

Sometimes distress to a stranger is easier to say, no one knows you, after listening, talk a few words, show sympathy, and then go their own way.

Shang Xiaoning followed the old Yimu came to her house. It was an old wooden house with a living room,a bedroom and a kitchen.The doors and windows were open,and in the bedroom sat a girl.This must be the girl who tried to kill herself,right?Shang Xiaoning saw her have a feeling like seeing relatives. She forgot the horror of her own face,and the girl showed no surprise when she saw her.A change in appearance only affects acquaintances.Who knows what a stranger really looks like?Just think she was born ugly.

Old im poured tea to Shang Xiaoning,Shang Xiaoning drank it,and told his story.The girl called White Chrysanthemum,also told her own story.She came out from her hometown to work,lived with her boyfriend for 2 years,and beat the fetus for him,but when she was lying in bed and suffering physically and mentally,she felt that she killed the child,her boyfriend disappeared for a week,and her mobile phone was turned off.Later her boyfriend appeared,she argued with him,and finally,the boyfriend said the truth:"Look at your breasts,like a man,who is interested in you?"White Chrysanthemums are humiliated!Extremely humiliated!It is like meeting freeloaders,not giving money after eating,and saying:"What rotten food you have!"So,White Chrysanthemum to die,to make her boyfriend guilty for a lifetime.It was his words that killed her!

"Well,he doesn't feel guilty.You died for nothing.If he were guilty,he wouldn't say things like that."Old Im told them own story.A story that could not be simpler.On her wedding night,the groom ran away because she was a stone girl(born without a vagina)!She lived on her own all her life,working for other people,doing some manual work,collecting and selling seafood on the beach.

6

"It's good to be alone,comfortable.I didn't want a man.I lived till now. Women who come here to jump into the sea are for men.How many have I saved?These women are stupid.We women are not made for a man.We are better off without him."

Yes,Shang Xiaoning listened to this,suddenly feel that she that things are nothing,not for a man?It's not worth risking your life.And he wouldn't think her life was worth anything,even though she thought it was a treasure.No wonder the White Chrysanthemums don't die.That's how it works.

Then the three women opened up to talk,until the east hair white,only to squeeze into a big bed to sleep.

Wake up,Shang Xiaoning found the old Im gone,White Chrysanthemum is still sleeping sweet.She got busy and ran to the kitchen,where she saw old Im cooking.Shang Xiaoning is very embarrassed to help old Im do something.In fact,there is nothing to do,old Im has cooked porridge,fried the small salted fish.

Shang Xiaoning found this meal extremely delicious. She wasn't sure whether it was because her mood had suddenly improved or the food was truly that savory. At that moment, Shang Xiaoning fell in love with the life here. No wonder White Chrysanthemum had given up on dying and was even reluctant to leave this place. Life here was truly like a fairyland, free from all the troubles in the outside world. Shang Xiaoning regarded this place as her home and started to follow Old im around, helping with various tasks. She hadn't brought much money with her, so she knew she could only work hard. By earning more money, she wouldn't have to freeload off Old im.

Three women dig in the sand of the beach for conch and shellfish;After the tide of the sea,many pits are left too late to escape the fish,shrimp,crabs and so on,they picked up,the big will be taken to the hotel to sell money,the small to eat. Every morning,after two low tides in the afternoon,enough for them to be busy for a while.The rocks were also covered with oysters and mussels,the size of nail clippings,and the larger ones they used shovels to cook soup.

    Shang Xiaoning is willing to spend a lifetime to live such a life.Here,they only work hard for a living,a completely primitive life,sleep when they are sleepy,eat when they are hungry,there are no mirrors,makeup,fashion,shopping,TV,advertising and other fashionable things,and there is nothing outside that can control their lives.Shang Xiaoning forget her face,she is ready to go back in a few days to get some money,put home here,here for a lifetime.Old Im is right,eating,sleeping is the foundation of life,love is full of sustenance.

    But Shang Xiaoning has not had time to carefully experience this beautiful life,shi was persuaded to board the White Chrysanthemum fishing boat-fishing at sea.White Chrysanthemum see fishing boat back to play so many fish and shrimp,it is very envious,must go to the fishing boat to experience life.Fishing boats won't take her because women don't go out to sea.White Chrysanthemum finally find a couple of fishing boats out to sea,said to help them work without money,is to come up with the sea.Fishing boat agreed,White Chrysanthemum will drag Shang Xiaoning to go.

    Two people made a good preparation,with food and drink,but also bought a lot of seasickness medicine,did not go on board to eat.Fortunately,they were so prepared that they did not vomit all over the ship.The fishing boat was far less fun than they had expected.The boat was rocking so badly in the sea that they could hardly stand.They had taken too much medicine for seasickness.

7

To the fishing ground,is the net at night,the net at night,two people can not do,a little fresh and stimulating sense is not,two people wearing life jackets,half asleep and half awake to work mechanically.If they had not begged for free work in the first place,they would have gone to sleep and cared nothing.

By the end of the busy,the day is also light,two people desperate to hide in the cabin to sleep.Tthey don't know how long it took for the two of them to wake up with a great shaking,and before they knew what was happening they were thrown to the ground.Shang Xiaoning instinctively wanted to catch a thing,but there was nothing to catch.The White Chrysanthemum screamed,holding its head,like a robber coming.Shang Xiaoning to find a chance,a grasp of White Chrysanthemum,White Chrysanthemum also like grasping a lifesaving straw to her,two people tightly hug together.

Then the two rolled around on the ground like a piece of corn.However,the increased weight provided some stability,and the two of them formed a cylindrical shape,which was easier to roll and reduced the collision,and although they were now black and blue,they did not feel pain.

They remained in this position until the shaking subsided.The two sat up and looked at each other.

"At first I thought it was an earthquake,but then I thought it was on a ship."White Chrysanthemum said.

"It must have been a storm."Shang Xiaoning said,and then started up again,"Oh,where are they?It didn't fall into the sea,did it?"Shang Xiaoning said to rush out.

Ran to the deck and saw that everyone was still there,the woman was working on the cable,and the man was in the cab.The two breathed a sigh of relief.Shang Xiaoning said to the woman:"Just scared me to death,is there a storm?"

The woman nodded thoughtfully.Shang Xiaoning looked up,how terrible the sky is,how terrible the rolling dark clouds are like a hundred thousand soldiers,will soon be forced to the front of the eyes,pressure people can not breathe;The waves are like countless monsters jumping with sharp knives,like at any time to tear the ship apart.The ship is still shaking badly,Shang Xiaoning has been used to this kind of shaking for a few days,otherwise it is not stable.

"Shall we hurry back,have we caught all the fish?"Shang Xiaoning said in horror.She already regrets getting on the boat.

"Yes,but the ship can't sail against the wind."

"So what?"

"Let's follow the wind and hide somewhere."

"Is there a place to hide?

The woman nodded.

Shang Xiaoning rest assured,fishermen must have experience,otherwise they can not get out of the sea.

8

"Let's help if there's anything you need."

"You'd better go back to your cabin,or you'll fall into the sea."

Shang Xiaoning looked at the White Chrysanthemum White Chrysanthemum nodded.The two men went back into the cabin.Before they could catch their breath,the violent shaking began again,and this time with experience,they immediately hugged each other and rolled to the ground.

The sky is dark,the earth is shaking,and the two people are like beans in the sieve,rolling with the master's hand,without a little of their own propositions.

Shang Xiaoning concluded that he can not go back this time,her mind repeatedly flashed the image of her son.Why is she getting a good divorce?If her husband has an affair,it is good to have an affair,at least she can live a stable life and be with her son every day.Plastic surgery failed to fail,looking for what to die?Just be alive.Ben and Old Im are alive and well.On what ship?This White Chrysanthemum is killing people.But also blame themselves not firm,is not on board,she can not...

It seems that after thousands of years,tens of thousands of years,they have forgotten to eat,sleep,forget that there is other life in the world,and only hope that the storm will pass quickly.

When the ship was restored to normal,the two men also collapsed,unable to lie,extremely tired and excited,and unable to sleep.After a long time,Shang Xiaoning said:"No,I want to go up and see,I don't know how they are."

"I went to see them too.They are like relatives now."

With difficulty,the two women climbed up,supported the walls of the ship,and went to the deck.The deck was empty,and they were on their way to the bridge to look for it, when the ship suddenly tilted and they both fell into the sea.

Shang Xiaoning in a flurry of confusion, after drinking several mouthpieces of sea water, and surfaced at the sea, she remembered that she was wearing a life jacket. Good thing she did, or she'd be dead. She can't swim. But she's pretty much dead now, and no one's gonna save her, and even if they do, can she wait for that moment? She is like a child's ant, at any moment may be ground to powder.

Suddenly, Shangxiaoning saw a red dot not far away, that is the White Chrysanthemum! Shang Xiaoning a burst of excitement, like seeing the lifesaving personnel, she shouted desperately, waving her hands, White Chrysanthemum also saw her, also excited. The two women rowed towards each other on all fours.

Soon they met in triumph at sea, and held each other tightly. They remembered the boat, and when they looked for it, they found that although it was not far from them, there was no one on it. They rowed as hard as they could toward the boat, but the boat always seemed to keep an equal distance from them, never to be approached. Both of them began to break down. They had no strength to swim anymore. After a day without food or sleep, they began to lose consciousness.

When Shang Xiaoning woke up, found himself in a very small room, according to the structure of the room and the feeling of shaking, coupled with a strong smell of fish, Shang Xiaoning concluded that she was in a boat, she saw all around the unfamiliar faces, knew that she was saved, and instantly shed tears. People brought water and bread, Shang Xiaoning felt that he was too thirsty, too hungry, busy eating and drinking.

She was told to take a fresh water bath in the bathroom and change her clothes.

9

When Shang Xiaoning recovered enough to speak,she told her story.As she talked,she thought of the White Chrysanthemums and asked them if they had saved another girl.They said no.Shang Xiaoning cried again.

"Hey,my daughter can't cry lightly."

Hearing this strange talk,Shang Xiaoning was taken aback,she found that it was a woman about her age.Shang Xiaoning look around again,just found her side are full of women

"You all go to work.I'll stay with you."The woman said to the other women.

Looking at the woman to leave the figure,Shang Xiaoning asked puzzled:"Is not the woman does not let the sea?"

'It's the men who won't let go to sea!"

'What?Shang Xiaoning clearly remember that they want to go on the fishing boat people do not take them,is it really her mind is bad,remember wrong?

Women said"Men aboard taboo.When you think about it,there's nothing they can do on board,and they make things worse."

'You have no men on board?

"No."

'And the captain?"Shang Xiaoning look around again,this is not a small ship,should belong to a class of ocean fishing boats.For ocean-going fishing boats,Shang Xiaoning is to the seaside to know.She can't say exactly,but it is big enough to withstand big storms,can hold a lot of fish,can bring a lot of food,use.

"I am."The woman said with a smile.

"Oh,that's remarkable."Shang Xiaoning sincerely admire.She thought of the female conductor,the purser,the minister,"I'm not cut out for it."

"Women should make a difference."

Shang Xiaoning listened,thought and nodded.She fell in love with the female captain.

"I'm not talking about you,you see you,for a man,almost ruined yourself."What matters to a woman is not her appearance,but her career.You've got a career,a house,a car,and men?What kind of man can't you find?"

Yes,the words of the female captain,is simply a wisdom,hit the key,make Shang Xiaoning suddenly wake up.Shang Xiaoning lamented that he did not meet the female captain earlier.

"So I am very strict with them,do not allow emotional entanglements to affect the work and career,and do not allow star chasing."Look at me on this boat,there's not a single star picture,those pretentious things are not interesting."

Shang Xiaoning kept nodding,feel that the female captain's words are very reasonable,in fact,think that it is such a thing,feelings and life plans to compare,count nothing.But she would not have been able to listen to this before,because she had been frustrated and had lived on the coast for some time,and now the lady captain summed up the meaning and found it incisive.

10

Shang Xiaoning thought of those people who had just seen. They all called each other "sister, sister". Including the female captain, they all had short hair in its natural color. None of them wore heavy makeup, and their skin wasn't meticulously maintained either. It was hard to describe, but they were like Chinese women thirty years ago. However, even back then, women would make use of all available means to adorn themselves. Even the heroines in model operas would style a row of bangs on their foreheads to make themselves look more beautiful.

These women were truly unadorned, exuding a sense of resilience and composure that left Shang Xiaoning feeling refreshed and invigorated. She couldn't help but think of the "Iron Girls Teams" from the past. When she was a child, she had always been filled with admiration for those capable girls. Perhaps it was due to the trials and tribulations they had weathered that these women had become more unpretentious and less delicate. Or maybe it was the influence of the female captain's leadership style, making everyone else follow suit. Shang Xiaoning really took a liking to this way of life. Apart from the demands of work, women here could be completely at ease and casual.

"Take a rest while I go and get busy.""Stop by my house when the boat lands.I like to make friends,it is not easy to find a friend in the sea,fate.Mainly I like your temperament,quiet.When you don't want to live in my house anymore,I'll send you back."

Shang Xiaoning heard someone speak of her in this way for the first time. She had always felt that she wasn't gentle enough, feminine enough, or skilled at being coquettish. In the past, if someone had praised her like that, she would have thought they were being sarcastic. But this time, it was a woman, the female captain, who was saying these things to her.

The female captain got up and left. Shang Xiaoning had some bread, drank some water, ate some fruit, and then fell asleep. After that, she didn't see the female captain again. Although Shang Xiaoning woke up several times, she was too lazy to move and just lay there, lost in her thoughts. By the time the captain reappeared, the ship had already docked, and it was already dark outside.

"Here are your clothes. They've been washed. Change them." The female captain held a stack of clothes in her hand and handed it to her.

Shang Xiaoning took her clean clothes, very grateful, and said: "Thank you, thank you." Since the female captain told her to change, there was no reason for her to keep wearing other people's clothes.

The captain went out for a while, and then came in when she had changed. Looking at the clothes Shang Xiaoning was wearing, the female captain frowned slightly: "How can your clothes be like this?"

Shang Xiaoning quickly looked down to check her clothes. She didn't button wrong, and there was nothing out of place. She looked at the female captain in doubt: "...It's OK..."

"No, I mean, why are your clothes so tight? How ugly is it to have your boobs completely exposed? And your pants, they're so tight, you can see the groove. ."

Shang Xiaoning looked at the captain. She really wore a neckerchief. So did the rest of the crew.

"Exposed?" Shang Xiaoning heard for the first time that people said she wore revealing clothes.

Shang Xiaoning looked down at her clothes again. No, this couldn't be called revealing? She was wearing a plain floral shirt, but it was tucked in at the waist and fitted perfectly; She touched her pants and buttocks again. The pants were a little tight. They were jeans. Skinny jeans were all the rage these days. This was Shang Xiaoning's favorite clothes. She just wore it ready to jump into the sea to die. Since she didn't die, and she lived at old Im's house, she had no clothes to change, so she just wore old Im's clothes. Anyway, it was summer, and it was convenient.

11

Old Im has a lot of clothes,enough to wear,White Chrysanthemum is also wearing old Im's clothes.Did she always save suicidal people,keep them for a while,and then pack extra clothes?Shang Xiaoning thought,should be like this. Later,her clothes were washed and she did not wear them.She wanted to say goodbye to her old life and did not want to look at her old clothes any more.

Before going to sea this time,White Chrysanthemum advised her to wear her own clothes,don't make it like begging.

"Then I don't have enough clothes to change."Shang Xiaoning said.

"You can't wear your own clothes during the day and old Im's clothes in bed,and use them as pajamas?"

And then they actually wore it on the boat.To their own clothes dirty,wash at night,dry,wear during the day,a set of clothes is enough.

But since the arrival of the fishing ground,this law has been disrupted,there is no day,night,dirty clothes for clean,also lazy to wash,really can not wash.They wore their own clothes,day and night,until they were thrown into the sea.They're so tired,they fall asleep,and what else is there to wash or change?You can't change it.It's all dirty.

If she hadn't been thrown out to sea,soaked in seawater,rubbed automatically by a storm,and rinsed for days in an endless array of the world's largest washing machines,her clothes would have stinked.Now,after natural cleaning and artificial cleaning,this dress has restored its true color and is emitting a unique fragrance.

Shang Xiaoning thought he heard the voice of her grandmother who had passed away.Grandma was against her wearing such a dress.She thought it was indecent for a woman to have her breasts curved out and her pants wrapped around her body.The female captain doesn't look too old,just like herself.Why is she so old?

Shang Xiaoning recalled the characteristics of the ship,feel that the female captain is too feudal,this kind of clothing is also called tight?Did she pass out when she saw girls wearing suspenders,tank tops,mini-skirts,shorts that showed a little butt underneath,pants that hung in the crotch,pants that exposed the butt ditch when they bent over,and three-point outfits?No wonder,probably all day floating at sea,busy work,not home,not shopping,do not know what era is now. Shang Xiaoning also did not have time to shop,but she kept the shop,no matter when,look at the people coming and going on the street,will also notice the dress up of these girls.

"That's what you're wearing.It's a fancy dress.Stand in front of a man more than that?Okay,let's go.One person,one habit."

The captain took her off the ship.The lady captain had already picked up her car from the garage on the shore,drove over,and stopped at the dock to take her to her house.Shang Xiaoning did not even have time to take a look at this strange place,on the car.In the car Shang Xiaoning want to see the night scene on the street,but the female captain drove the car fast,almost to become a racing car,the scenery outside the window are spent into a piece,Shang Xiaoning heart also mentioned in a voice.

12

The car stopped in front of a small building."This is my house."'said the female captain proudly.Shang Xiaoning got off the car,the female captain put the car into the garage,and then led Shang Xiaoning into the home.

Open the door is a very handsome young man,he tied a horse tail,chin with a long beard,lip beard cut with the upper lip,also wearing a neckerchief,Shang Xiaoning was surprised.He was also wearing pink pajamas,and he was gentle and shy,a typical white horse prince and new dood man.Shang Xiaoning almost fainted,fainted in this myth before.

Shang Xiaoning like flying clouds,unreal into this luxurious home.The two children rushed at them,and the captain put her arms around them and kissed them for a long time.The man poured them tea,unpacked the captain's travel bag,took the contents out and put them away,took the dirty clothes to the washing machine on the balcony,and then went into the kitchen.

"Is this your son?"

"No,it's my husband.His name is Wen Biyu."

Shang Xiaoning stared at the female captain in disbelief:"He seems to be much smaller than you."

"Much younger,18 years younger.He was 18 when we got married."

'What?

"I didn't get married until I was 36 because I wanted to have a career."

"And still get married?"

"Why can't you get married?Didn't I say that?With a career,a house,a car,what kind of man can't find?"

"But women are too big to have children..."

"I froze my eggs when I was 20 years old and planned ahead.I am very career-minded,why would I hold my family and children back?"

"What did you say?What egg'freezes'?"

"You don't know that?You are so ill-informed.No wonder you had a baby so early."

"I wasn't young to have a baby.I was 28."

"Isn't that early?I didn't graduate college until I was 24.I had to be a sailor for five years,first mate for five years,and captain for two years before I could get married.Every level up,the competition is very fierce,and they have to go through rigorous examinations,written tests and operations.Not everyone can be a captain.Many women are sailors all their lives."

"So they never marry?"

"No,no,there is only one chance for the exam,if you can get it,if you can't get it,then they can get married."The marriage leave is three years,including maternity leave.I'm gonna do something big anyway,so I put my eggs in the egg bank and freeze them.If I don't pass,it doesn't matter,then I'll have my own baby,not those frozen eggs."

"What is an egg?"

13

"Hey,the man's that is the common people say testicles.We're talking about a woman's actual eggs.Don't we have a uterus inside us?That's where children grow up;And the ovaries,where the eggs grow.How do you grow a baby without eggs?Eggs are tiny,tiny"eggs"that we can barely see with the naked eye.We have two ovaries,and they alternate each month.Ovulation is the'laying of eggs',which are laid one month and another the next.Sometimes they go together and they give birth to twins.But these twins are not very similar,in fact,they are ordinary brothers and sisters."Identical twins are one egg that splits into two people."

"Huh?Do we lay eggs?"

"Why not?Every woman lays an egg,just like a hen,except that instead of laying it outside,it goes into the womb,where it grows into a child."

"Oh--that's right,so...Why do you have to be married for an egg to grow into a child?"

"Isn't it the same thing?Without a rooster,the eggs laid by the hens will not hatch into chicks."

"Yes,yes,yes,ha ha ha...You're not a doctor.How do you know so much?"

"It's common sense,we all learn it in school.How could I have saved my eggs without knowing that?"

"Ouch,we didn't learn that.But I didn't go to school for years,my family was too poor...Weren't you married at the time?How can eggs grow into children?"

"This is test-tube baby ah,in the outside,and then planted in the belly."But I used fresh eggs from my body,not frozen eggs,and I'm not that old yet.You don't have eggs until you're 50.After the old hen has laid eggs for a few years,she cannot lay them."

"Oh,you talk funny.that What if we didn't have this technology before?"

"After college,get married,have kids,and then work when the kids go to kindergarten."

"Hey,how do we know that?When the time comes to know love,marriage,do not know such arrangements.Are these all stipulated by your work unit?"

"Maybe,different professions may have different rules."

"Therefore,it is good or bad to have units;But people who do business like us are tied to business.If you don't do it,you'll lose your money.It's best to make money during the New Year holidays,and you can't rest if you want to."

"Not the same?Let's go out to sea,what weekend,what festival?"

"But you are very happy with such a good husband."

Shang Xiaoning a little sour,feel that fate is too unfair,she herself is like a flower,but found a husband,she would like to live in peace,but her husband will play a trick.Alas,people are more popular than men.How is the life of this female captain so good?But did the man really love her?It's just a woman's bread and butter,right?You can get something for nothing,be a gigolo.It's fashionable to find a rich old woman,to be kept,and then to find yourself a mistress.

14

In Shang Xiaoning secretly hurt,suffering from not so much envy as jealousy,the food is good.Wen Biyu smiled and called them to eat.Shang Xiaoning picked up the rice bowl and tasted the extraordinary delicious dishes that she couldn't even make herself,and couldn't help but praise Wen Biyu.

Wen Biyu smiled proudly,and the female captain looked very satisfied.

"Come,come,drink."The female captain has poured Shang Xiaoning a full glass of white wine.

"I don't drink."Shang Xiaoning busy decline.

"What woman doesn't drink?No,you must."

"I really don't drink,you two drink."

"He doesn't drink.I won't let him."

"I never drink,and she says it's not like a man to drink.I listen to her anyway."Wen Biyu replied,with a well-behaved look.

Shang Xiaoning think this man everything is good,is too soft,not like a big man.Shang Xiaoning had to drink hard scalp.

"Well,I haven't said my name yet,and you mustn't call me captain,that's what subordinates call me."Now that we're friends,you still say my name.My name is Yan Peanut,not pickled peanut,but serious Yan."

"Haha,that peanut is a"peanut"to eat?It's a funny name."

"Hey,it's just peanuts.There are several meanings in this.My mother's last name is flower.Of course I am Peanut.In addition,my brothers and sisters are"inserted peanuts",that is,a boy,a girl,separated,very regular.I'm the fourth.My name is Peanut.In addition,the vitality of peanuts is very strong,and the fruit is in the ground,not empty,very real.That's who I am."

"So it seems a very good name indeed.Like the name,it is also said that the word is also like a person.My handwriting is very big and very sketchy."

"Perhaps careful herringbone is always written in a proper way,and odd herringbone is also written in a strange way."

"I have good handwriting,too.The teacher praised me."The two children were also eating merrily,and the older one interposed.They also wear bibs. Anyway,all the people Shang Xiaoning saw were wearing bibs.

"You are very good and capable."Shangxiaoning kua child,can not help but think of his son,a tender feeling makes her carefully look at them.

"Your daughter is so beautiful,just like Daddy."

"No,he's not a daughter,he's a son.That's the daughter."

"No,I mean her."Shang Xiaoning pointed to the children with braids and dresses around them.

"Yes,he is the son,and this is the daughter."The captain pointed to the boyish child beside her.

'What?Shang Xiaoning couldnt believe his ears,she looked at Wen Biyu. Now even the son is dressed like this,and the female captain and daughter are like men,which makes Shang Xiaoning very uncomfortable.

They all wore the neckerchief.

15

"I think it's better for boys to act like boys."Shang Xiaoning said carefully, while glancing at Wen Biyu.

"Yes,I think so too.A man should do his duty.The atmosphere is so bad that I don't even put on TV in my family because I'm afraid the ads will poison my children."

Speaking of this,Shang Xiaoning is not good to say anything else,had to lower his head to eat vegetables.The female captain advised Shangxiaoning drink,Shangxiaoning had to drink hard scalp.The captain herself drank a few glasses of wine,and then,lighting a cigarette,put her hand on Wen Biyu's shoulder and said,"I have a good husband,skillful and beautiful."Many people envy me.I'm happy.But I don't treat him badly.I go out to make money,and I give it to him when I come back.He is good,the family does not want me to worry about,he is also very hard,pulling two children is not easy.But I'm also worthy of him.I'm decent on the outside.Here,cheers."

Shang Xiaoning and the female captain dry cup,"I want to live a day like you,dead also close my eyes."

"There will be,you are better than me,you will find a good man."You'll find it when you dry this one."

"Well,I beg of you,do it!But I would advise you to drink less alcohol and try not to smoke.They are not good for you."

"Ha ha,I am smoke,wine and tea,there is no way,not to drink at sea."But I don't gamble or prostitute."

After a pause,the captain said,"Your long hair should be cut off.What would you look like with a horse's tail?"

Shang Xiaoning is most disgusted with women who cut short hair,think that women should keep long hair,and can not tolerate women who cut men's heads or even shave their heads.

Shang Xiaoning although those days at home every day drunk,but she still will not drink,after a few cups,the head dizzy,the female captain helped her to the guest room to sleep on a big bed,"this is your room,you live here,love to live how long to live."

Shang Xiaoning lay down in bed and soon fell asleep.

Shang Xiaoning woke up at noon the next day.The lady captain is golfing and won't be back until late.The kids are at kindergarten.Shangxiaoning wash up,Wen Biyu has put out the meal,call her to eat.This makes Shang Xiaoning very embarrassed.

"I'll do it.I'm sorry to have to wait on you all the time."

"What is it?Used to it,it doesn't matter."

"That's very kind of you.I do all the housework in my family."

"Is it?The man's eyes widened."People like you are rare."

'What?Shang Xiaoning laughed,"Talent like you is really rare."

"No wonder,when I was young,my father taught me to be sensible,to be considerate of women,to manage the house,and to let women do a good job outside."

"Your dad was a really good dad.Why can't I meet these good men?"

"Yes,although the concept has changed,but my family is very traditional,my family is also very traditional."

16

"It's best that way,when two people care for each other and are considerate of each other,it makes life interesting."

"Is it?Do you find that interesting?But I find it very boring."

'What?

"You see,I'm cooped up at home all day,the children,the housework,and she's often away from home,I'm bored.I was eager to get out there,eager to work."

"Then go to work.Leave the housework and children to the nanny."

"No,she wouldn't.She just wanted me to be a stay-at-home husband and take care of the family and her."

"That's just selfish."Shangxiaoning blurted out,finished and a little regret. The captain treated her as one of her own,eating and drinking,living in,and speaking ill of her.

"She's fine,in every way.I'm lucky to have found her,too.How many people envy me.She's decent,she's educated,she's financially sound,she's got a family. There are not many good women like this now.Women are too flowery.Like me,I didn't learn much,and I didn't get good grades,but beautiful people are always wanted."

No promise!Shang Xiaoning thought,a big man by looks to marry a wife,is really the first time to hear.No wonder,then,that there is always a balance to be struck between couples,either in the form of parity or in the exchange of money,status and looks.It's not surprising that if she was looking for an idiot like a flower,she could find him,but she didn't want to.

After dinner,Shang Xiaoning quickly clean the table,wash the dishes,Wen

Biyu moved like,"You are really a good woman."

"Is it?Shang Xiaoning laughed,"What is this?I do everything at home,just like you."

"She doesn't do anything in my family.It's a bit feminist."

"I will enlighten her well later,women,how can you do nothing?"

Wash the dishes,two people and sat on the sofa to talk,have not talked a few words,came the voice of the key to open the door,Shang xiaoning thought it was the female captain back,looking at the door,was ready to come in and greet the female captain,the result is a flashy woman.

The woman saw Shang Xaoning obviously stunned,do not know better or better back.Shang Xiaoning looked back at Wen Biyu,Wen,Wen Biyu's face flushed,embarrassed look.Shang Xiaoning understand,can not expect her,such a young and beautiful man will keep an old woman?If nothing happens!She complained again for the captain,thinking of finding such a young man,and being so kind to him,without knowing what he was like behind his back.Isn't that like having a mistress?When the old man was not at home,the mistress had a tryst with her lover.Captain,Captain,why are you as foolish as the old men?Can you rely on your mistress?Can you count on the pretty boy?

Perhaps Shang Xiaoning should not be a good wife and mother at all,such education to kill people,she is under such education,determined to be a good woman.Perhaps she should have kept a close watch on her husband,seized all his money,never let him leave the house,or he would have fought him forever. Those men who are afraid of their wives,don't they all have such a"tigress"at home?How good are those men?My only wish is that my should not quarrel and live a peaceful life.She sympathized with the men,but many men were"dirty embryos,"and she knew that now,but too late,she had lost her husband

This woman who comes in must be a woman who can satisfy the emptiness of a man's heart.Shang Xiaoning thought of his marriage.Fox spirit!She was furious,as if this woman had been the seducer of her husband.

17

The woman's name is Shaw Swan. At this moment, after a moment's adjustment, she entered with great dignity. She has a wavy hair and a neckerchief. The tights showed curves. "A visitor to the home? Why isn't your key on the door?" Then she smiled at Shang Xiaoning and said, "I am his neighbor, come and sat down."

"Oh," Wen Biyu immediately understood what Shaw Swan meant, and immediately took the message and said, "I forgot to take it down when I came back."

But he's obviously lying. His voice was hollow and dry, and the pitch was half a degree higher, which is characteristic of lying. Shang Xiaoning is based on this characteristic and concluded that her husband lied, and in fact her husband is lying. Why would a person tell a lie? For example, if he did not go to a place and said he did not go to a place, he must have something to hide, and why can't a man say something to his wife? Especially for such a good wife as she is, that he has another woman! Because the husband is free at home, no matter where he goes, what kind of friends he makes, how much money he spends, she never asks, so there is no need for him to hide anything from her.

Before the Shaw Swan could get close, a pungent smell wafted over.

The woman was a social butterfly, with dark, curly hair, light makeup, well-kept skin, and perfect dress. If there is no hostility to look at her, she should be very beautiful, like Hong Kong super beauty Zhang Xiaohui. Age aside, she should be a good match for Wen Biyu.

"Come, sit down, I'll get some tea." Wen Biyu ran to the kitchen in a panic.

Shang Xiaoning sulkily not to pay attention to Shaw Swan. It is difficult for women to make friends with women who are more beautiful than themselves,not to mention Shang Xiaoning's husband was abducted by such a fox spirit.Both enmity filled her with righteous indignation.But the social butterfly did not mind her attitude,but sat down beside her,and looked very appreciative of her,and was very kind.she don't know if she really appreciate it,or because she came to cheat,was caught and flattered her.

"You're the most tasteful woman I've ever met.Just the hair and the outfit."

"Huh?"

The same costume,the female captain is so disgusted,but this woman appreciates it.It was Shang Xiaoning's turn to squirm,she blushed,couldn't help but touch her hair,and looked down at her dress,which is very ordinary clothes ah.A woman can't stand praise,she was listening to her husband's sweet words before she surrendered to him.

18

Shang Xiaoning remembered that she did not look in the mirror for many days,nor did she dress up,her hair was unkempt and tied behind her head,and she did not wipe anything on his face.She's forgotten she's a woman.Her beauty failure made her almost die,afraid to meet people,and now she has the appreciation of this super beautiful woman.Shang Xiaoning thought she heard wrong,guilty,but she would rather she heard wrong.

All Shang Xiaoning's hostility to her immediately collapsed,and the woman was not hostile to a woman who was more beautiful than her,but hostile to a woman who was more beautiful than her and looked down on her.If women more beautiful than her find her beautiful,then there will be no animosity.Shang Xiaoning had this experience for the first time.

"I'm not criticizing women today.They're too casual,they don't take themselves seriously,and few of them dress up."

Wen Biyu had already brought out the tea and handed it to Shaw Swan,while whispering to her,"My wife has come back from the sea."

"I know,I saw her out,playing golf.Hey,but it doesn't matter if she's not home.Isn't there another woman here?Women talk to women more."

"It is."

"People of the same sex have more to talk about together."

"HMM."Shang Xiaoning nodded.

"Where do you work?"

"I had a small shop."

So Shang Xiaoning put their own things simply said.Women are easy to have a good impression on people,and when they have a good impression,they will say everything.She had forgotten her indignation and her sense of justice,that the woman had come to have an affair with the female captain's husband.She turned her into a friend because she appreciates her!

"You,really too silly,is it necessary?"It's hard to find a three-legged toad,but what about a two-legged man?Why are you staring at him and seeing nothing else?It's not worth dying for him.You know,life is so beautiful,we haven't enjoyed enough,how can we die?"

Shaw Swan set up his legs,took out a box of Moire smoke from his arms,and pulled out one from it with his blue fingers.Wen Biyu immediately picked up the lighter and lit it for her.Wen Biyu could not get a word in now. In contrast,Xiao Swan has a sense of pride,like a hero among women,without losing the charm of a woman.Not like a female captain,too masculine;And this husband,too feminine.

"Yeah,I wasn't that open then,and I'm not dead now."

"You're not open yet?It's all facelifted.It's trendy,it's bold.As stylish as I am,I have thought about plastic surgery but haven't done it yet."

"You're so beautiful that you need plastic surgery?I was not forced into it."

19

"Beautiful,people are not satisfied with their own places,all want to achieve the realm of perfection.You are good in everything except your feelings. Shaw Swan again to Shang Xiaoning from beginning to end to see again,"Where do you want to whole what?"Is that so bad?Born beautiful."

"Really?"Shang Xiaoning touched her face,"However,I was not ugly before,otherwise how could my husband chase me?"

"I've never seen a woman as beautiful as you.No matter what you looked like before,at least you make me feel beautiful now."

"Really?Shang Xiaoning's eyes were full of doubts.

"No wonder your husband has changed his mind.People don't care if they are beautiful,but care if they look at themselves as beautiful.But this has to have a big premise,that is,the appearance is passable.If ugly did that,they'd laugh their heads off."

"Well,that's true."Shang Xiaoning face embarrassment,because she has now become an ugly person,to ugly people confidence is very difficult.

"Have you never considered yourself a stunning beauty?"

"No.There never was,and there is no more now."

"Look at you."The woman pointed her finger at her."You are Cleopatra."

'What Cleopatra?

"There was a queen in ancient Egypt who was very beautiful,and she married Julius Caesar.Now when people say beauty,they compare her to Cleopatra;When a man is handsom ,he looks like Pan An or Song Yu."

"I look like Cleopatra?"

"What's not like?You see,high nose,bronzed skin as smooth as satin, black eyes,sexy lips,big hair.Don't you look in the mirror?"

"No,I look in the mirror?Why look in the mirror?This face scares me.I just want to get on with my life and forget about this face.Are you trying to make me feel better?Afraid I'll be sad."

"Oh,you!I insist you look in the mirror." Shaw Swan stood up,put the smoke on the ashtray,and then dragged Shang Xiaoning to the bathroom like a dead pig;Shang Xiaoning is also like a dead pig and refuse to go.

"Just spare me,please."

"No,you must take a look at it,and if it is not as I say,you will beat me and scold me,and I will accept it."

All said to this,Shangxiaoning had to go into the bathroom with Shaw Swan,but she stood in front of the mirror with her head down,or dare not look.

"You show me."Xiao Swan pull Shang Xiaoning head up,force her to look in the mirror.

20

Shang Xiaoning had to look at himself in the mirror,it does not matter,a look really scared.My reflection in the mirror is exactly what Shaw Swan said. Why isn't your nose crooked?One and a few double eyelids have returned to the former phoenix eyes;Her eyebrows and eyelashes had fallen off.The mandibular Angle may not have been sharpened at all,because the face shape is still the same;The sun by the sea had tanned his whole body,so the soy-sauce color of his face was also covered up;.She has always been thin skin and bones,not to grow meat,in old Im's home for a while,but fat.

Not only was she not ugly,there were no disfigurements left,but she was more beautiful than ever,and younger,at least twenty years younger!Shang Xiaoning could not believe that this face was hers.She had a trance and thought she was dreaming.Or this mirror has magic.

She remembered a story about a very ugly queen who had a little mirror in her hand and liked to look at it every day.After her death,it was discovered that the mirror had magic powers to make beautiful people ugly and ugly people beautiful.Is this the mirror she's looking into now?But she clearly saw in the mirror that the Xiao Swan was still beautiful.

"You see,we're just black and white together.A pair of stunning beauties." Shaw Swan put her face together,and Shang Xiaoning next to.

Shang Xiaoning looked for a long time,after being sure that it was neither a dream nor a magic mirror,suddenly broke out into cheers,"I became beautiful,I became beautiful!"Then she turned around and hugged the Shaw Sswan,jumping,jumping,"I'm not ugly anymore,I'm not ugly anymore!"

"Well?Am I right?"

"Ha ha,great,great.You're right,that's what I am."

"Now you have confidence,can you go out?"

"Out?Where to?"

"Go out and play.There's a fashion show,will you watch it?"

"Look!I can't wait to get out there and show the world."

"Then go?"

"Go on."

Two people out of the bathroom,happy,but see Wen Biyu pursed mouth,sitting there.

'Why are you so unhappy? Shaw Swan asked casually.

Wen Biyu glanced at her plaintively and twisted.

"I'll go with her and come back later." Shaw Swan was a little absent-minded.

"How can you remember me?"

Shang Xiaoning see this scene is very uncomfortable,she is afraid that they will make what scary move to embarrass her,and busy interrupt said:"The captain does not take me out to play,I had to go out to play with her."

"The captain will take you,aren't you drunk?"Wen Biyu a little blame Shang Xiaoning look.

"Come on."Shang Xiaoning also ignore so much,urging Shaw Swan,head back to the door.

The Shaw Swan turned and walked out the door.

"You haven't finished your cigarette yet."Wen BIyu shouted behind her.

21

"No more smoking,no more smoking."

Shaw Swan head did not return,catch up a few steps,put his hand on Shang Xiaoning shoulder.

"Do you know why I am called Shaw Swan?Because I was pretty and white when I was little,everyone called me Cygnet,and that became my official name."

"You look beautiful now,too."Shang Xiaoning turned to look at her face and said.

"Hey,not now,old,not even close.It is because they are so ugly that I am beautiful."

"They're not ugly.They make you pretty."

"Hey,compared with you,I can't beat you."Shaw Swan mouth modest,heart is very proud.

"We are two different types.You are prettier than me."

Shang Xiaoning now also dare to admit that she is beautiful,because she is really beautiful,people naturally have confidence.What beauty isn't full of confidence?Everyone around her is a mirror that reflects her beauty. In addition,Shang Xiaoning was bewitched by Shaw Swan.She had never met anyone who dared to admit that she was beautiful.

People always like to find fault with others,especially when this person likes to brag.Internet celebrity"Sister Furong"has been attacked for boasting about her beauty,and is said to be extremely narcissistic.Experts say that extreme narcissism comes from childhood insecurity,first favored,then out of favor,resulting in psychological imbalance,low self-esteem,in order to attract others'attention,they began to brag,and finally to extreme narcissism,unable to extricate themselves.But she was also famous for being attacked,and then they offered her a TV show.As the saying goes,"Learn from the good,learn from the beggar."Shang Xiaoning at this time also feel their beauty should be able to boast.She was completely on Sister Fleur's sie.

"I value my looks very much and cherish this beauty,self-appreciation.Look at them.They're all unkempt.So they didn't like me and said I was different."

"Not unusual,not at all.Just like that.Like a woman.You see, female captain,I don't speak ill of her.she saved me and served me,and I shouldn't speak ill of her."

"Yes,I think so too.The female captain is too stuffy and feudal."

"It's not that I'm stuffy,I think..."

Shang Xiaoning searched for words in her mind,and wanted to use an accurate word to describe the captain's family,but she could not find it,she had never seen such a family,and her knowledge and experience made her some difficulty in understanding such issues.She's not a sensitive,suspicious person,even a little sloppy.Why else wouldn't she know her husband had a seductress?By the time everyone knew,it was too late.

"I went to see him because I felt sorry for him.The captain is often not at home,and a handsome man who looks like a flower stays at home all day,wasting his youth and beauty,wasting the resources of nature,and wasting the pains of nature.Why does nature make colorful flowers and butterflies?Is to let their beauty be enjoyed.If flowers and butterflies were kept in a small room,they would lose their purpose.It's called aesthetic waste."

22

"Yes,but he is taken and married.They're no longer compatible,they have baby,and they should still focus on each other.And they have a good relationship."

Shang Xiaoning thought of her home again,a pain in her heart.How does she end up with this family wrecker now?She should stand firmly against her,on the side of the female captain.The female captain was as happy in the dark as she had been.She should have revealed all this to the female captain.

But what was the result of the Revelations?The family is broken,the pain is eternal.No one wants his family to betray him,and everyone hopes to have a stable home forever,even if he turns over outside,he still wants to go home.A man without a home is a failure,no matter how successful he is.

What if you don't?That is still happy,Shang xiaoning if you do not know,she is still living the original life,not to come to this step.Her husband refused to divorce,and said that he loved her,probably also reluctant to give up his own home?She was sick to her stomach when she heard it.Love your wife and have sex with someone else?She could hardly have imagined it.I don't know what kind of animal a man is.

But Shao Swan and big husband gas,dare to admit that he is active,unlike Shang Xiaoning's husband,dare not to do,insist that the fox seduced him. Seduce?One bowl does not ring,two bowls jingle!Others to seduce her Shang Xiaoning try!She doesn't believe anyone can seduce her!

She's not gonna put up with what's going on with her family.Whenever her husband made love to her,she would think that he had done the same with the fox;When eating together,she will also think that he has eaten with the fox spirit;Together on the street,she will also think of him and the fox prowling together.Whatever she did with her husband,he probably did with a fox.The thought of it sent a wave of nausea and goosebumps through her body.Her husband's presence was a constant reminder of the fact that she would be restless and miserable forever.So,divorce is out of sight.The husband is not her husband anymore,whatever you do,it has nothing to do with her.

"Here we are,what are you thinking?"

"Huh?"Shang Xiaoning hurriedly raised her head.

"This is my home.We'll play when we get back.We'll go to the fashion show first."

It was also a small house similar to the captain's,with a large garden and lawn.It was true that the Shaw Swan and the Captain lived next door to each other,but this was still two gardens apart.It's not like her apartment,right next to each other,the two homes share a wall,and you can hear each other.Alas,money is good ah,although she Shang Xiaoning do a small business,but also can only afford to buy a unit.

23

Shaw Swan opened the garage door,out of the car,greet Shang xiaoning on the car.Shang Xiaoning naturally went up,and did not stand on the side of the female captain.It turns out that seeing someone else's third party is not as hateful as seeing your own.Oh,let it go,Wen Biyu also has bad.Shang Xiaoning thinking about other people's things is like watching a movie,others fight after all,they do not hurt.

Shaw Swan while driving the car and chat.Shang Xiaoning Shang Xiaoning is talking with her,while looking out of the window,want to know where this is.She always thought this was the city she lived in.The people here talked and lived like her,but so far she had not found the streets and the houses she knew well.Now the city is being built so fast that she can't recognize the road if she doesn't go out for a few days.She didn't ask.It was funny.

She guarded a small shop every day,took the shop as her home,and went back to sleep at night,and she really did not know what was going on outside. She had never heard of such things as sailors,sea captains,wedding leave,and egg freezing.It was as if she were living on a foreign planet.

Shaw Swan elegantly drove the car,Shang Xiaoning looked at her from the side,think she is great.Shang Xiaoning envy a woman can drive,a woman drive has a sense of heroism.Captain,that car is driving...They say women have to be wild,more wild than men.Shang Xiaoning home has a very small truck,it is her husband driving the car loading,she has not touched.Cars seem to belong only to men,and racing cars are all driven by men.Whenever she saw women drivers in taxis and buses,she would give them a few more looks and think they are very manly.

Shaw Swan car drive is not slow,call a moment in the past.Shang Xiaoning light saw the name of the store flash by,just can not see what is written.Looked at Shang Xiaoning's eyes for a while,she blinked a few eyes,no longer to look outside.Thought let it go,anyway,it is not in a foreign country,wait for a few days tired of going home.Now I don't want to go by sea,I'd rather take the bus,and I can sleep on it.

Shaw Swan tell Shang Xiaoning,she is engaged in fashion design,for this performance,she spent a lot of time.She came back very late last night and had to go when She woke up this morning.She was ready to call Wen Biyu to go to the show,take him out to relax,he was too stuffy at home,did not expect to meet Shang Xiaoning,she temporarily changed the plan.

"Well,then you should bring him out,and we'll see him together,because we don't want him alone."

"Oh,well,he's here,and there's a lot to say.He's so used to this kind of life anyway,he doesn't mind being left without him once or twice."

"Well,that's not so good,is it not I who influenced him?"

"It's okay.You're more important now."

The car turned a few big corners,shaking Shang Xiaoning around,fortunately she put on a seat belt,or it will hit the glass.Just now Shaw Swan asked her to wear a seat belt she still do not do it,or old driving experience.

"I haven't asked you yet,how old is your child?" Shang Xiaoning said.

"A child?My baby?Oh ha ha ha..."

"Why are you laughing?"

24

"Why should I have children?I don't even have a husband,ha ha ha..."

"What?You're not married?You're so pretty and nobody wants you?Or are you divorced?"

"Why should I get married?By the way,it's not that I'm not wanted,it's that I don't want to get married at all."

'Why?

"Single aristocrats,happy,free,do whatever you want.I'm not getting married for nothing?"

"What a pity,you have talent and beauty."

"My talent and appearance are not for others,but for myself,why share it with others when I should be enjoying it?"

"All in all,it is a pity."

"Actually,I was married once,just for a few months,and I couldn't stand it.Maybe I'm not the marrying type.I was relieved when I got divorced."

"Then my divorce would be very painful,equal to shedding several layers of skin,and dying several times."I don't want a divorce.Divorce is a woman's failure."

"How can you say that?Divorce is when we set ourselves free and escape from our cages.You want me back in the cage?Absolutely not."

"It's strange that there are women who don't want to get married."

"Not at all.Single women have a really good life."

The car came to a theater.Shao swan park the car,led Shang Xiaoning into the theater.

The stage is set up,but people are still busy and noisy.Several people saw

Shaw Swan coming and greeted her.But they all looked at Shang Xiaoning strangely.The male crew members all had long beards and horse tails,just like the husbands of the female captains.

"I brought the most beautiful woman here today!"Shaw Swan called out to them.

Shang Xiaoning felt a little embarrassed,just looked at them at a glance and lowered his head,walking hurriedly behind Shaw Swan, Shaw Swan take Shang Xiaoning to the dressing room in the background.Here is more chaotic,many tall and handsome young men are making up,changing clothes,walking on the platform.All the people were wearing neckerschief.

"Miss Shaw is here."

"Hello,Miss Shaw."

Young people and Shaw Swan greet,but the eyes are all staring at Shang Xiaoning.

"This is the beautiful woman I brought you to meet."

The young people gathered round with a chorus of praise.

"Wow,it's beautiful."

"Never seen it before."

"Almost catching up with Miss Shaw."

25

Shang Xiaoning has not seen this scene,had to grin at everyone.She did not dare to look into the eyes of these young people,though she could be their mother,but their eyes were too hot to bear.If you go back 20 years,Shang Xiaoning will be very intoxicated.

Shang Xiaoning a little escape like turn around,look around,touch the makeup table,touch the mirror,and touch the clothes.Then watch people put on makeup,try on clothes,and walk.She was curious about it all.

"It's hard for them,too.They all live here and have to get up early in the morning."

"There are dormitories here?"

"No,just find a place to sleep.I didn't dare to eat anything all day for fear of getting fat."

"That's pathetic."

Shang Xiaoning looked around and suddenly thought of it like saying:"Huh?Why don't I see any female models?"

"You mean female model?Why do we need female models?How ugly women are."Before the words stopped,Shaw Swan suddenly hit a finger hard,like discovering a new continent,his face was filled with excitement and excitement,and she pointed with her fingers and said to Shang Xiaoning,"Yes,you inspired me."Come,come,come."Then pull Shang Xiaoning,came to a row of clothes,holding a variety of clothes in Shang Xiaoning body to try.

"Why?Want me to be a model?"

"Yes,and me!If they're all so ugly,why don't we?I never thought about it.Hiya,this is a great idea!"

Then Shaw Swan looked at Shang Xiaoning all parts of the body,and turned her around to look behind,see enough,one hand held in front of the chest,one hand holding the cheek,thinking about the problem.

At this time,a female staff member took two boxes of lunch and said:"Dinner,dinner.""Said the two boxes of lunch handed to Shaw Swan.

"Lunch already?Ha ha,I haven't had breakfast yet."Shaw Sswan pass a box lunch to Shang Xiaoning.

"I got up late,and had my breakfast not long ago."

"Eat,or you'll be hungry this afternoon.Until late at night."

"You do this work is very hard,life is not regular,stomach will be ruined."

Shang Xiaoning took the box lunch,and then they found a place to sit down,eat while talking.

Shaw Swan and let Shang Xiaoning when the model thing,Shang Xiaoning see her so serious,smiled and said:"You will not joke with me?Who am I cut out for?When I get up there,I panic.I can't even walk.I can't sing or dance at all."

Shaw Swan waved his hand to stop her from saying:"No one is born a model,and they are ordinary people before they become models."Don't define yourself.I can't do this.I'm not cut out for it.I asked you to be president right away,and you did just as well."

26

This let Shang Xiaoning a little surprised,also very not used to.As a child,she was scolded by her parents for being stupid,ugly,worthless,etc.If she fights with others,it must be her fault,and all the children are better than her. But when she really wanted to have some ideas and do something,her parents laughed at her and regarded her as mentally abnormal.Everything she did,her parents would tell her what she was doing wrong and teach her how to do it.In any case,she has not won the praise of her parents,she is a fool in their eyes. But are parents that capable,that right?The parents themselves fought every day,with their neighbors.They complain every day that life is more difficult than a mountain,and they always say that people bully them because they are poor and honest.

Shang Xiaoning was very inferior when he was a child,and felt that he was the ugliest girl in the world and the most incompetent.Not good at study,not humble,stubborn,quick temper.Until a young man had something to do with her,someone proposed to her,and she got married,she knew that she was OK,not so ugly.Then she feel that life is very simple,not so complicated,and people are also very easy to get along with.Then she looked at her parents with adult eyes and thought they were a mess and some of their things were childish and ridiculous.

But she still hated their complaints,complaints from relatives is the most unbearable.She doesn't ask for praise,only criticism.That's why she hasn't told her parents about the divorce.She knew what would happen if she told them,and that was she couldn't even tie down a husband;She's unattractive,she's dry,she's not plump,she's not gentle,she's not capable of that,and that's why her husband's having an affair.It's all her fault.

She had also vaguely mentioned to them,men outside flowers,can not all say that women are bad;The woman is the fairy,the man wants to spend the same flower;The woman is ugly,the man wants her still want her,can not say that this woman is capable.What about disabled people?What about the paralyzed?What about a vegetable?What about neuroses?So they're all getting divorced,and their husbands are all out there?It's a man.It's not a pig.Is to raise a cat,a dog,throw it away,but also the boss reluctant to give up.

Now the Shaw Swan valued her so much and praised her so much that she wanted to cry.She knew that the Shaw Swan was not a fake,and there was no need for her to flatter her and say nice things on purpose.From the moment Shaw Swan saw her,he had been praising her like this,seeing her as a great beauty,and also believing in her ability.To tell the truth,Shang Xiaoning's ability is not bad,but no one has ever told her.Shang Xiaoning feel with Shaw Swan together,she is really seen as a person.

"Maybe I'm really cut out for it?But I'll try."

Shaw Swan said:"I am bold,willing to endure hardships."As long as I like it,I'll do whatever it takes.How's that??This is the temperament of a successful person.I can't be wrong.How many people have I met?You just lack an environment and training."

"Also cultivate,do not scold is a good thing."I still get nervous when I see my parents because I'm never right."

"Just look at how many children have their self-confidence and ability snuffed out by their parents and turned into drunken bags waiting to die."

"If I had a mother like you,I would sleep and wake up laughing."

27

"It's not too late,you just wait for me to find your talent."The Shaw Swan ate very quickly,whether it was hungry or just the habit.Shang Xiaoning also accelerated the speed of eating,do not speak.After the two people finished eating, Shaw Swan said:"In this way,we do not talk about things now,there are many things waiting for me to deal with,before the show is the busiest."She took out a ticket from her pocket and gave it to Shang Xiaoning,"You first go to this seat and sit down and wait to see the show."You're going to fall asleep.Just take a nap in your seat.Or give you a magazine of some sort..."

Shaw Swan looked around and saw the woman who had just delivered the lunch box.She was reclining on a cardboard box,shaking her legs and reading a magazine.

" Shaw Zhang,do you have any more magazines?Show she one."

"There are,uh,several."Xiao Zhang took some books from the cardboard box.

Shang Xiaoning took the magazine and said,"Thank you.I'll give it back when I'm done."

"You're welcome,I've seen all these.I don't want it either.I bought it for fun. You can do whatever you want with it when you're done." Xiao Zhang finished talking and lazily went back to the cardboard box and continued to read her magazine.

"So I'll just go to my seat?"

"Well,go ahead,I'm going to get busy.Oh,and remember,you don't leave after the show,just sit there and wait for me.Don't go,we have work to do."

Shang Xiaoning found his seat.She wanted to read a magazine,but she couldn't.Everything here is so tempting for her,especially when she is going to be a model,and this will be her stage.She could not help thinking,thinking about all sorts of things,and then watching the staff busy,watching them try lights,try sound,running around,climbing up and down.She had never seen anything like it and thought they were buzzing around like a swarm of bees.It turned out that the performance was so troublesome,she thought that the performance was the business of the actors.

    I don't know how long it took,but gradually the audience came and began to sit in their seats.Shang Xiaoning's left also sat a man,Shang Xiaoning only glanced at him,think he is about her age,shaved,cut short hair.She did not pay too much attention to him,she is not interested in men at present,she was too hurt by men,see men are a little afraid.She involuntarily moved a little to the right,where a girl sat.Long hair.Both were wearing neckerchiefs,aand anyone do it.

    Then the lights dimmed,the music began to play,and soft lights came on,hitting the long,narrow catwalk.Shang Xiaoning also pays attention to the catwalk,she is facing the center of the catwalk.

    A team of outrageously dressed male models emerged from behind the stage,all clean-shaven and with their hair cut to an inch.They stomped to the beat of the music and made gestures,but moved forward with deliberate ease.When they got a little closer,Shang Xiaoning had not had time to carefully appreciate their bodies and faces,she gasped in horror,and then tightly closed his eyes,never to open them again.

28

Male models are wrapped around the neck of the transparent neckerchief,but their bodies are also made of the same transparent gauze made of all kinds of clothing,underwear are not wearing!Shang Xiaoning knows that the fashion is now see-through,she has also seen the performance of female models on TV,they do not wear underwear,the meat is swaying inside the clothes;And now what performance are wearing two sections of clothing,only the most economical cloth around the woman's body two sections of vital parts,men only surround the bottom.She was very unaccustomed to seeing these things.

"What a shame!The man on the left slapped the armrest of the seat.Shang Xiaoning could not help but pay more attention to this man,she listened carefully to what he was saying.

"Wow,all handsome men."The girl on the right claps her hands and cries,and says to the girl on the other side,"A man is handsome,no matter how he walks or dresses."The human body is handsome,why do you think it is ugly and secretive?This is the way to live up to nature."

Another girl is not much to talk,just listen to the girl kept praising the male model,"men are made of water,have spirituality,you look at them,one by one is born handsome,intoxicating,love;Women are made of mud,dirty,chaotic..."

The music changed,Shang Xiaoning estimated that the team performance has gone down,just opened his eyes again,exhaled a breath.

The man on the left has also been muttering,"Just strip off,don't wear anything,it's the most handsome!"Why don't these creators take it off themselves?All naked is best!Don't even wear any lights or choreography!"

Now the male models are on stage one by one,and sometimes two come out together,but the clothes are still that routine,Shang Xiaoning still dare not look,and close his eyes.

Shang Xiaoning in this way,a moment to open eyes,a moment to close eyes,nervous like peeking at others to take a bath,sweating.But the atmosphere in the audience was intense,with some clapping,some screaming,flashbulbs flashing and a gaggle of reporters,photographers and videographers going about their business.

If not for Shaw Swan told her dont go,Shang xiaoning must go at this time,she is very uncomfortable,but have to endure,no place to hide;I want to read the magazine in my hand to pass the time,and the light is too dim to see the words.Shang Xiaoning kept moving on the seat as if on pins and needles,a restless look.

"What's wrong with you?""Said the man on the left.

"Oh,no...I just...Not used to seeing them."

"Aren't you used to it either?Then you must be a decent man."

"Well,not so much.I'm not used to seeing it for the first time.I am a woman."

"Crooked people get used to it the first time they see it."

"Maybe I'm too backward to catch up with The Times.I'm old-fashioned."

"This kind of soil is good.If everyone could be old-fashioned,the social atmosphere would be better than it is now.Look what it's become.TV,commercials,performances are not for children.Children living in such an environment,how can not be bad?"

29

"I have the same opinion.An ordinary TV drama,did not say that children are not suitable,men and women as soon as they are well,they quickly take off their clothes."Shang Xiaoning just said"take off clothes"a little regret,can not help but face a red,this man is a man.Fortunately,it was dark inside and no one saw it.But Shang Xiaoning still bowed her head shamefully.

"Yes,don't children learn?If grown men and women take their clothes off when they're together,so do they.Too small not sensible,adults still think they are fun,but a little bigger?How about 11 or 12?Fifteen or sixteen?"

See someone also has the same view as her,Shang Xiaoning does not feel that he has seen more strange.At this time,she felt that the show's costume design Xiao Swan had a problem,not that she was too fashionable,but too alternative. Shang Xiaoning has never seen a fashion designer dare to open a man,let a man wear a see-through suit!The courage of Shaw Swan has far exceeded that of ordinary people.

Ah, Whaw Awan will not want her to wear such a see-through dress in the future?Then she won't kill her!Not to mention a see-through outfit.She won't show her belly button!She's not at the point where she has to make a living putting her body on display.She can go on stage in a pretty dress,but it has to be opaque!

"I have rarely seen a woman so ashamed as you who knows shame is almost brave."

"He who is not ashamed is almost brave."The girl on the right took up the conversation,she had long hair."Those who know shame are afraid of embarrassment,and if they do not come to power,they will not be brave;He who knows nothing is fearless,ha ha ha..."

The light suddenly bright,the show ended,Shang Xiaoning these three people also stopped the debate,all looked at the stage.A group of flashy male models came out of the backstage surrounded by Shaw.Swan The Shaw. Swan has been carefully dressed up,like a shining diamond,shining brightly in a piece of pearls.Don't say man,is Shang Xiaoning,also by her light can not open their eyes.

Shaw.Swan wore a white satin evening gown,studded with sequins,her hair pulled up high,and a crown on her head.She came out with a smile and white lilies in her hand,like a queen.

The whole audience stood up and cheered her,applauding warmly.The applause went on and on.

The Shaw Swan bowed gracefully to the audience,and bowed again.

At the end of the performance,many people ran to the stage to take photos with Shaw Swan and ask for her autograph.Shaw Swan also did not refuse,smiling to meet them.Some people look for their favorite male models to sign,take pictures.

Immediately after,the staff escorted Shaw Swan to the backstage.Shang Xiaoning left the man and the girl on the right also ran to the background.Shang Xiaoning did not know what had happened,and unconsciously followed.

Shang Xiaoning followed them into a small room on the side of the theater. The words"Press Conference"were posted on the wall facing the room.A long table was covered with flowers,and among the flowers were several microphones. Shaw Swan is also surrounded by people into the hall,sitting in front of the long table.

There were many chairs on the opposite side of the long table,and the reporters all sat down.Shang Xiaoning also found a seat in the last row and sat down.After the host made an introduction,the reporter began to ask questions.

30

"I'll go first."A girl with long hair stood up."I am Li Baiyu,a special reporter from the radio station of Haibin University,and I would like to ask that the style of the model has changed greatly this time,with a cold and strange appearance,a change from the past pure and soft.Does that mean you're transitioning,that you're going to follow this style?That's all,thank you."

Shang Xiaoning only saw the girl's back.But Shang Xiaoning according to the sound,can infer that she is just sitting on her right girl.

Shaw Swan smiled and said:"Art has no certain pattern.Today we can do this,tomorrow we can do that.If I always have only one style,then I am old and no longer creative.Thank you."

"Do you think it's handsome for a man to completely reveal his body?Thank you."

Shang Xiaoning looked at the sound,and only saw a man's back,but she was sure that this was the man just sitting on her left.

Shaw Swan raised his eyebrows and said defiantly,"Ah,reporter Jiao Liang,we are old friends.And your views haven't changed at all?On the question of what is handsome,I will not preach here,I think everyone knows.But what I want to emphasize is the excavation and liberation of human nature,harmonious breakthrough and innovation.This is art.Please do remember that."

Everyone laughed.

"May I ask if your personal life is so indiscreet?"

"Yes,I'm completely naked at home,can't I?Is it illegal to do this with my boyfriend?"

The crowd laughed.

"Go ahead."

"What does it mean that you yourself have changed your style this time and are wearing dresses?"

"That's what I'm most interested in." Shaw Swan smiled and said,"The inspiration for me this time is a special person,who will not think of it."She came to the show this time,and I told her to stay in her seat..." Shaw Swan whispered to Shaw Zhang,a staff member next to her,"You go to the yard and find her."

"I'm here,I ran here."Shang Xiaoning stood up and raised his hand to greet Shaw Swan.

31

The Shaw Swan her and waved to her,"Come,come here,let everyone see."

"No,no,you go about your business,I'll wait for you right here."Shang Xiaoning scared quickly shake hands.This is the first time she has seen this position,it is not too fresh,she wants to go on stage?But Xiao Zhang had already come over and dragged her up.

Shang Xiaoning stood in front of the long table,facing the crowd in front of her,she was at a loss.Eyes will stare at the flowers,dare not look up.Just see Shaw Swan so cope with the ease,put on the shelf,she also felt that Shaw Swan changed to another face,and she was completely different.When she is with her who really is If she Shang Xiaoning in the future,what kind of attitude should be put forward?Before these questions could be thought out,she was brought to the stage.

"It is she,Shang Xiaoning,this great beauty,inspired my thinking."My next fashion show will be an unprecedented show featuring us.I just couldn't wait for the day when I came out for the curtain call in this costume.I can't wait to perform like this."

Flash swish sounded,there are a few camera lens aimed at Shang Xiaoning,Shang Xiaoning eyes are spent.She wants to raise her head to face the camera and smile,but her eyes are blinking from the light,and the flesh on her face is not listening to the command,it is all twitching.She managed to grin,but her lips trembled so much that she bit her bottom lip between her teeth and held on to a quivering smile.Her eyes could see nothing,her ears could hear nothing.

Shang Xiaoning do not know how long after,the shaking figure in front of the receded,the noisy voice is also small,Shang Xiaoning seems to wake up from the sleepwalking.She sank down in her chair,her whole body aching and her back cold.Her clothes were wet and she was in a cold sweat.

"Come on,let's go to the celebration party."

Took Shang Xiaoning's arm,and returned to the usual state with her.Shang Xiaoning this just feel Shaw Swan really great,in such an occasion to respond freely,but also to counter all attacks of speech,quick response,answer all kinds of questions,do not make a fool of herself,do not give people a handle.Shang Xiaoning said:"You are really not simple,I always panic when I'm around people."

"It doesn't matter.It's like that at first.It'll get better."

"I'm afraid I'll never do it.I'm not cut out for it."

"Again,what are you afraid of when I'm here? Let's go."

"To where?"

"To eat,of course.Didn't I tell you to eat for lunch?How could you have made it this far without eating for lunch?"

Shang Xiaoning followed Shaw Swan,like she followed Lao elder sister,in fact,they were about the same age,maybe Shaw Swan was younger than her.It's a matter of ability.It's not acceptable.

32

On the car, Shaw Swan is still full of spirit,elegant driving,as if just got up;Shang Xiaoning can not,after the toss just now,she is like a defeated battle,the whole body can not lift the spirit.

The car was parked in the underground parking lot of a luxury hotel,and the two took the elevator directly to the lobby on the ninth floor.Entering the hall,the stage on the front of the hall is hung with a scarlet goose down curtain,on which there are three white foam carved out the word"celebration party".In and around the hall were tables filled with delicious food,fruits and drinks.A lot of people have come,people are busy carrying plates,looking for their favorite food.

Buffet Shang Xiaoning has eaten before,but such a large scale has not seen. Staff Xiao Zhang came to greet them.

"Shangjie--"a woman's scream scared Shang Xiaoning jump,where does anyone recognize her?Even the female captain is too old to sound like a little girl.Suddenly,Shang Xiaoning's heart jumped,is she?She's not dead.She's here,too?

Sure enough,Shangxiaoning expected,white chrysanthemum rushed over,a hug Shang Xiaoning.Two people like long-lost sisters,hugging each other kissing,rubbing,crying,laughing.

When they could be quiet, Shaw Swan said,"This is the White Chrysanthemum,isn't it?I am jealous of your intimacy;you have never treated me like that before."

Shang Xiaoning said a little embarrassed:"I was so excited,I thought I would never see her again.Didn't I almost die myself?"Said can not help but sad from it,and began to cry.

"Well, aren't you all alive?" Shaw swan for Shang Xiaoning wipe away tears, and help her hair, tidy up the clothes, "Come, let's go to eat." Then she told the waiter to get a table and some chairs and put them in a corner.

"The staff here are very hygienic and wear masks." Shang Xiaoning said.

"Yes, this is the most advanced hotel, of course you should pay attention to these, otherwise the beard will fall into the dishes, and the guests will complain."

Three people sit down, Shaw swan and asked the waiter to install a little food, and then Shangxiaoning and White Chrysanthemum said their own experience. The original White Chrysanthemum in the sea was also saved by a captain, she is now living in the captain's home, and her daughter formed a dry sister.

"She's coming, too. I'll go get her." White Chrysanthemum finished, hurriedly stood up and walked away.

Shang Xiaoning and Shaw Swan here have not lamented enough unfortunate life and coincidence, there are two girls have come.

Shangxiaoning and Shaw Swan here have not lamented enough unfortunate life and coincidence, there are two girls have come.

Shaw Swan looked up and paused a little, "Isn't this Miss Li Baiyu, a big reporter? Come, come, sit, sit."

Li Baiyu said pleasantly, "How can you remember my name? I'm just a stringer, temporary."

33

"Well, I've practiced. Besides, before the press conference, I already knew which departments were coming and who they were sending, and I had memorized their names to show that I had an amazing memory. That's not true at all. You think it's true? Politicians like to play this game. Of course, I'm no exception. I'll give you a performance. What other impromptu speeches are not pre-written and memorized? And the answers are all prepared, aren't they? Can you ask about foreign countries?"

"Oh--so it is." Shang Xiaoning thought . Shaw Swan not so god.

"I prefer not to fake, but on that occasion, I can't help it. People want that."

"Why didn't I see you at the press conference?" Shang Xiaoning asked the White Cchrysanthemum.

" Dry sister Li Baiyu asked me to wait here for her, saying it was a very important meeting, and I couldn't go in without a press card."

"Then how did you get in here?" Shang Xiaoning asked again.

"My dry sister Li Whitejade gave me a meal voucher."

"Should I come in and ask for a voucher?" Shang Xiaoning asked Shaw Swan.

"Of course, I already gave it for you."

The four women were chattering, laughing and eating and talking. By the time they had finished eating, everyone had gone to dance in the ballroom next door. Shaw Swan also led them to the ballroom. The ballroom was very dark, and they were not accustomed to it for a while, so they found a seat and sat down.

Loud music, flashing lights, people whirling, Shang Xiaoning dazzled. She could not dance or see the way, so she kept drinking tea and eating sunflower seeds.

"Ah, the light, the beauty..." Li Whitejade greedily looked at the people on the dance floor, and then half-closed her eyes, shaking her head, chanting, "Wine luminous cup, people face peach blossom red, all the eyebrows drunk, red sleeves add fragrance most enchanting."

"Don't be so sour, you'll come here after learning a few bad poems." Shaw Swan's face wrinkled, like drinking rice vinegar.

"Oh, I can't help it, I can't help it. I should have laughed at me in love, I was born as early as gray hair all for the king, the clothes gradually widened and eventually did not regret, for him haggard."

"Come on, come on, here we go. Say you're fat and you pant. You're not studying Chinese, are you?"

"Why not? Yeah, ancient poetry major."

"No wonder. I can't stand it."

"My name is Li Whitejade, Li White and Jia Jade."

"Acid plus color."

"Can't do without color, can you blame me? Everywhere is full of temptation. With so many beauties dangling in front of you, dressed so skimpy, and smelling so good, how can you control yourself? If you don't believe me, ask everyone, is that true?"

34

"Oh, lust is human nature, can not be called a man?" I got into fashion because I love beauty. You see, I come into contact with young and beautiful every day, it is difficult to think of color. How am I supposed to get married? Marriage and family are too oppressive. I'm best the way I am. I have passion when I meet beauty, and I have inspiration when I have passion. Just like Picasso, every good love has given him countless inspiration. Art needs inspiration, inspiration needs passion, passion needs love, and this is the source of all art."

"I agree. Love is the driving force of society. Man dies for sex and birds die for food." Li Whitejade said.

Shang Xiaoning said:"I found that the men here have beards, long hair, wear skirts, except for male models, no beard, cut hair, wear pants, and all wear makeup. The women have short hair, wear pants, dress casually, and don't make up.

"Isn't that normal?"

"Normal?" Shang Xiaoning turned to look at Shaw Swan, like dont know her, you say normal? How is that normal? For example, it is normal for women like you, me, White Chrysanthemum, and us to dress like this."

"Have you had too much to drink? This is what we're wearing now. Do you see a woman who looks like us? That's how I got noticed when I looked so different. People say I'm a pervert, that I've had work done, that I've bleached, that I shouldn't wear makeup, that I'm masculine."

Shang Xiaoning such as falling into the clouds in the fog, she frowns, look at Shaw Swan, look at Li Whitejade and look at White Chrysanthemums, and look at the men and women on the dance floor, and then look back at these women.

"White Chrysanthemum, tell me what's going on? Are we dreaming?"

"I...I don't know.I think it's weird everywhere.Is it different customs?Maybe it's a minority?I've been thinking about that a few days."

Shang Xiaoning turned to Shaw Swan again,"Then you say,what is a man,what is a woman?"

"You can't even figure that out?I think you're probably mad,too." Shaw Swan laughed.

"Or they were in a state of shock,like falling into the sea,losing their families,losing their memories..."Li Whitejade said.

"How come?Even if I am stupid enough not to eat,I still know the difference between men and women."

"What is a man and what is a woman?" Shaw Swan asked back.

"Isn't it just men with Adam's apples and beards and short hair?A little taller,a little stronger,a little rougher,a little darker,a,a little more angry,a little uglier,a little more lustful..."White Chrysanthemum grabbed to say.

"Women with long hair,breasts,less daring..."Shang Xiaoning added.

35

"You are only partially right,you are talking about the secondary sexual characteristics of men.The second sex characteristic is that in addition to the lower body,the second thing that can show gender characteristics,men have Adam's apple,beard,and thick voice is correct;Women,too,have breasts and small voices;But everything else is backwards.Women are taller,stronger,rougher,darker,harder,more angry,uglier,and more lustful."

"How come!"Shang Xiaoning must quarrel,debate a right and wrong.

"It's hair and clothing,there's a question of aesthetics and habits.Because women want to work,do business,long hair is not convenient,it has been short hair;As for clothing,there is also the problem of convention.Men are in a state of being aesthetic,men for their own tolerance,so wear skirts ah,makeup ah,wear high heels ah,to please women.We are a women's society,and of course we have to look at men through women's eyes."

"You've got it backwards.Women wear skirts,makeup and heels."Shang Xiaoning said.

"No,no,no,you have it backwards.Because men are comfortable with who they are,their characteristics,including secondary sexual characteristics and handsome men,are a good subject to play.For example,chest-length beard,shoulder-length hair,black and bright,it is very masculine;Adam's apple,the most able to reflect the curvy beauty of men,the looming Adam's Apple,it is very visual impact,give a shock.Now you know why I put a transparent veil around the Adam's apple?This,to the average person,is outrageous.Well,when am I going to take off my veil and show some skin.If everyone likes it,let them see enough."

"What is there not to expose?I think young people with long beards look worse.It's not ancient times."

"You see,you are more radical and daring than I am.You're thinking exactly what I'm thinking.Why argue?So this time, My models did not wear skirts and high heels,all short hair,beard is shaved,and the tone is cold,soft with firm,close to neutral."

"That's the way it's supposed to be.Women dress more like that."

"So I just put on a dress and dressed myself up.Just because women are short hair,I have long hair,Li Whitejade also has long hair,they are despised.We artists like to wear our hair long."

"Women do not engage in art also need to grow long hair,you see me,Li Whitejade and White Chrysanthemum are all long hair,women who do not like short hair."

"Maybe there's something different here.In general,our society is a male society,the root of everything is this,why women must have big breasts?You have to be pretty?Must be gentle,virtuous,loving husband and teaching children?You have to do the housework?Do you have to stay the same?So a man can have three wives and have four concubines?"White Chrysanthemum think of his experience is angry.

"You are talking about the past,how can you have three wives and four concubines now?"Shang Xiaoning busy correct her.

36

"Isn't the essence the same?Now it's worse.They are all plotting against us in the dark,and we are being plotted against before we know it.In the end,both our property and our people are moved away,and we are left with no money."White Chrysanthemum said.

"Yes,even before there was a first wife,she was still in charge of the family power,the fourth wife had to serve her;The first wife can't get a husband and still get comfortable."Shang Xiaoning said.

"Now some people say that young women have excess resources and should be given a way out,allowing them to be the concubines and concubines of successful people,which is better than them being prostitutes on the street and conducive to social stability."There is no reason why a teapot should be matched with many teacups.These successful people can support them anyway,and a good man should have more than one woman.It serves an unsuccessful man who can't find a wife."White Chrysanthemum said.

"Then do you want to be someone's 4th wife or not?"Shang Xiaoning asked.

"I don't want to.I don't like to share a man with others,especially after a few days he has his eye on who,and finally the nanny and servants at home have got on.Might as well get divorced,get some property,and find another one."White Chrysanthemum said.

"Well?I thought the same thing,and I left,didn't I?"

White Chrysanthemum said:"Yes,IF,I am the 4th wife,who can guarantee that I will be the last one? Unless he dies tomorrow,I'll marry him today.But to be honest,I don't like the old ones,I like the ones around my age.I would rather die to be with those old men who could be my father,grandfather,and great-grandfather.Don't blame blue flower every day curse old man dead,she wants to steal out will lover.These old men don't want to think,who could fall in love with them?So old,so ugly,but not the money?But if I had any money,I wouldn't want any of these little,dangerous,time bombs that might one day go off and kill someone.I might as well pay to hang out and be done with it."

"But the blue flower did not do it right,the people received the bride price,the money was collected,the things were cheated,and the people kicked off and ran away."If you don't want to do it,don't do it in the first place."Shang Xiaoning said.

"Maybe the family is poor,forced."White Chrysanthemum said.

"Forced?Then you can run,but you can't run in the first place?"Shang Xiaoning said.

"How can you get money if you run away in the first place?This isn't like cheating on a wedding and standing you up,is it?First sell the woman to someone else as a wife,sleep with him for a few days;Some also do not sleep with them,put the groom down with wine,and run away in the middle of the night;Some brides are dressed as men."

"Ha ha ha..."

The two women talked to themselves,and left the two next to them hanging.

"How is it that you're talking about gender in the wrong way?Now it is said that a woman can have multiple men so that men do not become male prostitutes or break up other people's homes...Wait a minute...Why are you saying the exact opposite of what we are saying...Uh-huh...I see.You are from a foreign country."

"What foreign country?Aren't we all Chinese?"Shang Xiaoning said.

37

"The Chinese?The Chinese are foreigners."

"I think you drink too much wine,aren't you Chinese too?"If we are foreigners,what nationality are you?"

"We are our daughter's countrymen."

"The land of women?Don't be ridiculous,I've never heard of it."Shang Xiaoning said.

"Ah,I know,matriarchal society,walking marriage,the Mosuo people by the Lugu Lake.I read a book written by a woman named Yang Erchenam.She was a Mosuo,and then she escaped and became a singer.Now married to a foreigner,a diplomat."White Chrysanthemum is very excited.

"You're talking nonsense.What Mosuo?We are not a minority at all,we are a serious country with our own sovereignty like every other country in the world."

"Seeing you bickering just now,I guessed that you are not from our country. Were you not rescued from the sea?"Li Whitejade said.

"Well,now it's clear.No wonder we never agree.It turns out it's not from the same country.""Said the Shaw Swan.

"Then since you are not Chinese,how can you speak,live in habits,and write the same as China?"It's just like our city.I didn't think I was out of it."Shang Xiaoning said.

"No,I studied geography.There is no such country in the world."White Chrysanthemum said reached over to pinch Shang Xiaoning,and pinched Li Whitejade and Shaw Swan,and finally pinched himself.All four of them cried out with an ouch.

"What,are you sick?"Shang Xiaoning asked.

"I'll see if I'm dreaming."

"Not a dream,definitely not a dream." Shaw Swan said,"I also heard Wen Greenjade say that his wife said that foreign countries are different from our country, His wife goes to sea a lot.That's why I thought you might be foreigners."

"Yes,I've heard my mother say that too,and I think about that too.Now the problem is clear,we are not from the same country,so don't quarrel,different countries,customs and habits are different."

"No,there is only one country in the world similar to China,Singapore,language,writing,life are the same,there is no other country."White Chrysanthemum still insist.

"I don't know exactly what the situation is,and I'm not studying this.Don't worry about it either.Since you're from a foreign country,we'll treat you like hosts.So that you can see the splendor of our country of women.Let us go to the dance before we waste our time and fail our beauty with all these great questions of right and wrong."

Just as the song began,Li Whitejade could not bear it any longer,grabbed the hand of the White Chrysanthemum,and dragged her to the place where the male model was clustered.She invited one of the most handsome male models to be her partner,and then she pushed the glazed White Chrysanthemum.

38

"Why do you stand still,like a fool?"Turning to the male models," Brothers,would you like to dance with this pretty girl?"

"Yes,yes..."The male models were screaming.

Before the WhiteCchrysanthemum could respond,a young man who looked just like big star Hu Bing stood up and said,"I'll do it,I'll invite her."

"Oh-"the male models coaxed.

The White Chrysanthemum turned red with shame.She thought that she was experienced,can be indifferent to these young people,did not expect that she now like really met the big star,heart plop plop jumping non-stop,people also shy,mechanically followed the young man into the dance floor.

But their hands and dance moves are not coordinated,the two peple seem to be doing tai chi.What's going on here?White Chrysanthemum is strange,suddenly mind a stirring,think of the country is the reverse,that is,the young man is jumping the female step,then she should jump the male step,fortunately she has learned,when there is no man in the dance floor,she jumps the male step.Sure enough,when she did the man step,the problem was solved.

"Sister,is this your first time to dance here?"The young man asked gently.

"Aah,"he said.White Chrysanthemum a little flustered.

"My name is Yellow Flower."

"Daylily?"White Chrysanthemum burst out laughing and forgot to be nervous,"But my name is not much better,my name is White Chrysanthemum."

"The White Chrysanthemum from the chamomile tea we drank?"

"Yes,every word of it."

"Hey,hey,interesting.Two flowers,one for vegetables,the other for tea."

The two were walking around on the dance floor,not dancing at all,as if they were taking the road,or taking a walk.

"I prefer shy women."

"Is it?

"Shy women have flavor and are very attractive."

"HMM."

"Shy people tend to have very deep,very detailed inner emotional experiences,which is also a concrete manifestation of their tenderness and ability to love others,so there is a special urge to love them."

"How can you be so knowledgeable?Also,when a woman is in the presence of her loved ones,she is shy and coy."

"That's a good addition.Only a few women are like this.Most women are careless."

"Am I a shy woman?"

"Yes,why else would I say that?"

39

    White Chrysanthemum's heartbeat intensified again,her legs were weak,her head was dizzy.It was as if it was really the big star Hu Bing who was saying such things to her.But she had not yet lost her mind,and it should be said that at this time her brain's thinking speed and reaction speed had reached an unprecedented peak.No matter how stupid people are,they are the smartest at this time,and they are all geniuses.She wanted to re-establish the meaning of the man's words,the truth of them,to rule out any other possibility of ambiguity.

    "As I said earlier,some women are shy around the person they love.I know that.Do you know why I'm saying this?I've loved you since you came."

    "Really?Me too."

    "Is it love at first sight?I've never felt anything like this before,and I'm going to hold on to it and not let it slip." Daylily said clenched the White Chrysanthemum hand,the head also leaned on her shoulder.But he was half a head taller than the White Chrysanthemum,so he had to bend his head sideways to touch the White Chrysanthemum's shoulder.

    The heart of the White Chrysanthemum is about to jump out,she feels difficult to breathe,out of breath,and her face is burning.She gently closed her eyes,took a deep breath,and leaned her head against the Daylily's as she hugged him.

    Here Shaw swan must pull Shang Xiaoning dance.

    "I won't."Shang Xiaoning refused to stand up.

    "No,I must teach you today,you can't help it." Shaw swan half pull half drag Shan Xxiaoning left the seat.

    "Why is that so difficult?Isn't it just like walking?You can't even walk?Stand,we toe to toe,when I retreat you enter;When I come in,you go back."

"It's that simple?"

"It's that simple."

"Did I not see him jump in a straight spin,and do tricks?"

"That's what dancers do.People just walk."

"So how do I know when to go forward,when to go back,when to turn?"

"I command you,my right hand pushes you behind your back,and you go forward;my left hand supports your right hand,and I push your hand,and you go back;When I take you around the corner,you turn."

"Oh,it's that easy?

"It's that easy.You just won't try."

Two people under the dance floor,Shang Xiaoning bowed his head,staring at his feet,so often stepped on the feet of Shaw Swan.

After one song,the two returned to their seats.Shang Xiaoning too tired,she is too nervous,palms are sweat.To the music sounded again, Shaw Swan and pull Shang Xiaoning jump.A few songs down,Shang Xiaoning actually a little entry,she relaxed a lot,but also more easygoing up,really can be like taking the road,not thinking.

At the end of another song,they sat down,drank some tea,and took a breath. Just then a man came along.

"May I sit here for a moment?"'asked the man.

40

Shaw Swan looked up and immediately said in a sarcastic tone:"Yo,this is not the famous male rights movement,the men's United adviser,the famous Jiao Liang jiao reporter?"How did you end up in this horrible place?Is your private life such a mess?"

"It is because my private life is as pure as a child's that I am immune.It is called untainted by mud."

"Good point.Then how can you see that I am not out of the mud and not stained,I have no immunity?"

"You don't need immunity.You're in your element."

"Well said,why should I be immune?I can't be friendly enough."

"Well,let's not argue,I'm not here to see you,I'm here to see the lady."

"You want her?You know her?" Shaw swan pointed to Shang Xiaoning asked.

"Yes,we just sat together at the show and had a long conversation.We hit it off."

"Oh?It's rare.I thought you were a die-hard,you'd stick it out till the end. Is it time for a change?So your current extreme patriarchal views will have to change?"

"Why should I change it?No way!I will defend my views to the death."

"Well,brave,admired."The Shaw swan clapped her hands.

As they spoke,Shang Xiaoning looked at the man carefully.He's very masculine,unlike any of the men here.Shang Xiaoning also took him and the female captain's husband Wen Greenjade compared,that is really one in the sky,one on the ground.The female captain's husband is everything,but too sissy,too soft.Alas,in this country of women,it is rare to see a man like reporter Jiao Liang.

"So you cut your hair and beard short,dress casually,don't apply powder,don't trim,everything looks like women,do you think this is male power?"

"It is only a sign that I have the determination,the courage,to break this Ring and declare my insubordination to the world."What I'm fighting for is equal rights,of course.When women and men are truly equal,my masculinity will automatically disappear."

"Do you know kung fu?"Shang Xiaoning could not help but ask.

"What martial arts?"

"Didn't you say male boxing?I only know that there are southern boxing,North boxing,and south leg,North leg.Oh,I don't know.I saw it in martial arts movies."

"Oh,you mean like that?Ha ha,interesting.In a way,if I'm a fighter,I have to be a fighter man That's a good word.It's to hit them hard!But the male power we just talked about is not this male boxing,it is men's rights,men's rights."

"Oh--this male power.Men still fighting for rights?Oh,yes,you men are fighting for rights here,just as women are fighting for rights there."

41

'What did you say?

"Has our great reporter encountered a new problem?This lady is a foreigner,not from us,make no mistake about it."

"What?Foreigners?"Jiao Liang stared at Shang Xiaoning,carefully watched her from head to toe,"No wonder I said,how the lady thought quite traditional,dressed like a hippie?I'm glad I didn't give up."

"Aren't you afraid that this kind of woman will be more feministic?"

"She won't be living a decadent life like yours.Her duty is one of integrity and kindness.This is important in either gender.Only then can women and men be equal."

"Yes,yes,yes,I believe in equality between men and women.Male chauvinism is not good,male chauvinism is not good."Shang Xiaoning quickly said.

"I knew you were that kind of person.My eyes will not be wrong,40 and not confused.If I can't see people at my age,then I have lived in vain and will never mature in my life,because I have passed the growing period."

The music sounded,Jiao Liang stood up,left hand behind,right hand forward,bowed to Shang Xiaoning,and asked:"May I ask you to dance?"

Shang Xiaoning was about to answer, Shaw Swan said:"Yo,even dance this kind of thing to take the initiative to invite it?"

Shang Xiaoning quickly stood up,she was eager to have such an opportunity.Since this man appreciates her so much and she has a crush on him,why not go hopping and make contact?Shang Xiaoning's heart is alive again,no longer exclude men,on the contrary she thinks this is a good opportunity.

"Wait,you haven't asked my permission yet.""Said the Shaw Swan.

Shang Xiaoning and Jiao Liang were surprised to look at Shaw swan.

"This is my partner,and I dance very well,how can you take love from me?"

"Why,you have commandeered so many members of the opposite sex,and played with so many people,I'm afraid you can't count yourself?"

"Snap!" Shaw Swan slammed the table and stood up,"I put up with you,you are too presumptuous."You ugly bastard that no one wants,one of the few ugly bastards in the world,stick to your chastity arch and live the life of an old virgin!Are you jealous when you see me hanging out with pretty boys all day?I still have it.You don't.What,now you're attracted to a beautiful woman?I mean,you're all about celibacy,because no one wants you,so you pretend to be celibate,and now this hot lady's being nice to you,and you're crazy.You think she's interested in you?Go ahead and dream your big dream!I'm just being polite!"

"Forget it.Don't fight about me."Shang Xiaoning in the middle of the two people said,think and turn to Jiao Liang,push him out,Jiao Liang turned back and said loudly:"Please feel the conscience to think.how would you feel if your brother or son were played with?"

42

"I don't have a brother or a son,so I wouldn't want to!"

"Forget it."Shang Xiaoning tried to push him away.He said,"Call me."He took out his business card and gave it to her before he left reluctantly.Shang Xiaoning quickly put the business card into the pocket.

Shang Xiaoning pushed him away and returned to his seat,"Why are you so angry?"Don't you care?"

"I don't care what he says about me,but not if he wants to touch you!"

"Well,if you think of me as a treasure,people may not take me seriously."

"No,you don't know your worth.This man is interested in you."

"Let him have fun,then."

"No,he is such an ugly old virgin,his mind is not normal,Well,if a toad wants to eat swan meat and not pee on himself,no way!I wouldn't be able to say anything if I was like Wen Greenjade."

"Ok,OK,don't be angry,let's go dancing again."This is Shang Xiaoning pull Shaw swan under the dance floor.

They dance song after song, Shaw swan later gradually also not angry,see Shang Xiaoning dance has become skilled,began to teach her a variety of tricks. Shang Xiaoning also jump more happy,but the heart always thinking about the reporter.

By the time they could jump no more,it was almost dawn.They were lying on the table like two mangy dogs.

"Ouch,my feet are swollen."Shang Xiaoning said.

"Are your feet swollen?I'm still wearing high heels,which I'm lucky to have taken off and danced barefoot,or I would have broken a bone.The good thing is that the dress is long and covers the feet so no one can see it."

"Where are those two dead souls?I haven't seen them since the dance."Shang Xiaoning looked at all corners of the ballroom,male models are almost gone.The staff member Xiao Zhang has fallen asleep on the desk.

"Shall we get a room and sleep?I can't go any further,I won't go back.Call Xiao Zhang too."

Shang Xiaoning lurched to the front of Xiao Zhang,shaking her,"Get up,get up,we go to the room to sleep."

"Huh?"Xiao Zhang opened her red eyes and looked at her stupidly.

"Let's get a room and go to bed.It's morning."

"Oh,all right."Xiao Zhang stood up and staggered over.Then the three of them stood up to each other and asked the waiter to show them to their rooms.As soon as they entered the room,they all fell down on the bed and fell asleep.

43

In the afternoon, Shang Xiaoning was the first to wake up, and after determining where she was and who she was with, she couldn't help but think of this unusual country. Is there such a country in the world? Why haven't she heard that? Why does the White Chrysanthemum not believe that? She is a college student, very learned, should know this kind of thing, she said that there is no country in the world, perhaps there is no. But without such a country, what is this place now? Shang Xiaoning dont understand, and here men and women strange look, call her really cant stand.

Ah, great, Shang Xiaoning jumped up from the bed. She promised to call the reporter. He must be waiting. Shang Xiaoning looked at the two people on the bed again, and both slept very well. Probably haven't slept in days for this fashion Shaw show. Just fell asleep, Shangxiaoning think of Shaw Swan hate this reporter, if she knew she wanted to call him, maybe will not let her play it.

Shang Xiaoning hope they dont wake up soon, so she also alone to deal with their own things. She hadn't been alone since she fell into the sea. She thought of the White Chrysanthemum again, and the dead ghost did not know where to go.

If she hadn't insisted on going to sea, why would they be here? Don't come over, Shang Xiaoning has become a beauty, it is also worth it. Eat the bitter, the master.

Shang Xiaoning gently to go out, but again thought, his body no money, how to call reporters? Oh, it's a foreign country. What kind of money? Even if she has money in her pocket, she can't use it. Whatever. Just take their money. Whatever it is she can use it. Shang Xiaoning secretly smiled and walked back gently to see where their bags were. She remembered that the three of them didn't bring a bag last night,so they came to sleep,then where is the money?No,if they don't have money,why would they let them sleep?

Shang Xiaoning came to their side,looked left and right,just did not find a bag or purse kind of things.Could the purse be in their pocket?But Shaw Swan or last night's queen dress,did not change down at all,this kind of clothing is impossible to have pockets.There are more pockets in Xiao Zhang's clothes,ten or so on the top and bottom,but which pocket has the money or the wallet?Shang Xiaoning considered for a long time,decided not to pick people's pockets,in case people wake up,how to say?Even if she does not mind,Shang Xiaoning still want to say the call,this thing is not to say.

Shang Xiaoning standing there,and then start thinking,also can not think of a way.Let's get out of here.Let's get out of here.They wake up,they're found,there's no way out.Thinking of this,Shang Xiaoning quickly turned around and tiptoed out for fear that they would suddenly wake up.She went to the door and gently twisted it open,looked back,and then gently closed the door again.

After coming to the door,Shang Xiaoning looked at both sides of the corridor,saw an exit on one side,and went to the exit.After passing a service desk at the exit,Shang Xiaoning thought for a moment and came back and asked a girl at the service desk.

"Is there a public phone near here?"Shang Xiaoning think well,if she answered yes,then Shang Xiaoning said her lost her wallet,want to call home,but no money,she can borrow some money to her?Even if Shang Xiaoning play an IOU to her,later to return.

44

The girl was reading with her head down,and when she heard the question,she looked up and had a long beard.It's a lad.

The young man was also clearly looking at her with puzzled eyes,deciding whether she was a man or a woman.If he's a man,why doesn't he have a beard,his neck is half exposed,covered by a collar,and his voice is so crisp?If it's a woman,why is she wearing long hair and dressing so well?

See the young man staring at herself,Shangx Xaoning and talked about the design of the second sentence.But she had just mentioned that she had lost her wallet and had no money when she called,the young man spoke:

"There's a pay phone in the lobby,and it's free for guests staying there."The young man pointed to the information desk in the lobby.

It's that simple?Also too out of Shang Xiaoning's expectations.Shang Xiaoning also prepared a variety of entreaty,going to perform well,the results all in vain.But it's better this way,she can call right away,she don't have to ask,and it's not easy to cheat a phone bill.Shang Xiaoning immediately rushed to the phone,dialed the reporter's phone.Sure enough,the reporter had been waiting for her,thinking something had happened to her;Or forget it.After explaining the reason,Shang Xiaoning said emotively:

"How could I forget?"

"I'm afraid that psychopath has locked you up."

"No,she's very nice,and she's very nice to me."

"Let's meet sometime.We'll talk when we meet."

"This?I don't know...I wonder what the Shaw Swan will do."

"Stop listening to her and leave her at once!"

'Leave her?Where am I going?I have no money.I can't go home."

"Where are you now?"

"Isn't that the same hotel where we danced yesterday?I'm in room 705.Wait for me at the gate."

Shang Xiaoning happily hung up the phone,and looked over to the guest room,there was no figure.They're not up yet?Shang Xiaoning hesitated again,think this is not very good,people are so good to her,like found a baby,she said betrayal betrayal,leaving such a good person,to take refuge in an unknown man.

Let's go to the gate first,and then we'll talk.She won't betray Swan Shaw,and she won't just go with some unknown man.Shang Xiaoning still went to the gate.

45

Outside the door,Shang Xiaoning has a chance to see the country.To this day,she hasn't had a chance to take a good look at it.But before that,how did she know it was another country?

The hotel seems to be in the center of the city,and the outside is very busy and busy,just like in China.The fashionable girls on the street,no,the boys,they're all in the same wave.They dressed up,wearing high heels,while walking,eating snacks,laughing,very happy,very carefree look.Shang Xiaoning could not help but think of the Chinese girls,they are not so?Wasn't that what you used to do?The best years of your life!At what point do you lose it?And become a woman?And then there's the old woman.

These girls,no,these guys,some of them were wearing miniskirts,some of them were wearing jeans,some of them were barefoot and they had slip-on sandals,and their toenails were painted.Were it not for their beards and Adam's apples,Shang Xiaoning must have thought she saw a group of girls in hher own hometown in China.

Beard style that can be a lot,some hot,like a curly dog,this is generally a little older people,more than thirty years old people;Some float vertically,chest length,this is generally more than twenty years old,relatively stable kind;Some dyed yellow,but also cut seven long or eight short,and China now popular broken hair almost it;Some comb into a braid,there is a middle braid,there are two separate braids,there are countless braids,and some with a bow tied,equivalent to China's"horse tail",but this"tail"is in front of ah,should be called"goatee",and some are tied on both sides;Some are held with clamps,clamps are also colorful,different shapes;There are hair in the ear side tied together,make a shape,this Shang Xiaoning can not be classified.

These are the beards under the lips,and the beards above the lips,which the young man separates on each side of his mouth,shapes with mousse,and hangs down;Some are held with clips,tied with bows,and braided;The older man cut his beard flat with his upper lip,just like the beard on Lu Xun's mouth.The beard on the top should be treated like this,otherwise it is difficult to eat.The rest doesn't matter.Ha ha ha,Shang Xiaoning thought of here,laughed out of the sound.

A few of the lads had long beards,but they still wore heavy make-up,jingled earrings,and looked every bit like women.The older men had beards half a foot long,but they did not do anything about it,but many of them had their beards dyed black,like their hair.Shang Xiaoning judged that they were dyed because there were also many people whose hair and beard roots were gray or all white.

But when teenagers are too young and their beards have not yet grown,it is difficult to tell whether they are boys or girls.Hey,why are you so stupid?Isn't it the other way around?If you see a girl,it's a boy.If you see a boy,it's a girl. Although Shang Xiaoning has long known to think this way,she can't help but sometimes use the Chinese way of thinking.

46

Their clothes are also very funny,the back can be exposed,but the neck is wrapped in a neckerchief.Fashionable people,clothes are translucent,there are many people with short shirts,belly buttons exposed,pants hanging on the buttocks,and a bend to expose one tenth of the buttocks.Half the people wear skirts.

If not Shang Xiaoning always remind themselves that this is in the women's country,she would think that those men neck injury,like throat cancer people,after the knife,the neck are surrounded by a gauze Oh,no wonder.Their Adam's apple can't be shown,like our women's breasts,right?But they're also desperate to show off,so they wear necklaces,or stretchy turtlenecks,which is like tights for us women,right?Shaw Swan said,Adam's apple is curved.

Shang Xiaoning laughed again.Shang Xiaoning found that people are trying to walk with their necks,so that people can see the protruding Adam's apple from a distance.Some people's Adam's apple is particularly large,Shang Xiaoning all think it is a long bag,like the country people before the big neck disease.

Hey,what's so nice about that?It's not fake,is it?Shang Xiaoning thought of plastic surgery,and thought of himself,couldn't help but face a red.Wasn't she fake,too?Got some kind of plastic surgery?It's funny now,you know,not like these guys?

Also from time to time there are pedestrians to Shang Xiaoning cast strange eyes,and looked at her up and down,Shang Xiaoning calmly let them see,anyway,her dress normal,she will feel at ease.Perhaps they looked at her as strangely as she looked at them?People would also be surprised to see a man on the streets of China wearing a flowery suit,skirt,high heels,earrings and a neck that exposes most of his Adam's Apple.

This thought,Shang Xiaoning can not help but touch his neck,her Adam's apple is exposed.It's just normal clothes,isn't it?She was still wearing a shirt,with a half-height collar,only the first button was unbuttoned.However,even if the buckle,there is still half of the Adam's Apple on the outside,or"weird",which is intolerable!Equivalent to the Chinese girl's underwear to wear,and walk!Men go shirtless in the street.Hahahaha...Shang Xiaoning smiled again.

A group of girls,no,a group of lads,passed in front of Shang Xiaoning and entered a nearby shop.Shang Xiaoning eyes chase them,but see the side of the shop sign,is"beauty beard shop".What is a beard shop?Shang Xiaoning a little curious,followed the past.

At the door of the store,Shang Xiaoning saw photos of various men posted in the window,all of them as beautiful as heaven,their beards were made into various styles,and the advertising slogan was:

"Blowing,cutting,ironing,combing,baking,pasting,planting,tattooing,VIP service,public price."

"111 raw beard water,effective after 1 week,invalid refund."

The couplet has:"The new cause starts from beard and the old phenomenon must be spared."

47

The beard is also fake,planted and tattooed?Shang Xiaoning and look at those photos,sure enough,there is a group of pictures,is a few men after the use of"111",from the mouth bare beard,to grow a full brush beard,to the chest flowing beard comparison photos.Another set of pictures showed various fake beards.

Hey hey,Shang Xiaoning feel very funny,no wonder most of the men on the street have beards,but also very thick,the original is so!Shang Xiaoning did not dare to go in,she did not have a beard.She was just outside the window looking in,trying to see what those people were doing.No,soon there was a girl,no,the young man came out,smiled at her,and asked in a soft,gruff voice,

"What do you need,Miss?"

Shang Xiaoning was surprised by him,her instinct to run,if in the past she thought she met the shemale,now she always have to remind themselves that this is in the women's country.Shang Xiaoning settled down a little and said,

"I don't need anything."

"We can pick them here."

"Pick what?"

"It's the people in these pictures."

"Why pick on them?I don't have a beard."

"No,"said the young man,seeing that she was a layman and suppressing a laugh,"it's a special service,it's...It's for you."

"Why with me?I don't know them.They are certainly not like Lei Feng,accompany me shopping,accompany me to eat,are charged,right?"

"No,you can get a room..."The young man's face has not taken off,has no beard,just hairy,can not call him a young man,should be called a teenager more appropriate.His clothes were low in the neck and translucent,with the neck, neck clearly visible underneath.He's not much older than his own son,is he?Well,it's amazing how young you are to be working.Shang Xiaoning thought of his son again.I don't know how he is,without his mother around,the stepmother must be bad for him,maybe he doesn't go to school now,go to work.

The young man saw Shang Xiaoning was silent for a long time,and added,"That is,it can be introduced,and it can be taken home,and it can be here."

'What?"Shang Xiaoning still did not react,but the words" introduction" and "take home" stimulated her,and she suddenly thought of something,opened her mouth wide and was stunned.Her husband came home with a hair salon girl,and she ran him over.

She had a bad cold and a bad headache that day,and her husband had gone to stock up again.She asked the owner next door to keep an eye on the shop while she went home to get her medicine.Entered the house,opened the bedroom door,just saw her husband and hair salon sister in bed.In a rage,she rushed in,slapped the hair salon sister several times,and then slapped her husband's face,and then grabbed the hair of the hair salon sister,hard to scratch her face.

This salon girl she knew,in a small salon not far from her home,also washed her hair,blow over her hair.The husband protected the salon girl and forced her to pull away.This made her more angry,she grabbed something to hit them,caught what is what,two people hiding in the corner shaking.Then she started smashing things in her house,picking up a chair to smash the TV and throwing everything on the table to the ground,screaming and crying as she threw it.

48

"No,no,I will die with you,I will burn you dog and woman,and I will let you go to the grave to be husband and wife."I will go to the King of Hell and Sue you,and he will fry you in a pot of oil,with a saw,with a mill,with a mountain of knives,with a sea of fire..."

To her jumping tired,scold dumb,tears dry,things also smashed,she sat down on the ground,feel to faint.Her husband was busy to pinch her,she woke up,saw her husband,and wanted to slap him in the face,but she had no strength,fan can not move.The husband carried her to the bed and knelt beside the bed with the salon girl,begging her forgiveness.

"No,divorce!How am I ever gonna live with you with this?Just thinking about it makes me throw up!"Shang Xiaoning cried with a hoarse voice.Then Shang Xiaoning struggled to sit up,her husband did not know what she was going to do,rushed to help her,Shang Xiaoning broke away from his hand,"Don't touch me,I think you are dirty!"

"What are you doing?"

"Am I going to sleep in this dirty bed?I will die at once and not sleep!"

Shangxiaoning staggered out of the house,let her husband how to shout in the back,do not promise.Later Shang Xiaoning has been living in the store,the store is not open.Her husband came to her many times,but she wouldn't open the door.And then everything was sold,and the store was sold.She got the house and part of the money in the divorce.She didn't want a son because she didn't want her husband to feel too comfortable.No matter who the husband marries in the future,dragging a bottle of oil is not so satisfactory,and the life of any stepmother is not easy.The son will only hate them,will not give them a good look.It's harder to keep them alive than dead,let her son take it out on her.

As soon as Shang Xiaoning and her husband divorced,her husband bought a house and married the hair salon sister.Shang Xiaoning at this time and good regret,why so help them?Now they were secretly,but now they were openly and proudly,entering and leaving together,and it was she herself who removed her stumbling block for them,removing the thorn in their side and the thorn in their flesh.Otherwise,the hair salon girl will never be a regular,only to be an underground worker,at most,a dick.Loss,loss.

But to call Shang Xiaoning and husband again,it is absolutely impossible. Broken mirror can not be round,in fact,how the circle has cracks.Because husband and wife is the matter of men and women,betrayed in this matter,Shang Xiaoning can not tolerate.

"If it's a boy,it's five times more expensive."The young man misunderstood Shang Xiaoning's silence and said further.

"What do you say?"Shangxiaoning from the past back to reality,anger is still burning in the chest,"really shameless!What do you take me for?"Shang Xiaoning's face was distorted by anger and pain.

The young man looked at her in horror,not understanding what he had said. At this time Shang Xiaoning and feel a little hard to bear,after all,the child is not sorry for her,he and her son is almost old.What a crime,to do something like this at such a young age.Shang Xiaoning shook her head,closed her eyes,sighed and left the shop.

49

Next door to the beard shop is a neckerchief workmanship shop.Shang Xiaoning gas has not calmed down,no mood to see these things,but these things do attract her,do not look.Shang Xiaoning step into,she did not Adam's apple,see still not?

Ah,that's right,no wonder some people on the street see Adam's apple so big,it turns out to be fake.Oh,Shang Xiaoning smiled again,she has forgotten the grief and anger,become very happy.This is not surprising,Shang Xiaoning thought of Chinese bra shops,the same thing!

Shang Xiaoning see beautiful neckerchief,cant help but touch with hands.Such exquisite crafts,put anywhere will be loved,her praise and love is overflowing.Her move terrified several teenagers next to them,they quickly fled to one side,like looking at a monster to see Shang Xiaoning,while whispering:

"Well,she's not a pervert,is she?"

"I think so,isn't it true that some women like to collect men's underwear and neckerchief?"

"Yes,some people steal it."

"Yeah,some people steal underwear and bibs from celebrities."

"Be careful that she doesn't come after you."

"The newspapers say that women are often following teenagers into homes to rob them of money and sex."

"Another kidnapped a teenager and then killed him."

Shang Xiaoning listened to these words is really laughing and crying,when she turned her eyes to these teenagers,they were all scared to lower their heads,and some pretended to look at the neckerchief,but in the corner of their eyes to peek at her.Alas,Shang Xiaoning only smile bitterly.

The boss's eyes have never left Shang Xiaoning,he looked her up and down,trying to figure out her intentions,observing her actions.These young people's words also gave him a wake-up call,he was alert,but he was not willing to give up a good business.He looked from Shang Xiaoning,she is very fond of these things,then there must be a great business opportunity.

The boss came over with a smile and said softly to Shang Xiaoning:"What kind of neckerchief did the lady fancy?"Is it for your boyfriend?"With an ambiguous smile,as if he knew this kind of woman very well and was very amicable,"The cushion inside this one can be taken out,"the boss took down a neckerchief hanging on the shelf,and then took out a group of things from its mezzanine,"When the summer is hot,you can take it off;You can also take it out when you wash it.This mat is a high-tech product,absorbs sweat,does not hurt the skin,and can also play a health care role.Long-term use,and the effect of increasing the larynx.It's much more convenient than that bubble."

50

"Ha ha,it's really beautiful.I didn't want to buy it,but now that I've told you,I really do."Shang Xiaoning suddenly want to buy a son,this is what a fun thing?

"I knew this lady had an eye.I don't get regular people in my shop.A woman dressed like you must be very fashionable.Many boys must love you. Buy this as a present.It's the best thing ever...Cluck."The boss is like a pimp or a madam,smiling ingratiatingly,while flirting himself,hoping that the lady will suddenly take a fancy to him and eat his old grass.

But Shang Xiaoning touched her pocket and remembered that he had no money.Not only did she remember that she had no money,but she also remembered that because she had no money to call the reporter,I went to the lobby to call the reporter,and then made an appointment to wait for the reporter at the hotel gate.

"Oh,oh,oh,I almost forgot all about it."Shang Xiaoning said to herself,he started to rush out.

"You haven't bought anything yet?"The boss called after her.

"Come back and buy later.I'm in a hurry,and I don't have any money.I will definitely buy it later."Shang Xiaoning running while answering the boss,she really want to buy.

Shang Xiaoning ran back to the hotel gate,no one.She looked around again to see if the reporters had also wandered nearby and saw no one.He didn't come and see her gone,did he?Shang Xiaoning regret,should not go to see those shops,what is the meaning?Delay the big thing here,maybe even the big thing in life.Shang Xiaoning became very anxious,restless,walking back and forth at the hotel door.

Maybe he had to come up to something?Or a traffic jam?Or she run into someone she know,and she can't get away.Shang Xiaoning ruled out all possible situations one by one.Ah,did he suddenly lose interest in her and stop coming?This is the last thing Shang Xiaoning wants to think.Yeah,why would she trust him?She doesn't know anything about him.Is a man a reliable thing?She was never supposed to trust a man again.Shangxiaoning and chagrin up,hate themselves useless.A few sweet words had taken her prisoner again,and not much had been said,not nearly as much as her husband had said.

"Can I help you,ma'am?"A man's voice woke Shang Xiaoning from his meditation.Shang Xiaoning looked up,a young man is smiling at her,"I have been looking at you walking around here,the mood seems very bad,do you want me to play with you?"

Shang Xiaoning soon understood what he meant.At the door of the hotel there are three or three pairs of heavily made up young men in the swaying,Shangxiaoning did not pay attention,now a look will know what they are doing.Shang Xiaoning gave him a hard stare and turned to walk away.

Shang Xiaoning walked to the hotel,because she also missed a possibility that the reporter could not find her,and rushed directly to the room she lived in.

51

Sure enough, when Shang Xiaoning came to the door of the room, he heard a fierce quarrel inside, a man's voice and a woman's voice. A man's voice is a journalist's voice. Reporters will not not come, Shang Xiaoning did not see the wrong person. Shang Xiaoning excited, he opened the door and went in.

"You crazy, psychopath, I want you! Shang Xiaoning slept here, and now there's no one there. You must have kidnapped her, staged it like it had nothing to do with you. I tell you, I'm not that stupid!"

"You are the madman, the pervert, the pervert. If you don't hand over Shang Xiaoning today, I'm not done with you."

"That's strange, who is Shang Xiaoning to you?" What right do you have to have her? What thick skin!"

"Stop it, stop it. Hurry up and find someone before anything really happens." Xiao Zhang said.

'Yes, call the police!" Said the Shaw Swan.

"Call the police! Jiao" Jiao Liang said.

"Hello, 011." Jiao Liang has opened the phone, pressed the number, and shouted at the phone.

"Don't call the police, I'm here." Shang Xiaoning shouted quickly.

"Oh, you're back!

All three people in the room shouted those words at the same time.

"Where have you been? Without saying hello?" Shaw swan hugged Shang Xiaoning complain.

"Are you all right?J"Jiao Liang holding Shang Xiaoning hand, secretly made a strong.

Shang Xiaoning knew what he meant,and said it to her,but also said it to everyone,but the content was slightly changed,leaving out this section of the meeting with the reporter:"I can't sleep when I wake up,see you sleep so well,I didn't wake you up."I'm just gonna walk around the door and check out the shops.It's a pity I didn't bring any money,or I would have bought a lot of things."

"Why,why didn't I think of that? Shaw Swan patted hier head,"You were rescued from the sea,there must be nothing on you.I should have given you some money;And cell phones.You don't know anyone.You wouldn't be able to find them if you got lost.Xiao Zhang,give your all the money in your pocket,and I'll pay you back later;And your mobile phone,too.I'll get you another one tomorrow. You have my number on that phone,too,for convenience."

Xiao Zhang took her pocket,took out his mobile phone and money,and was ready to give Shang Xiaoning,Jiao Liang said:"Give me to you,and my wallet."And he reached for his pocket.

"Don't take anything from him,he's up to no good.Maybe he still has a bug in his mobile phone,and he hears something and he puts it in the paper.They can sell any information for money,even at the cost of family,friendship,law,and morality."

"Are you moral?If you want to be moral,you shouldn't put Shang Xiaoning under house arrest."

52

"I put Shang Xiaoning under house arrest?" Shaw Swan rushed to beat Jiao Liang,but a run,was her mop queen dress to a trip,almost fell.This made her more angry,she simply lifted the skirt,divided the hem into two corners,and used them as a rope,tied up the buttocks,so that it was smooth.

"Why?Want to fight?I tell you,I was a wild boy when I was growing up,and I'm not a big boy.I beat a lot of girls to tears.You want to try it?Come on then?I wanted to be a cop.I know martial arts.There are many bosses who want me to be a female bodyguard."

Jiao Liang took his hand out of his pocket,did not pick his mobile phone and wallet,and squatted down on his horse,his hands standing upright in front of his chest.

Shaw Swan said:"Huh?I'd love to.I've never been in a fight or a fight in my life.I've been a good student since childhood,a good baby,people call me cream girl,say I'm daddy,not feminine.I'm going to be a real woman today and show you what I can do."

See these two people want to go together,Shangxiaoning hurriedly sandwiched in them.

"Noise again?Did you call again?Can you not do that?Is there anything we can't just sit down and talk about?"

"That's impossible." Shaw Swan said with his chest.

"That's not possible either."Jiao Liang also learned her look to say.

Shaw Swan and want to rush up to beat him,Shang Xiaoning open his hands to stop her,"Oh,how are you two?"

"I will not give up!""Said the Shaw Swan,shaking his fist.

"Me too!Jiao" Liang also shook his fist.

"Oh,you two are so annoying.You go!"Shang Xiaoning pretended to angrily push Jiao Liang to the door,gently said,"I have time to call you."After pushing him outside the door,Shang Xiaoning slammed the door shut.

Jiao Liang banged on the door again and shouted,"I won't stop.I'll come again."

'Die,you!The Shaw Swan called to the door.

"Now,now,don't be angry."Shang Xiaoning comfort her way.

"We had so much fun last night,and we slept so well today,and I'm in a good mood."There are activities later,give him so,really not in the mood."

"Take it easy,take it easy,what activity?"

"We'll know when we go,keep it a secret for now.Xiao Zhang,right?"When Shaw Swan mentioned the activity,he smiled again and was somewhat proud.

"What's the big deal?It's not a no-panties show,is it?I've seen your boldest. What am I afraid of?I have a resistance."

"Ha ha ha,you are so..." Shaw Swan lovingly touched Shang Xiaoning's head,"I will say you are bold,trendy,I am far less than you."

"I don't think I'm trendy at all.I'm old-fashioned."

"If you are old-fashioned,there will be no new people in the world."

53

Shang Xiaoning sat on the bed,swinging his legs,happy in his heart.She likes Shaw swan praise her,and Shaw swan is not a lie,is really like her,from the heart like out.To tell her to abandon Shaw Swan,go with the reporter,she is really reluctant to give it up.She had never met anyone in her life who liked her so much.That's why she had to push the reporter away.

" Xhao Zhang,go get my clothes.I've worn enough of these dresses.I don't know how men get on in them.I almost fell and made a fool of myself.You didn't see that,did you?I'm barefoot all the time."

"I see it.With your bare feet and your skirt tied up your ass,you look ridiculous."

"Yes,you remind me again.It's a good idea." Shaw Swan clapped his hand,"This shape of me,on the stage,will cause a sensation?"

"It certainly will.Ha ha ha..."

"Well,you always fill me with passion and inspiration.You are one of the rare women in the world." Shaw Swan holding arms,shaking his head,Shang Xiaoning praised.

"You say I'm good,you're the only person in the world who likes me.I don't really have any skills."Shang Xiaoning puckered up her lips,sprinkled with Jiao Liang .

She never knew what it was like,and she didn't act like a coquette.Since childhood,she has been inferior and submissive.Will not deceive people,will not deceive,will not be clever,will not play tricks,in the constant complaints and scolding sound to correct their behavior.She would endure everything again and again,and when she could not bear it,her family would not be able to bear it,saying that she was stubborn and eccentric.

She only knew how to be a man,and after marriage,it was still so,until she found the hair salon sister,the fire that she had never emitted since she was small,finally erupted to the maximum extent.In that moment she turned into a demon and a hag,and she wanted to cut them with a knife and burn them with fire!She had also thought of all kinds of excruciating,excruciating tortures to teach them.

Now Shang Xiaoning know that when someone loves,people will naturally be confident,naughty,lively,smart,clever,of course,will be spoiled.It feels really good.It wasn't that she couldn't do it,it was that no one had given her the chance. It's nature.It's not taught.Shang Xiaoning is now fully enjoying the joy of being spoiled,the naughty princess on the TV series,which is not spoiled?Tell her to be a child bride.Try a bad mother-in-law.Then you become a dull,cranky,annoying person.

Shang Xiaoning thought here,tilted his head,can not help but burst into a smile.

"Look at you,I don't know how cute you look." Shaw Swan sat down beside her and said,"Really,I've never liked a woman as much as I like you.I also thought of my nephew.He was my favorite child.It's a very strange thing."

"Is it?I like you,too.Because you praise me every day."

"Look at you,all naughty with me." Shaw Swan with a finger point Shang Xiaoning's head.

54

Two people so intimate chat,a little Xiao Zhang came back,carrying a large bag,this is taken during the performance.There were clothes,shoes,socks and handbags.Then all three washed and made themselves,and went out.

"We don't need to drive.We'll just walk.It's downtown."

"Well,I'll take a look,too."

Three people walk and talk while watching,because Shang Xiaoning just saw enough at the door of the hotel,surprised enough,and now it is not strange,can be as calm as they.But the huge billboards hanging all over the street still attracted Shang Xiaoning's attention.Basically are men's advertisements,very few women,to have,but also what brand-name clothes,brand-name cars,brand-name computers.Women are handsome,arrogant,brooding,or lounging on their shelves.Mostly middle-aged women,with the look of successful people.

Most of the men's ads are for young handsome men doing ads for nec kerchiefs,underwear,bedding,kitchen items,beauty items,toiletries,etc.When they do the neck advertising,the body is a three-part style,the neckerchiefs,the underwear,and even the transparent coat is not covered.It is no wonder that Shaw Swan simply removed these three things from their bodies and created a see-through costume.It's better to be naked and just wear underwear than to be naked and just wear outerwear.Now Shang Xiaoning fully accepted the idea of Shaw Swan,in fact,this is the case!If you want to take it off,just take it off.That's bold. It's strange that people can accept these ads,but they can't accept Shaw Swan's underwear less see-through dress.

Passing by a shop,I saw a sign that said"Hibiscus body",and then looked at the window,above it was posted"painless increase Adam's apple,a touch of effect."Secret family recipe,green plants,natural essence."

Shang Xiaoning couldn't help laughing and said,"Can I put some of this on?"Make my Adam's apple swell up too?"

"Then you'll be a shemale and instantly famous.""Said the Shaw Swan.

"So terrible?I'll leave it at that."

Shang Xiaoning passed a telephone pole,see the above posted with many small advertisements,and came to see,I saw the above read:

"Specializing in andrology all kinds of inflammation,infection."

"Gynecological treatment of various venereal diseases,a needle effective."

"Are you going to see an STD?"XShaw Swan saw this and asked maliciously.

Shang Xiaoning is a little embarrassed,"I just want to see what is written on it,where am I sick?"

The three women came to a square in the center of the city.In the middle of the square was a platform with a huge banner that read"Original Performance Art Exhibition."This place is under siege.

"It's not too late;it's going to take all afternoon anyway.We'll just go up there and see it."Said the Shaw Swan.

The three walked behind the stage up the steps,and onto the stage.The artists met Swan Shaw and said hello to her.The artists were all men,their hair disheveled,their clothes disheveled,and they were all holding pads and pens in their hands,painting on the bodies of young men.The boys were all in their underwear,sitting or lying down for them to draw.

55

Of course the Adam's apple is completely naked.But these Adam's apples are artfully painted as flowers,eyes,volcanoes and so on.Two artists went even further,holding a young man in their arms.He wore a neck,a corset,and underpants,and,using his long hair and beard as a paintbrush,stuffed his head into buckets,covered it with ink and colored paint,and painted it on a large cloth that lay on the floor of the stage.

"Is that it?I've seen it.I've seen it on TV.It's called body painting."

Shang Xiaoning's words let Shaw Sswan a little disappointed,"This I was specially to take you to see rare,originally you have seen,that is not interesting."

Just then,an audience boy climbed onto the stage and immediately took off his clothes,leaving only three pieces of underwear inside and no longer taking them off.

"What's going on?They also participated in the painting,so open-minded?"Shang Xiaoning asked.

"Look at it,look at it."

Only a young male host shouted at the audience:"You see,this brother is very brave,he dared to take off his clothes in front of everyone."His body was so handsome,so handsome,so curvy.Now that he's wearing the"Gao Mei Health tight underwear,"the$1,000 underwear is his.Let's applaud him!"

The male host himself held the microphone and clapped,and the monotonous applause was amplified countless times by the loudspeaker and wafted across the square,much like empty thunder.

There were a few more boys climbing up the stage.

"Ah,we welcome,there are several handsome brothers up,they are very confident in their bodies,dare to take off their clothes,this underwear is all theirs. We applaud them."

Shang Xiaoning skimmed his mouth,"Just this?I've seen it on TV too."All she didn't say was that she'd seen big girls doing it on TV,and here it was just boys.

"Oh,it's boring,you're so new,you've seen everything.Why don't we go to dinner?We haven't eaten anything since we got up.I'll take you to one of the most special restaurants.Yesterday's meal doesn't count,it's a working meal.Today's meal counts."

"All right."Shang Xiaoning really feel hungry now,want to eat.

The three women went down from the stage again.

Shaw Swan led them through a few streets to a magnificent hotel.As soon as they entered the door,a row of welcome boys in cheongsam bowed to them and said,"Good afternoon."Their beards were tied up in a bun on their chin and pulled over in a black net with a very beautiful red bow,corresponding to their red cheongsam.And,of course,all the hair at the back.

56

Shang Xiaoning is used to seeing these waiters and thinks they are also very beautiful in this way,but some people should not be old and have no beard?But can't a beard be fake?Shang Xiaoning and think of their plastic surgery,can not help but face a red.

Immediately a young man,who looked like a foreman,came over and asked:

"How many?Where would you like to eat?There are private rooms upstairs."

"Then go upstairs.""Said the Shaw Swan.

The head waiter led the way and took them to a private room called Peony. When the three of them sat down,a young man brought them tea,and as they drank it,the head waiter took the menu and asked them to order.

"Hey,do you still have any specialties here?""Asked the Shaw Swan.

"Yes,it's our specialty."

"What specialty?"Shang Xiaoning asked.

"It has the function of supplementing,and women eat best."'said the foreman.

"Oh,that's blood activating?I often have back pain."Shang Xiaoning said.

"Hey,hey,that's more to fill,Yin deficiency.You may be overworked.The food here is strong Yin."The swan smiled darkly.

Shang Xiaoning see Shaw Swan smile is not a general smile,that means…Shang Xiaoning understood,this is like Chinese men like to eat aphrodisiac things.

"I'm not as bad as you.I'm a good person."Shang Xiaoning coy hit Shaw Swan.

"I'm sorry,good people and bad people,we'll prove it later." Shaw Swan looked at Shang Xiaoning,giggled,and then said to the head waiter:"That's it,have beef Yin stewed sugar cane,sheep Yin lychee pot,green moth soup,steamed emperor fish,snow clam stewed papaya,braised abalone."Three more beers,one for each of us."

"Oh,don't order such expensive things.Abalone is very expensive."

"Abalone is the strongest Yin,especially your Yin deficiency."The Shaw Swan laughed again.

In a moment the dishes came.

Shaw Swan used a spoon to stir in the soup,while giving Shang Xiaoning scoop into the bowl,and asked:"Where are so many cow Yin,sheep Yin?"Isn't there only one in a cow or a sheep?" Shaw Swan said with a smile.

"What ox's eye,goat's eye?There's a bull's eye,a goat's eye?Oh,I dare not eat,I am so afraid of people,and I dare not eat again."Shang Xiaoning side body,far away from the bowl,very afraid to look at the things in the bowl.

"Ha ha,this is cow Yin,sheep Yin,understand?A cow or a ewes is like a bull's whip,and a sheep's whip is like a bull's or a ram's."

"Huh?Is this the thing?How dirty is that?How do you eat it?"Shang Xiaoning is still hiding from the bowl.

"Say you are trendy,you are sometimes very old-fashioned,why so inconsistent?"This thing is good.Look at me.How fit I am?I can handle having an 18-year-old with me every day.That's what fills it."

57

"I don't need it.I'm not that kind of person."

"Why,how can you say that?Food and sex also.If a woman doesn't like to eat pussy and doesn't like men,is she still a woman?"

"So I'm not a woman?"

"Yeah,so you need to catch up on that and learn from me."

"I won't learn."

"It doesn't matter,stay with me long enough and you'll let go. This is human nature,why suppress it?Come,eat,eat and you'll feel different."

But Shang Xiaoning still can not eat these things,"this I slowly adapt to later,I eat fish first,I like to eat fish,a day can not leave the fish."Shang Xiaoning picked up a piece of white and tender meat of Emperor fish with chopsticks,dipped a little soup,and sent it to his mouth,saying:"You say how this fish can't be done at home?"At home is also steamed,but not as tender,not as fresh."

"This time should not be too long,just ripe.There are also ingredients to pay attention to,cooking wine must be put,to fishy."

Little brother came to pour them drinks.His mouth is fuzzy,and his beard hasn't grown yet. Shaw Swan smiled and asked little brother,"How old are you?"

"Seventeen."

"Working so young?"

"Well,I have a sister at home who has to study."

"What's your name?"

"Tang Wantsister."

"Oh,there must be many boys in your family,and your mother wants girls,doesn't she?"

"HMM."

Shang Xiaoning looked at Shaw Swan with joy looking at Tang Wantsister know she is not only concerned about him,he said:"These children come out to work so youngnot easy."My son is still very spoiled at home.He should really learn how to stand on his own two feet."

Shaw Swan or look at Tang Wantsiste ,didnt put Shang Xiaoning words in mind. Tang Wantsiste although Shaw Swan smile Ying Ying,but answer while busy with his own,but the eyes clearly have a kind of expectation.

"Eat,eat your girsl."Shang Xiaoning greet Shaw Swan, Shaw Swan this came back to God,began to eat vegetables,drink,and chat with them.

Xiao Zhang seldom spoke,only eating food and drinking.

After the wine and food had been satisfied,the three women got up from their seats and walked out.

Shaw Swan walking while looking at Tang Wantsister,Tang Wantsister also lovingly sent them out of the private room,"go slowly,welcome."The Wantsister anticipation in his eyes was more pronounced.

After walking out of the private room, Shaw Swan also looked back at Tang Zhaoyounger sister,and then said without hesitation:"This little brother is very good."

58

"It's good to be your son."Shang Xiaoning said.

"Hey,be a cousin,I have a lot of cousins."

"I can guess."

"But I have a nephew who is really nice,not only handsome,but also good for me."I treated him like a son.He's 26 years old.He's not married.So,what's the use of getting married and having children,a nephew is enough."

Out of the hotel, Shaw Swan stopped her pace,"It's still early,where are we going?"

"When I got home,I was so tired that I just wanted to lean on the bed and watch TV and read a book.I danced so much yesterday that I hurt all over."Shang Xiaoning said,and then suddenly remembered something,"Yo,I left those magazines in the theater."I saw people running backstage,I didn't know what was going on,I also ran,I forgot to take the book."

"It doesn't matter,I don't want it either.I have a few more in the car if you want to read them."

"All right."

"Get your car from the hotel first and then go home," Shang Xiaoning said.

The three walked in the direction of the hotel.When they passed through an alley and passed a building,suddenly a ball of paper was thrown from the upper floor and hit the Shaw swan on the head.

'What is it?

Shaw Swan looked down at the ground and found the spitball.She immediately picked it up and opened it.It read"Help me."The paper was torn from a schoolboy's notebook,and the words were written in pencil,crooked and hasty.

"Someone has been kidnapped,.."

Shaw Swan looked at this building,this is a 7-story building,where the paper ball was thrown out? Shaw Swan noticed that only the Windows on the second and seventh floors were open and lit.Everything else is closed.

"People on the second floor,let's go rescue!"

"How did you know it was on the second floor?"

"It's not so accurate to throw something from the seventh floor.All the other Windows are closed and nobody's there."

"Call the police."Shang Xiaoning took out the mobile phone that Xiao Zhang gave her and asked,"What's the number?"

"011."Xiao Zhang replied.

"No,just us." Shaw Swan took the phone,the phone turned off,and then returned to Shang Xiaoning.

"Oh,I don't dare.What if the robber has a gun?"

"What are you afraid of?Look at me." Shaw Swan lead to the building,Xiao Zhang immediately follow her,Shang Xiaoning also had to follow behind.But Shang Xiaoning suddenly had an idea,she deliberately took a step slowly,turned around,quietly opened the mobile phone to call the reporter,the phone number she has already memorized.She feels too scared to have a man around,just three women.

The phone went through,Shang Xiaoning covered her mouth with her hand,gently and hurriedly said to the mobile phone:"You come quickly,we are rescuing the hostages."

"Hostages?Where are you now?"Jiao Liang asked anxiously.

59

Shang Xiaoning took a few steps back,stepped outside the building,saw the door number,read:"Tianxin Street No.54,second unit,second floor.I turned off my phone.Come quickly."

After the phone call,Shang Xiaoning feel calm in the heart a lot,this just trotted to catch up with the two people in front.

When the three of them reached the second floor and reached the door that corresponded to the spitball window, Shaw Swan motioned to them to get out of the way,asking them to press against the wall next to the door,and pointed to the cat's eye in the door.The two of them understand,and immediately tiptoe to do so.

Shaw Swan gently knocked on the door,after knocking,immediately put on a seductive posture,one hand soft fork waist,one hand put a lock of hair into hier mouth to bite,face is turned sideways,eyes coquely looked at the cat's eye.

Sure enough,after a while,a rough woman's voice came out of the door:"Who are you looking for?"I think she saw the Shaw Swan from the cat's eye.

"Oh,I don't know you,do ?I'm a little brother." Shaw Swan learn a man's voice,coaxing to say,while still twisting.Shang Xiaoning looked on the side almost laughed out loud.

"What do you want?"

"I just miss you,I haven't seen you for a long time,where are you dead?I made a little money in the lottery today,and I,I came to see you...Can't I do it today?"

The woman inside the door apparently hesitated for a moment and asked,"Just you?"

"Oh,who else would I bring?It's not convenient to bring it."

After a while,the door opened,and soon, Shaw Swan kicked the door open,waved his hand at the two women attached to the wall,and said:"Up!"She rushed into the room and shouted,"I'm a police officer,don't move!"Said the Shaw Swan,stretching his arms,clasping his hands together and holding them against each other,with two index fingers stretched forward,much like a policeman holding a gun in both hands.

When the woman in the room was stunned,Shang Xiaoning and Xiao Zhang rushed into the room inside,there was a boy tied up on the bed,and his mouth was covered with tape.Shang Xiaoning quickly tear the tape on the child's mouth,the child wow a cry.

"Don't cry,don't cry,it's all right now.We've caught the bad guy."Shang Xiaoning held the child in his arms and patted him gently.Xiao Zhang was quick to untie the child's rope.Yes,it was in this room that the window opened onto the alley."You were clever enough to save yourself.We looked at the spitballs before we came to rescue you."

Xiao Zhang is carefully examining the child's clothes,"She didn't do anything to you?"

The child shook his head and dried his tears with his hand,"When I took her to get the rope,I quickly wrote a note and threw it down."She had just tied me up when you came."

"What does this woman mean?Why take a girl?Do you want money?"Shang Xiaoning said.

"I'm a boy."

60

Shang Xiaoning lost her head again,wearing flower clothes is a boy.

"Was she trying to abduct children?"

"Abducting children,how can you abduct boys?No one wants the boy,to kidnap is to kidnap the girl.That's usually under the age of four or five.No one wants a boy this age."Xiao Zhang said.

Shang Xiaoning was about to argue with her,said which boy no one wants?No one wants a girl.Then she remembered that everything here is the opposite,and she suppressed her words.

"Then the boy must be from a very rich family."

"Do you see him dressed like he's rich?"

"Then why did she bring him here?"

"Don't you understand?This woman must be a bachelor,a pervert,a womanizer,and she wants to violate this child."

Shang Xiaoning try to turn this to think,otherwise thought will fight with each other,do not understand these words.Don't they have men like that in China?Kidnapped a little girl to do something bad,then killed her to keep her quiet.Such a thought Shang Xiaoning will feel more smooth,can understand.

"Luckily we got here in time.Swan Shaw was right.There's no time to call the police.We have to do it ourselves.I'm still too scared to come.If it doesn't,the kid's dead.Sometimes everything lasts only a few minutes.Oh,good luck."

Shang Xiaoning hugged the child again.

From the outhouse came banging and banging fighting,and Xiao Zhang ran out. Shaw Swan and the woman are at loggerheads.The woman saw that Shaw Swan did not have a gun in her hand,and his courage grew,and she threw things at her to smash her.The Shaw Swan threw something at her too,but he couldn't get near her.After all,Shaw Swan has not learned this,how can not subdue this woman.

Xiao Zhang rushed to hug the woman,but the woman kicked Xiao Zhang in the chest,and Xiao Zhang fell to the ground.When Shaw Swan that she was angry,she rushed to catch her.At this time,Xiao Zhang also endured the pain,got up and forced her.The two pushed her into the corner,and seeing that there was no place to run,she suddenly rolled over,jumped through the window,and jumped downstairs.

"Catch the bad guy-"cried Shaw Swan to the downstairs,and Xiao Zhang also cried.Then the two men turned and rushed out the door again,just as the siren wailed outside and the police car stopped with a clatter under the window. Then there was the sound of hurried,confused footsteps on the stairs,and a group of policemen rushed in.

"Go and catch the bad guy.The bad guy is gone."Shang Xiaoning shouted at the police.

"Someone's already gone.How's the child?"A male policeman with a half-beard came toward the child,and the other policemen scattered around the room,searching for useful clues.Through the voices and beards of these policemen,Shang Xiaoning judged that they were all women,and only this one was a man.

Jiao Liang also rushed in at this time,"The child is okay?"We're not late,are we?"Said from Shang Xiaoning's arms pulled the child,very lovingly held in the arms,and then from the arms to open the child,look at him,straighten his hair,said:"not scared?"You are very brave."Then he put his arms around him.

61

Some doctors came in with stretchers."Where's the baby?Hurry up."

Doctors,nurses are wearing hats,masks,Shang Xiaoning can not see whether they have beards;The white coats they wore were very wide and did not show the characteristics of women.Shang Xiaoning was unable to determine their gender,now only by voice.Shang Xiaoning has developed a bad habit,meet people,must identify him is male or female.she didn't know they were all women until she heard them speak.

The child looked at the doctor and said with a little fear,"I'm not hurt.I'm not sick."

"That,too,should be checked."

"I won't go."The child hugged Jiao Liang tightly.

"Child,I will accompany you,it doesn't matter,don't be afraid,there will be no injection.We're waiting for your family in the hospital."

"My brother works here."

"Where does he work?What's his name?"

"I don't know where he works.His name is Tang Comesinstert."

"Don wants a sister?Is that the one we met at the hotel today?"

"He said he worked at the hotel."

"That's right,that's him."

"What hotel?I'll make the call."Jiao Liang took out his phone.

"It's called something...I only remember that the private room where we ate was called Peony,and it was near the central square anyway."Shang Xiaoning said.

"I see,the Golden Yan Hotel."Jiao Liang got through the phone,told Tang

Comesinstert what happened,and said to the child:"Let's go,your brother is waiting for us in the hospital."The child is willing to lie on the stretcher,Jiao Liang holding the child's hand,with the stretcher to go out,Shang Xiaoning also followed them to go out.

The security cordon outside the house full of people,a group of reporters to see them come out,immediately mobbed the,flash"click click"lit,microphone all stuffed up,mingled with the reporter's question:

"Was the child harmed?"

"Was the villain caught?"

"How many of you fought the scoundsisters?"

"......"

So many people ask,Shang Xiaoning dont know who answer good,she is not in the mood at the moment.She just wanted to accompany the child to the hospital as soon as possible,and wait for the child to see his brother,settle down,and then ask why the child would fall into the hands of this woman.

The male policeman replied briefly:"The robber has not been caught,the child is not hurt,and there is nothing else to say."Shang Xiaoning,Xiao Zhang and the police followed the stretcher together on the ambulance.

To the hospital emergency room,doctors,nurses busy for a while Tang Wantsister also came.Tang Wantsister came to hold the child crying,and touched him everywhere,and then asked the doctor:

'Is she all right?

"She was fine.she healthy.she was just in shock."

The male policeman also copied down the medical records recorded by the doctor and began to take notes,first asking from the parties.Through the child's intermittent description,plus the brother Tang Wantsister in the side of the constant supplement,they know the whole incident.

62

The child is called Tang Comesinster third boy in the family.The boss is Tang Wantsister,a waitress in a restaurant;The second,also a boy,has run away from home.Because her mother really gave birth to a girl after giving birth to the third Tang Comesinstert,the family all think that this sister is brought by him,so he is also more respected,allowing him to study,and promised him that as long as he reads well,he can go to college.

But this year dad suddenly got seriously ill,hospital operation spent a lot of money,but also find others to borrow debt,the family can no longer let the two children study,so decided to let him drop out of school,at home farming,go out to do small work,to ensure that his sister read.This let him stand,his grades are very good,and the monitor,he was determined to go to college,this his dream was shattered.

He cried and made noise at home,the result was beaten by his mother,his father advised a few words,and was beaten by his mother.Dad is going to die,was stopped by relatives,he took advantage of the chaos,on the back of the bag,secretly ran out,into the coach,came here to find big brother.He thought that his eldest brother had gone to work and had money for him to study.

But when he got off the car,he found that he did not know how to find the big brother,he did not know the address of the big brother.It was getting dark,too,and he was afraid and anxious to cry.Just then,a woman,the bad guy,asked him why she was here alone.she said she was from the country,looking for his brother.The woman said.:"I know your brother,I will take you."

So she followed the woman to her house.As soon as she entered the house,she asked where the big brother was.At this time,the woman closed the door with a fierce look on her face and said,"Who knows your big brother?"she was crying and screaming to go.Then the woman said,"If you keep crying,I will kill you,and then kill your brother,and then kill your whole family."He was too scared to cry.

The woman said,"Do what I tell you,and I won't kill you."But she was not at ease,and said:"I must find a rope to tie you up,or you will move.And she went to the kitchen to find the rope.Tang Comesinstert wanted to climb out of the window,but the window outside is facing the alley,there is no place to settle,he did not dare to jump.

She was in a hurry,when she saw three people coming,he gently shouted"Help",but they did not hear.In a rush of wisdom,he thought of throwing spitballs.he once heard a teacher tell a story about a boy who was kidnapped and threw a spitball to survive.

At this time,he quickly opened his bag,took out a book,tore a piece of paper from the book,wrote two words quickly,rolled the paper into a ball,and threw it at the tall person in the middle,hitting, it is Shaw Swan than hurried back and put away notebook and pen just as the person found the rope and came back.

63

Tang Comesinstert was doing,he said nothing.The woman did not think much,put her mouth with tape,and tied him hands and feet,just then,someone knocked at the door.It was the three person from the street who had come to his rescue Tang Comesinstert gussed .

After listening to her story,everyone worked .p a sweat for him,and praised her for hier wisdom.If she had not thought of using this trick to get someone to save her,she would have been finished.

The male policeman took the record,let Shang Xiaoning look at it,signed it,and left.

Shang Xiaoning call Jiao Liang and ,said they are in the hospital. Shaw Swan had just gone down to catch the bad guy,then came panting,"Ah,the bad guy has been caught."She ran so fast that I couldn't catch up with her,and if the police hadn't come and shot her in the leg,they wouldn't have caught her.Oh,my legs are breaking."

Shaw Swan's clothes were sweaty and her face was tired,but she still came to see the child first,smiled and asked:"Is it OK,is it OK?"We're not late,are we?"

Tang Comesinstert shook her head.

Shaw Swan's face immediately rippling with a look of pride and pride, "How?I say we go save it?By the time the cops get here,it'll be too late.Don't you,little brother?"

"HMM." Tang Comesinstert nodded.

Shaw Swan touched Tang Comesinstertr's face,"This child is really cute."What's her name?"

"Tang Wantsister."

" Tang Comesinstert said:" there a Don looking for women?"

"This is his brother."Shang Xiaoning said.

"Really?What a coincidence?Then we are destined."

"Sister,I am here,thank you."Tang Wantsister walked to the front of Shaw Swan,eyes full of love and awe,but also very shy.

"Oh,hehe hehe,you brothers are both so cute.I am also a hero to save the beauty,ha ha ha,little brother,isn't it?"

At this time,the coke light came.A few more people arrived,followed by some reporters and people from Typhoon TV.As soon as Jiao Liang saw them,he immediately greeted them:

"Director Yu,are you here?How do you know?"

"A reporter called me,and I knew the basics."

Jiao Liang introduced to the younger brothers:"This is the director of the men's Federation,he is a special manager of boys,boys can find him to solve any difficulties."He turned to Director Yu and said,"This is the boy and this is his brother."

More than director came and Tang Comesinster shook hands,and touch Tang Comesinstert's head,asked:

"You are safe now,little brother.In the future,if you have any problems,you call me,okay?Our men's Union is your strongest backing!"

Tang Comesinster seemed to understand and nodded.

Cameras have been following Director Yu shot,reporters are also around her to take photos.Director Yu reached out her hand to several people who followed,took the fruit and supplements in their hands,handed them to Tang Comesinster,and pulled out a red envelope from his pocket,and said to Tang Comesinster:

"Here is a grant for you,1,000 yuan,to solve your current living difficulties first,and then we will solve your specific problems later."

64

Then Director Yu and Tang Comesinster stood side by side,one hand on her shoulder,one hand holding the red envelope,facing the camera lens. Tang Comesinster labored to hold the things in her hands.After shooting,Tang Comesinster took over her brother's hands and took it for him.

"So I can go to school tomorrow?"

"Yes.If your mother and father don't let you go to school,you can find us again and call us."

"I'm going back?No,I'm not going back.If I go back,my mother will kill me."

"Your mother often beats you?"

"HMM."

"Is it serious?"

"Serious."

"Still hitting others?"

"Yes,she beat my father a lot.Once broke her father's leg."

"Have you ever been hurt?"

"No,when she hits me,I ran."

"She's the one who made me run away to work."Tang Comesinster said beside,eyes red.

"Alas,domestic violence."Director Yu shook his head.

The camera was pointed at Director Yu alone,and Director Yu held his hands in front of his stomach and began his speech:

"Boys out of school in poor areas is still a serious problem,although through our efforts,has been improved,but for every individual,it needs to be solved immediately,and reading has become their biggest desire."Knowledge changes the fate,struggle to achieve the future.We can't let our kids lose at the starting line.Although this is related to economic backwardness,the traditional idea of valuing women over men also plays an important role.In the same difficult circumstances,it is always boys who miss out on the opportunity to study. Therefore,in addition to working hard on policies and regulations,we should also vigorously promote the idea of equality between women and men,improve the social status of men,and let boys out of school no longer happen.It is also hoped that those who have the means can give them financial support,so that they can enjoy the same educational opportunities as girls.

"Domestic violence often occurs in backward areas,although it is still related to poverty,but the female ideology is the most important factor;Low literacy is also a factor,which prevents them from communicating well with their families;The victims of domestic violence often do not know the help,think that being beaten by a woman should be,the husband and children belong to the wife,and it is her right to beat and scold.It's a family matter.It's not for outsiders.

"Now I want to tell the men,you should stand up and be a man,women are human,men are human,you also have the same status,they do not let you go to school,beat you,is illegal,you can go to Sue them."The men's League is your mother's home,there are your relatives here,when you encounter grievances,domestic violence,you will come to complain,we will help you solve the problem.Our hotline number is 12345678.Thank you."

65

After introducing the whole incident, he called for more attention to be paid to the out-of-school boys:

"We have set up a funding line and if anyone is donating, or wants to help, they can call 87654321. In addition, our reporter Jiao Liang, he is not only a senior senior reporter, has reported many major social issues, responsible for the writing of newspaper columns, but also a man who is enthusiastic about men's rights, he is a senior adviser of the Men's Federation. In the future, if you have any difficulties, you can also contact him. His number is 13912345678."

The camera lens then aimed at Jiao Liang, Jiao Liang waved his hand to the camera:

"Hello everyone, I am a fighter and will always fight for equality between women and men!" "Call me if you need me."

Then Director Yu asked the doctor again:

"Is he all right? Do you need to be hospitalized?"

"No, you can go home now."

Director Yu asked Tang Laimei again:

"And where are you staying tonight?"

"I'm staying with my brother."

"You have a place to stay?" More than director turned to ask Tang Comesinstert recruit.

"I live in a dormitory."

"That's not a long-term solution. Take him home today to rest, and then we'll figure it out."

"I have to go to work, leaving him alone in the dormitory I don't trust, in case he is abducted by some bad guy..."

"Well,why don't you stay at my house first?"Director Yu said.

"Live in my home,my home condition is good,I can afford to raise him."Shaw Swan grabbed to say.

"No,absolutely not.Don't walk out of the tiger's mouth into the Wolf's den."Jiao Liang step out,block in front of Tang Comesinstert if Xiao swan want to take him away.

Shaw Swan's face suddenly changed,and she was angry and waved her fists,rushing toward Jiao Liang,"I knew you deserved a beating,you this lack of women's love,only taste a woman's fist,in order to make you awake!"

People are pulling Shaw Swan,Director Yu is not very happy to say:

"Just now we were talkig about chauvinism,domestic violence,and now we're talking about it."

"I am not a violent person,I also have culture,culture,but when the good intentions are misinterpreted,everyone will be angry."A man like him deserves a beating!"

"You're the one who needs beating!"Jiao Liang said,then took Tang Comesinster in his arms and said to him,"Just stay in my house,OK?"

Tang Comesinstert looked at his brother,and looked at Shang Xiaoning,and then looked at Director Yu,and finally looked at Shaw Swan,said,"I still live in a man's home is better."Say holding Jiao Liang,and put his head on his chest.

66

"Oh,kid,very fine,eat once,learn good."So be it,respect his opinion,stay at Jiao Liang's house for the time being."Director Yu turned to Tang Comesinster," You will go to school here in the future."I'll find a way to help you with school."

The party was leaving,and everyone shook their hands.After they left,Jiao Liang took Tang Lai sister away.Before leaving,he took a deep look at Shang Xiaoning.Shang Xiaoning heart a hot,she really want to talk with him,is has not got the opportunity.But there will always be opportunities,and now Shang Xiaoning has a mobile phone.Shang Xiaoning secretly nodded to him,this action is almost invisible to others,but Jiao Liang saw it,he also nodded to her secretly,she also saw.

Because Tang Wantsister also want to go to work,and Jiao Liang,brother went out.When Jiao Liang turned around, Shaw Swan waved his fists behind him again,and after he left,cursed:

"This old,ugly,chunky,tall guy is always full of himself and absolutely psychopathic.They say old boys get cranky.Live alone,what is the strength,of course to pervert."

"Don't you and I live alone?We're not perverts."Shang Xiaoning refuted her.

"Hey,I hit too big.I mean,he's going to be out of his mind all alone.We're alone,but we're happy."

'How do you know he's unhappy?

"Yes,perhaps he is.But he always acts so angry that I can't stand it.Well,let's not talk about him.Let's go back,too.I'm too tired."Xiao Zhang said:"we'll take your car,I can't drive any more."

"Where am I going?"Shang Xiaoning asked.

"To my house,of course,do you know?You haven't been to my house yet."

Three people walked out of the hospital,hit the hotel where they slept the day before,Xiao Zhang took the car,and they sat in.

"Oh,I'm so tired,I want to sleep,but I'm too excited to sleep.""Said the Shaw Shaw an,leaning back in his seat.

"Me too."

"I just want a bubble bath."

"I just want to take a shower and lie in bed and watch TV."

"Isn't that easy?After you wash first,I'll soak slowly."

"Ok."

Car to the door of Shaw Swan,Shaw and Shang Xiaoning walked out.

"Oh,and magazines."Xiao Zhang grabbed a handful of magazines on the floor in the driver's cab,handed them to Shang Xiaoning through the window,and drove away.

"Xiao Zhang is really a nice person who remembers others.She doesn't talk,but you can count on her."Shang Xiaoning looked at the car away,can not help but say to Shaw Swan.

67

"Yeah,how else can we get together with such different personalities?" Because she's honest and reliable.You don't look at those people with me hot,sweet mouth is very,maybe behind my eight generations of ancestors.When it comes to interests,it's harder than anyone.I've seen that a lot." Shang Xiaoning said.

Two people said into the small building.Although this small western building looks similar to the female captain's home,but inside,I know that it is completely an artist's style,romantic,luxurious,casual.Shang Xiaoning had never seen such a position and was overwhelmed.She walked,she looked,she didn't have enough eyes.

Downstairs,in the living room,hung a huge chandelier,all made of glass that glowed with strange brilliance.In the middle of the living room there is an expensive carpet on the floor,a painting on the wall,a piano in one corner,a fireplace on one side,a rocking chair in front of the fireplace,and precious flowers and green plants in front of the window.When they went upstairs,paintings were hanging on the walls of the corridor.

Shaw Swan showed Shang Xiaoning the bedroom,which was also like a royal palace,with a yellow satin curtain hanging down and a huge bed under the curtain.The curtains were also golden goose down,with tassels and lace. The dressers and closets in the bedrooms are also antique,with floral wallpaper and paintings of naked men hanging on the walls.Shang Xiaoning at first glance these men who do not wear clothes are not used to it.The only modern thing in this room is the TV.

Shaw Swan took out a light green silk pajamas from the closet and threw them to Shang Xiaoning,"You go first,then I bubble."

"Any underwear?I'm sweaty too.I can't change."

"What underwear?What does it matter at home?"

"Give it to me if you have it.I'm not used to not wearing underwear."

"You're so conservative sometimes." Shaw Swan found two pieces and threw them to her."I'll take you to the bathroom."

The bathroom is next door,Shang Xiaoning a look,obediently,that luxury. Shang Xiaoning saw when she bought a bathtub before decoration,it seems to be more than 10,000 pieces,which have the functions of massage,water column,etc.,can be washed by two people in it,it is square.This one is infinitely superior to that one.The bathtub seemed to be made of jade,translucent,and was placed right in the middle of the bathroom.Shang Xiaoning can not help but touch with his hand,is indeed jade.Shang Xiaoning has a jade bracelet,so she knows a little about jade.But the jade bracelet was also lost in the water this time.

"Well,you wash it." Shaw Swan left Shang Xiaoning,take the door away.

Shang Xiaoning also want to bubble in such a bathtub,but she has said :"that the bath,it is not good to change temporarily,."Shaw Swan still waiting to bubble it."We'll do it later.There's plenty of opportunity.It's gonna be a little longer at her house?"

Shang Xiaoning rushed out of the shower,came to the bedroom.

Shaw Swan is on the computer:"So soon?"

"All right.You like to play computer,too?"

This should be the second modern thing in the room.Shang Xiaoning thought.

68

"This is a good thing,who is not fascinated?"

"My son can't get off the computer every day."

"You don't play?"

Shang Xiaoning shook her head,"Interest is not very big.In the shop every day,when do you have time?Besides,my son works on the computer all the time,which is not my job."

"In my future here,must make up this lesson,let you also become a computer fan."

"The Internet is not a good thing,and we have invited experts there to talk about how to quit Internet addiction."

"Strange thing!You want to quit this high-tech stuff?Well,let's all get a hoe and go to work.However,the hoe was also high-tech at that time,and it should also be stopped,ha ha ha..." Shaw Swan took the clothes and went to the bathroom.

Shang Xiaoning lay on the bed,turned on the TV,the TV is advertising.

A young man with a chest-length beard clasped his legs and said,"If there is no problem,use clean water."

Another,older man with a half-long beard,said,"What if there's a problem?"

Another older man,with a hot beard,came out and said:

"Twenty."

"Thirty."

"Forty."

The three men spoke in succession,and finally said in one voice,"All shall be washed."Ha ha ha..."

On the other side of the AD,a young man holds his neckerchief highlighting his enormous Adam's apple,although the Adam's apple is surrounded by a neck,but the neckerchie only the bottom half,the top half is completely naked. The young man,with great pride,stroked his Adam's apple with his hand and said:

"What could be more important than being a man?"

Then the picture turns,and the young man appears in the street,his neckerchie is casually wrapped in a transparent gauze scarf.At once many men cast envious and surprised glances;A lot of women looked at him in awe,and one woman ran headfirst into a telephone pole.

Then the picture turns again,the young man appears proudly in a restaurant,as.he passes a table,a woman keeps looking at him greedily.But the young man suddenly turned around and it was her husband,and now his Adam's apple was huge.The two laughed happily.Then a picture of a hospital appeared on the TV,and a voiceover introduced:

"Beautiful Neck beauty salon,world class level,to create unmatched,firm neck curves."

The original young man wore a uniform again,hands akimbo,leaning Adam's apple,making a posture,"With this neckerchie,I am more confident."

69

In the next commercial, for hair remover, a young man crouched down in the street in a hurry, covering his legs and shrinking his shoulders. Another guy came up and asked,"Why don't you use a skinny-looking hair removal cream?"

Then close-up, a hairy leg like a monkey, was coated with a little milky cream, and then with a touch of the hand, hair all gone. The young man jumped, his arms outstretched, showing his white armpits and his white legs.

Shangxiaoning for a station, the station advertising more rare, see Shang Xiaoning dumbfounded.

A young man in tight underpants with his lower body swollen like intestinal gas. If Shang Xiaoning had seen such a person on a Chinese TV commercial, he would have thought it was an advertisement for a hospital to perform lower body tumor surgery.

The young man said:"Wearing such underwear, my hip circumference has increased by 10 centimeters."After saying that he looked at his lower body with satisfaction, he immediately surrounded two young men who were also wearing tight underwear, but the lower body was not swollen too much, and looked at his lower body with envy,"Wow, what method do you use?"

The young man proudly said:"I use pumpkin health underwear, which has the effect of promoting blood circulation, massaging important acupuncture points, and converting outer space information into necessary energy for the human body, so that the lower body is full and upright. you can wear it and it will increase in size over time."

A computer-generated picture appeared on television, and the lower body really expanded rapidly in the underwear, immediately turned into a small pumpkin."See,this is what it does."The voiceover emphasizes.

The young man was holding a swollen lower body like a small pumpkin,a middle-aged woman came over,hugged the young man from behind,and lovingly put her face on his face,the young man said happily:"What can I give my wife?"That's where happiness comes from."

Shang Xiaoning changed another station,this time it was really a hospital advertisement,but there was a huge lower body wearing underwear,which was a little bigger than the small pumpkin just now.This must be an advertisement for the hospital doing cancer surgery.Shang Xiaoning looked at the advertisement with a bit of schadenfreude and bet with himself.

Voiceover:"Winter melon beauty hospital,adopt the latest high-tech enlargement method,no surgery,no medicine,no bleeding,no pain,10 minutes to do well,will let you have a very proud lower body."

Shang Xiaoning changed another station,this time finally a woman to advertise,a middle-aged woman held up a box of medicine,said:"female treasure female treasure,essential."A guy came up and stuck it to her chest and said coyly,"Girl girl girl girl,she's good,I'm good."

Shang Xiaoning changed a channel,she dont believe all these things on TV,she must find a general TV to come.Turns out it's a beauty pageant. A row of tall boys wearing only three-section clothes,neck circumference has no any barrier,but also exposed a small Adam's apple outside;Almost equal to not wearing underwear,of course,is tight,the lower body outline incomparable"curve",underwear hanging a brand,indicating their code name;They are already very tall,but they still wear heels at least half a foot high,putting their full weight on five toes and the"one finger Zen"heel.

70

They were skinny,as if they had just been released from a concentration camp,and you could clearly see the ribs,but they did not have any signs of exhaustion,and they walked and twisted with vigor on the stage.In the end young,can support a while,Shang Xiaoning to so,afraid also can not climb up.

Next to the host introduced the 4 circumference of each young man:

"Number 9,height 1'80,weight 55,neck 50,chest 80,waist 60,hip 70."

The boys will come out in evening dress,will wear their own designed clothes,will wear a wedding dress,anyway,toss enough,and start the quiz.

"Who is the author of Compendium of Materia Medica?"

A young man rolled his huge eyes with false eyelashes,thought for a long time,and said:"Jin Yong."

"No,it's Li Shizhen.What is the molecular structure of water?"

"Ice,water vapor."This time the young man answered quickly and affirmatively.

"No,two hydrogens and one oxygen."

Shang Xiaoning yawned,and changed a channel,this time is a TV series,Shang Xiaoning to the spirit.

This is a costume Shaw show,only to see an old woman surrounded by a group of young men.The young men are all heavily made up,light yarn and thin clothes,hand pinch fragrant pa,and the old woman laugh.The old woman is also happy to squint left and right to enjoy this from all sides of the handsome surrounded.Shang Xiaoning,based on her experience watching TV dramas in China,guessed it would be in a brothel.

Sure enough,after a while,an older man appeared with a smile.He was no less coquettish than the lads,and he was just as well dressed,but the age had turned his obsequiousness into ugliness,and he was not even aware of it.This must be the whore house.No,the head of the whore house,the madam.

"Oh,what brings you here,sister?Ponceau,tea."

The old woman grinned:"No,I think,so handsome people,how can I not come?"

Madam with a handkerchief in front of empty play,the body to the left twisted 90 degrees:"Think I this drunk incense building national famous,the emperor will patronize here,which woman does not want to yo?"Then he covered his mouth with a handkerchief and laughed.

"Do you still have your card?"

"Oh,sister,today,I have to wait for a noble person,not to receive guests."

"Is that me?"

"That depends on whether your sister is a noble person,if you are more generous than a noble person,do not say ."That is ten Shang Xiang are willing to serve you ah."

71

"Ha ha ha..."The old woman lit the madam with her hand,smiled heartily,and then took out a bag of silver from her arms and put it on the table,saying:"Is this enough?"

When the madam saw the silver,her face immediately lit up,she grabbed it and put it in her arms,while Shouting upstairs:"Qiu Xiang,don't come to serve my sister."

A young man upstairs agreed,floating down with a palace fan half covering his face.

Shang Xiaoning changed a platform again,this time it's a modern play,a couple walking in the quiet night,not out of how far,suddenly,the girl hugged the young man,on his mouth to chew,while still breathing heavily,while unbuttoning his clothes.Then there is a close-up of the side of the young man's neck.The girl untied his neck,exposing a quarter of his Adam's apple.The girl's hand also touched it.Then,one by one,the clothes were thrown out of the picture,and then the whole naked back of the young man,and the girl hugged the young man and rolled to the ground.

Shang Xiaoning ready to turn off the TV,but inadvertently touched another button,the TV automatically changed the channel.An old lady was talking:

"I believe in gay toilets.Don't women like to spy?That's because she's so curious.If it's a gay bathroom,it'll take away her curiosity,and she'll stop peeping. Being open and demystifying men is the best cure for voyeurism.People who have never eaten meat,always want to eat meat.Let her eat,every day,and when she has eaten enough,she no longer wants to eat."

There appeared a reporter with a beautiful chest-length beard,the beard on his upper lip was fixed with mousse on either side of the top of the mouth,the neck was attached to the clothes below,and his long hair was held behind his head with a beautiful clip,so that the back of the neck,connected to the back,all the way to the waist was visible.Shang Xiaoning remembered this bare back,the last time in Shaw Swan's press conference,she had seen,because the last time she looked at his back,did not know what his face was like.The last time I remembered his name was"May",and he was a reporter for some TV station.

"Today,we have the honor to interview Zhu Xishou,the famous master of Chinese studies.We can not only hear the wonderful theories of the master of Chinese studies,but also have a glimpse of her extraordinary style and understand her daily life.Now,Teacher Zhu has entered this beauty shop,let's go in and have a look."

A handsome young man was massaging Zhu's face on TV.Zhu Xishou thin closed his eyes and lay there.

"Excuse me,do you often do beauty treatments for this sister?"

"Er,yes,she comes often."

"May I ask Teacher Zhu,are you particularly fond of beauty?"

"I'm here to cure the disease.Not very often,either.But for one thing,I want a nice young man to give me a massage.It's a pleasure,otherwise I wouldn't have come."

72

Then,the TV picture turned,Zhu Xishou thin face coated thick face mold,eyes pasted two cucumbers,has been snoring loudly."She sleeps every time she comes."The young man said with a sneaky smile.

"She loves men,and her eyes light up when she sees a handsome young guy. It shows that she is still capable of love,that she will never grow old in the face of love..."

Shang Xiaoning turned off the TV,lay in bed,stayed for a long time,and picked up a few magazines that Xiao Zhang left her just now.The covers of these magazines are full of close-ups of handsome young men's faces,.Shang Xiaoning opened one and read on:

"Late at night,there was a naked body floating on the water of the lotus pond,and a young man walked here and screamed in fear.

"It all started two years ago.A young man named Gong Luzhu,is the bay University of outstanding student.He has a tall figure,a full throat,a straight lower body,fair skin and a good face.At school,he was the one everyone chased. By chance,he met Wang Chengcai,a rich girl,and became her boyfriend.

"Their first time,Wang Chengcai will always remember.It was a dark night,Wang Chengcai took Gong Luzhu to an unoccuated villa in his home,after a passionate kiss,Wang Chengcai unbuckled his clothes,revealing his embroidered neck,a burst of delicious fragrance hit,so that Wang Chengcai's heart shook,she tore Gong Luzhu's neck recklessly,a white stiff Adam's apple jumped out,Wang Chengcai was shocked,she could not help but pounce...

Shang Xiaoning is not interested in looking at it,and turned the back of the magazine,but also turned several other magazines,the content is nothing more than "little husband cheating", "college students,second grandpa,murder case", "young love Internet cafe", "80-year-old professor married 20-year-old guy".

  Shang Xiaoning threw these magazines,out of breath,finally really bored,a glance at the computer is still open,can not help but walk over.Maybe Swan Shaw is right that high-tech stuff is good and should be fascinated,not banned. Fortunately,Shang Xiaoning was dragged by her son on the net several times before,roughly know how to open the article,how to look.

73

The computer screen stopped on the home page of a website,and Shang Xiaoning looked at the titles of these articles:"10 tricks under the skirt of a peeping brother""Famous movie stars show their necks ."""Famous male sports stars run naked.male models show their dew."The world's top 10 male stars enjoy the beauty of the throat"...

Now Shang Xiaoning see"man's Adam's apple"words are annoying,she hopes to see a little different things.After one title by one screening,Shang Xiaoning found a man's inner monologue.Maybe that's what's really inside a man?Shang Xiaoning clicked on the article.

Shang Xiaoning first caught the eye of two photos,an ordinary looking young man without clothes,cut a short beard,but the neck hastily wrapped a scarf,basically no Adam's apple.The scarf drags over his chest,covering two points.His hands covered his lower body.Another photo is lying on the sofa,legs open,although wearing a thin as cicadas dress,also wearing briefs,but this position is really inelegant,like in the maternity bed.

Here's what he wrote:

"I want to strongly accuse this society of inequality between women and men,why can women talk about lust,and men can't?"Why should women be able to write extensively about sex in literature and men not?Why should we not play them if they play us?After I've slept with so many women,I'm tired of..."

There are many replies under the article,basically all women back,some scold,say that now there is no system,how can you send such articles and photos online?...

Shang Xiaoning quickly closed the article.I just want to catch her breath,and then she sees a name that seems familiar,Tang Thinksister. Oh,is it Tang Wantsisteri's brother,Tang Comesinstert 's brother?Shang Xiaoning remembered his family is three brothers.If the little brother's second brother is here,why doesn't he come to him?Shang Xiaoning will understand.

The title is"Body Art photo of Tang Thinksister taking younger sister."Although Shang Xiaoning knew what it was,he could not help but be curious to see how far his art had gone.Because this guy seems to have some kind of relationship with them.

A series of photos,is a scrawny teenager,sitting,lying,standing,posture is quite artistic.That is,the posture is better,the key parts are covered,and of course the Adam's apple is completely naked.Shang Xiaoning now looked at a man,also looked at his Adam's apple,although she was very reluctant,but naturally looked at the past.

74

Shang Xiaoning inadvertently look at these artistic photos,she wants to see the introduction of the teenager's article.Sure enough,the teenager ran away from home early,learned to dance,and became a nude model.This made the family in the countryside feel very humiliated,and the family broke away from him and did not recognize him.Now he is going to devote himself to art and show his beautiful body to everyone.The article ends by saying that he misses his brother and his brother and wants to go home,but he knows that once he takes this step,he can never go back.

This must be him,the second of the three brothers,and he looks similar in face and age.

Shang Xiaoning is looking at,thinking about the family problem, Shaw swan washed out of the bath.

"What are you looking at?The Shaw Swan said softly and came over.

"Well,look around.Look,is this the brother of the kid you saved?Look at the name."

Shaw Swan in Shang Xiaoning shoulder looked at,a strong fragrance to Shang Xiaoning hit.Shang Xiaoning again hard to smell,really good smell,Qinqin.

"Oh,it's him?I know.It's been on the Internet forever.Yeah,why didn't I connect him to the kid?Yes,it's him,it must be him,yes."

"And that one..."

Shang Xiaoning is ready to put her just see"a man's inner monologue"to see Shaw Swan,but Shaw Swan has reached out to take the mouse to turn these off,and finally the computer is off.Shang Xiaoning felt a little embarrassed,how could she be interested in these?She's not a dirty person,she's not a lecherous person.Don't look at the Shaw Swan flower.She's pretty decent about that.Shang Xiaoning could not help but respect Shaw Swan said again."That's what makes a horny man more decent than he thinks,and a decent man more horny than he thinks."

Shaw Swan turned off the computer,with the tide around Shang Xiaoning's neck,face against her face said:"Now is our'two world',nothing else exists."

Shaw Swan learned the advertising words like this,and used them in the same place.Shang Xiaoning smiled,but she still felt that being held by a woman like this,so close to the skin is not used to.She stood up and tried to pull away from the Shaw Swan.

"Ha ha,God knows,Earth knows."Shang Xiaoning thought of her husband's cheating behavior outside,when he probably also thought so?{*Snort*}Shang Xiaoning subconsciously replied to this sentence.

When Snort Swan hand loose,Shang Xiaoning left the embrace of Shaw Swan.Shang Xiaoning just want to take a breath,a look at Shaw Swan clothes,and scared to close their eyes.

"Why are you wearing such a dress?"

"What's wrong with the dress?It looks good."The Shaw Swan opened her arms and looked down at his clothes.

75

"It's too transparent."Shang Xiaoning's eyes dare not look at Shaw Swan.

"Ha ha ha...You,I can make men wear see-through clothes,but I can't?It's in my bedroom,not on the street."

"That...Someone else was there,and you weren't alone."

"Outsiders?Are you an outsider?I'm wearing it for you.I'm not treating you like a stranger."

"This..."Shang Xiaoning temporarily speechless,"at least to wear a underwear underwear."

"How inconvenient is that?It's too unromantic,too unexciting,so as to arouse the infinite good feeling."

"Oh,two women together,do you need it?It would be better if you were with a man."When Shang Xiaoning said this,his face was a little red.

Shaw Swan sat down next to Shang Xiaoning,held her hand,and said sincerely,"Have you often heard me talk about my nephew?"He's a really nice guy and good-looking.I brought it up from a young age.That's closer than a son. I've liked you since I first laid eyes on you,and I've liked you for my nephew.You see,I've been so busy lately,I haven't had time for you two to meet,and he's kind of like Wynn.I'm sure you two will fall in love at first sight.

When Shang Xiaoning heard this,she quickly waved her hand and said,"No,no,he is only 26 years old,much younger than me."I have a child,too."

Shaw Swan said,"In the face of true love,nothing is a problem."You haven't worked with him yet,so how do you know?"

"I don't like Wen Greenjade 's personality,and not a good man deserves my love."

"Look what you're saying, how could I hurt you? I wouldn't hurt my nephew either."

76

Shaw Swan said:"You two together will be a real love,this love is honey mixed with coptis,sweet and bitter,do not eat will go crazy."

"I have always regarded you as a sister,and your nephew is my nephew,how can I love him?"

"When two people fall in love,age is no problem,you see captain,so old,find a young husband,so good,what a happy family."

"But Wen Greenjade is not also with you."

"We were just having fun,not deep love."

"Why do you think your nephew and I have a deep love?"

"That's how I feel.I can't be wrong."

"But I don't feel that way."

"That's because you didn't see him."

At this moment,Shang Xiaoning heart only reporter Jiao Liang,can not accommodate others.If Jiao Liang had said so,she would have happily agreed. God really played a great joke with her,and this touching words were said by a sister.She had a feeling that she could not laugh or cry.

Unexpectedly, Shaw Swan suddenly changed her face and said:"I am optimistic about things will not be wrong."What you do with my nephew,it will happen,it will happen,it will not happen,I decide."

At this time,there was a fierce knock on the door,Shang Xiaoning rushed to the door like to see the savior,opened the door,the person standing outside the door made her surprised and happy,thinking of him,he came,it is God.The person who came were the reporter Jiao Liang,and there stood the child-Tang Comesinstert.

Shang Xiaoning quickly ran out of the door,hiding behind Jiao Liang,said:"She insisted on introducing my nephew to me."

"I knew it.She talked about her nephew everywhere,calling him a flower. Actually,her nephew is a compulsive gambler.Let's go."

Jiao Liang dragged Shang Xiaoning to run,one hand also dont forget latang to sister.The three of them stomped down the stairs

By the time Shaw Swan came to her senses,it was too late,and Shaw Swan rushed frantically to the stairs,Shouting at the top of her lungs:"Jiao Liang-you are not human!I'm not done with you."

77

Shaw Swan was about to rush downstairs,looked down at his full-view nightgown,rushed back to the bedroom,opened the cupboard,took off the nightgown,scrambled inside to find a dress to put on,and a pair of pants to put on,and then rushed downstairs to the door,but the three people had disappeared. Shaw Swan angrily stomped,and rushed back to the bedroom to find the car keys,she did not believe they would fly wings.She would find them as far away as they could go.

Seeing Shaw Swan car away,these three people from the flowers drill out,Shang Xiaoning shocked,Tang Comesinster clapped and smiled:"Haha,or my idea is good,she must chase."

"Luckily I parked far enough away that she couldn't see."

"Well,how did you find it?"Shang Xiaoning asked.

"Hey,you gotta see what I do.Journalists,to put it crudely,are nosy,and they can't hide anything from me.A celebrity like her,I know all about it when I ask the press.She's been on TV,she's been on magazine covers."

"Then why come at the right time?"

"Telepathy.After we went back to bed,I thought about you and the Shaw Swan,and the more I thought about it,the more worried I was.Her nephew is very famous,and she must have tried to match Lang,to force you to be with him,to get him to marry you.She won't leave you alone.You must be at her house.I immediately got up and called to get her address.I was going to come alone,but I left my little brother alone at home in case something happened again,so I shouted at him.As we were getting out of the car,I suddenly had a premonition that something had happened.I pulled him into the fast run,sure enough,something."

"Well,it's lucky you got here in time,otherwise I really don't know how to deal with the situation."

"Let's get in the car."Jiao Liang said.

Shang Xiaoning came to the car with them,just want to get on the car,but hesitated,she followed a she is not familiar with,do not understand the people go?And go to his house.Stay there?If something else goes wrong,who's gonna save her?Captain?At the thought of the captain,Shang Xiaoning's brain lit up,and she immediately had a high-sounding reason.

78

"Let's go to the captain's house.I'm sure the swan won't leave me alone.She'll be looking for me everywhere.Shang Xiaoning was happy to come up with a good idea at a critical moment.She is not the one who just came here,and she keeps an eye on everything.

"This..."Jiao Liang had no idea for a moment and had to ask:"Where is the female captain's home?"

"It's next door.We'd better go first before the Shaw Swan loses track of us and comes back to see us again."

Shang Xiaoning also wait for whether they agree,dragging two people to the female captain's home run.

It was Wen Greenjade,the female captain's husband,who opened the door.He saw Shang Xiaoning a little unhappy,said:"I thought you were missing,kidnapped,is going to the police."

"Hey,something like that?"Shang Xiaoning casually respond.

"Well,if you don't come back to eat and sleep,you have to say hello,so that we have to wait,and think that you have an accident?"Wen Greenjade pursed her lips.

"Well,it's hard to tell.Let's go in and talk."

Shang Xiaoning wait for Wen Greenjade invitation,he hurried to go.Wen Greenjade took a look at the bright,her face showed a very complicated expression.He didn't invite Jiao Liang either.Jiao Liang had to go inside with a hard scalp.Wen Greenjade silently closed the door behind her.

"Who is it?'asked the female captain inside.

"Me."Shang Xiaoning loudly promised,people have gone in.

"Hey, how can you go with someone like that? I heard about it as soon as I got home. I thought it was a big deal, and I went to her house to find you, who knew you were not at home. Where have you been?"

"Well", the female captain is wise and her eyes are poisonous."I thought she was a good person, but a little more beautiful, a little more fashionable, and like me, I don't know she..." Shang Xiaoning looked around and asked, "Are the children asleep?"

"You're all asleep, so say what you want."

Shang Xiaoning to the female captain price two comers: "This is the reporter Jiao Liang who saved me, this is the child Tang Comesinster who was saved by us." Come, sit down." Shang Xiaoning himself first sat down on the sofa.

The female captain looked puzzled:"What? Who saved who? What happened? It's not that risky, is it? Oh, you're still in your pajamas." The captain noticed Shang Xiaoning's clothes, and it seemed that something had really happened.

Shang Xiaoning looked down at his pajamas and could not help but smile ruefully:"Alas, can not say that she is a bad person, but we are not on the right way, she is wishful thinking."

"What? What wishful thinking?"

Wen Biyu Greenjade then took a tray and brought four cups of tea, placed them lukewarm in front of everyone, and then sat quietly at one side.

Shang Xiaoning drank a mouthful of tea, took a breath, and fixed her mind. Only then did she speak out all about what had happened to her. Finally:"She insisted on introducing me to her nephew She won't let me go until I say no. Isn't that wishful thinking?"

79

The female captain was dumbfounded,and at the end said,"How can this be,how can it be?A nephew of someone like her is no better.I hear her nephew is very famous."

At the end,Wen Greenjade 's expression changed and said,"How can she be such a person?Always thought she was a good person."

Shang Xiaoning glanced at him quickly,his face flushed,but soon,his face returned to the old look,no longer cold.

Shang Xiaoning said:"Think of her also strange poor,lonely a person,at home even a talk no one.She was only looking out for her nephew,and she wasn't wrong."

"Soft again,soft again."The female captain rolled his eyes disapprovingly."I suppose you pity her,too,and have illusions about her nephew."

"Why,how can I like her?I think of her as a friend,a sister.To be fair,she's not a bad person,she's talented,she's a nice person...Only I had no feelings for her nephew,and though I had not met him,I could guess that her nephew must be as pitiful as she was.She loved her nephew so much that my refusal must have been painful."

"Here we go,here we go.She has to kill you and eat your flesh before you turn back.Then it will be too late."

Everyone laughed,

"It's not that serious,is it?"Shang Xiaoning said with a smile.

Tang Comesinster is already asleep on the sofa.At the beginning,he was talking about what he knew,what he had witnessed,and he was still interested,but later,when he heard what they said about spending or not spending,he was no longer interested,and recently he had been tired and tired,so his eyes could no longer open and he fell asleep.

"Ouch,the child is asleep."Wen Greenjade discovered it first.

"I suppose the boy lives here.He follows you,you have to go to work,you have to take him,in case something happens,it is not convenient to run."Shang Xiaoning said to Jiao Liang.

"Yes,yes, you live here,where I can keep my children company."Wen Greenjade said female Greenjade made a hasty statement.

"Of course you live here,where else would you live?"'said the female captain.

"That..."Jiao Liang also want to say what,Wen Greenjade has come over,holding Tang Comesinster went to the bedroom.

"I slept with him today."And as they walked,they said,"What a lovely child."

The female captain said,"I'll sleep without you tonight."

80

After a while,the female captain asked Shang Xiaoning,"What are your plans now?Do you want to travel here first,or find a job and settle down?It's not a problem to hang around like this."

"Settle down?I never thought about that.I'm going back."

"Well,I'll play with you first."

"It's good to play...I was afraid to meet the Shaw Swan.."

"Why are you afraid of her?I'm here,she moves!See if I don't break her neck!You said she was good a moment ago,but now you are afraid of her?"

"No,I was afraid of getting into trouble...In fact,I'm not afraid of her,I can fight her,I just don't want to hurt her heart too much,after all,she doesn't mean any harm..."

"Speaking for her again!We don't talk about her anymore!You follow me and you'll be fine."

Shang Xiaoning feel practical,like really returned to their own home,couldn't help but relax down,a yawn.

"I must go,you rest."Jiao Liang said,and then said to Shang Xiaoning,"We'll be in touch."

"Ok,let me see you off."Shang Xiaoning stood up.

"Come over and play sometime."The female captain stood up,too.

Shang Xiaoning and Jiao Liang went to the door,Jiao Liang turned around and said affectionately to Shang Xiaoning:"Remember to call me...Actually,you'd be better off staying with me..."

Shang Xiaoning blushed,she busily avoided the topic,said:"You also need to have a good rest,let the female captain accompany me."I'll call you."

Jiao Liang took Shang Xiaoning's hand,shook it hard,just reluctantly to go.Took a few steps back to look at Shang Xiaoning.Shang Xiaoning sheepishly lowered his head,and when he left,he closed the door.

The female captain yawned,too,and said,"Let's go to bed,too.I'll arrange something for you tomorrow."

Shang Xiaoning and the female captain took a bath and came to the guest room,but after going to bed,the doze of two people seemed to be gone again,and talked for a long time to sleep.

The next morning,Shang Xiaoning and the female captain got up on time. Wen Greenjade had already cooked breakfast and the children had already washed.

At breakfast,Wen Greenjade said:"Little brother,you will play in my house today,and after I send them to the kindergarten,I will come back to accompany you."I'm gonna show you a good time.You will live in my house and go to school,OK?"

"HMM."Tang Comesinster vigorously pointed his head and ate her food very sweetly.

Wen Greenjade looked at him lovingly,"Come,eat more food,you are a little malnourished,you need to make up more."

Here the female captain's son and daughter pursed their lips.

81

"Will Dad like this brother and not like us?"Said the daughter.

"Why do you like him so much when he wasn't born by mother?"The son said again.

"Well,you can't be so rude.This brother's family is very poor,can not afford to go to school,temporarily living in our home.He also has his own parents,and his parents love him and miss him very much.They won't give us their son yet. He is a guest in our house now.Shall we treat him well?"

"Yes-"the two children answered in unison.

"Let's go out today.Let's take him with us.He's never seen the world,just like me."Shang Xiaoning said.

"What do you think?"Wen Greenjade asked Tang Comesinster,and then asked for the captain's opinion with eyes.

"Well,let's show him,too."The female captain made a gesture,and the matter was settled.

Play for a few days,Shang Xiaoning also did not get the opportunity to be alone.In front of everyone,she was also embarrassed to call Jiao Liang.Only when Jiao Liang sometimes called to say hello at night,she told him about the play.

That night,the children are asleep,Jiao Liang called again.Shang Xiaoning briefly and he said a few words and hung up the phone.

The female captain said:"Big square,love does not contact how to do?"

Shang Xiaoning blushed,"No matter,who fell in love with him?"

"Don't cover it up,I've known about your relationship since he came."It's only natural.He's not married,you're divorced,just in time."

"I see it,too.He is good to you,and you are good to him."Wen Greenjade said a little sourly.

"Tell you what,you make an appointment with him,see when he's free,I'll give you a vacation,you play with him."Relationships are about having fun.""Said the female captain,looking at Wen Greenjade winked,and said,"Isn't it?A wife?"

Wen Greenjade blushed and said sheepishly,"Who is in love with you?You chased him down."

"Ha ha ha ha ha...I'm sorry,it's an old wife..."

Shang Xiaoning holding a mobile phone,in front of everyone,not too embarrassed to call Jiao Liang immediately;Moreover,he had just called,she called immediately,also seemed too impatient,but she really wanted to make an appointment with Jiao Liang.She suddenly had an idea and dialed Jiao Liang's mobile phone.

82

"Hey, Jiao Liang, it's me...I need you to find out where the White Chrysanthemums are for me. She hasn't been there since we danced, and I can't reach her...Huh?Which White Chrysanthemum...Oh, I haven't told you. She was one of the girls I went to sea with, fell into the sea, and was rescued here...Yeah, yeah, yeah, we were at the dance the other day, and she was with me at first...We were at the buffet, and you saw her?Yeah, yeah, we were crying and screaming and we thought each other was dead...Yaaawn...Oooooo.I forgot to mention that she was also rescued by a female captain and now lives at her house...The female captain's daughter is called Li Whitejade, studying in some university...Oh, by the way, she asked questions at the last press conference...Do you have the impression...Yeah, yeah, I ate and danced with her, and then they dis appeared...Oh, well, goodbye, that's all.'

Shang Xiaoning is very satisfied with this excuse for himself. But she does care about the White Chrysanthemum, this person is really, how not to contact her!But how can White Chrysanthemum get in touch with her?She can't get in touch with the White Chrysanthemums either, right?Think of this, Shang Xiaoning smiled. This is good, to Jiao Liang will definitely have no problem.

83

Soon, Jiao Liang called, he had the news of White Chrysanthemum," Really?"Then I'll go and see her tomorrow."Shang Xiaoning blurted out, and immediately added a sentence,"You take me tomorrow, or I can't find her."This was obviously superfluous, for the female captain could take her too. She said the face a little fever, and then secretly looked at the female captain, the female captain seemed not to care about this matter, Shang Xiaoning heart fixed some.

Not long after, Shang Xiaoning's mobile phone rang. Shang Xiaoning a pick, is White Chrysanthemum. Shang Xiaoning jumped up with joy,"You this ghost, crazy to where?you still hasn't contacted me...Huh?Oh, I can't get in touch with you either...Must come to your place tomorrow?All right, I was planning on coming to your place tomorrow. Ask the reporter to take me. Yeah, the guy who called you...Well, it's a long story. I'll see you later. I have so much to say to you too...Okay, okay, you work, you work, we'll see you tomorrow."

"Hey, she's in love. I didn't think she had such a knack for talking about one."Shang Xiaoning said.

"It's human nature. What woman can stay away from a man?It's time to think about your problem, too. I think the reporter is OK. That's him."'said the female captain.

Shang Xiaoning sorry, is she also a woman who can not leave a man?The female captain was too straight.

"What's to be ashamed of?It's not your first time. Haven't you been married before?Still can't let it go."

"Well, I'm not sure, I haven't asked anyone yet. In addition, we should get along with each other more, and we can only decide later..."

"Yes, it's better to be discreet."

The female captain turned on the TV and kept changing the channel to see the news. These nights, she waits for the baby to go to bed before turning on the TV.

A shot flashed by, Shang Xiaoning suddenly pointed to the picture, cried,

"Stop, stop, that station...Yeah, yeah, that's it. I've seen this man before. his names Gold Pingmei Why is he dead?"

A dead man is being introduced on the screen, next to his photograph. The announcer was saying, "...He was found dead in his bed at the chief's house without any clothes on him. As to why he died naked in the Chief's house, the police are doing further investigation..."

'How did he die? I saw him the other day..."Shang Xiaoning murmured.

"How did you meet him? Where did you meet him?"'asked the female captain.

"It was at a press conference; And then I saw him on TV. Oh, what a pity, so young and handsome."

"It's bad to be young and handsome and to be a public figure. My son will never ask him to do such a thing in the future. It will hurt him."said the female captain.

They talked on the subject for a long time before going to bed.

The next day, Shang Xiaoning got up early. Wen Greenjade was already up before the children got up.

84

"Why are you up so early,too?you.Don't you sleep in the morning?"Shang Xiaoning asked.

"Make you breakfast.You can't go on a date on an empty stomach."

"Where is a date?Just go out with him."Shang Xiaoning mouth still do not admit.

"I get used to it in the morning,get up early and cook,and they get up and have something to eat."

"You are a good woman...Worthy of Our country is called the good wife and good mother."

"We call it'good husband and good father.'"

Shang Xiaoning froze for a while,and then laughed again,"Ha ha,yes,yes,it should be said."Ha ha,very funny."

At this time,a car horn sounded outside,Shang Xiaoning ran to the window to see,she saw Jiao Liang beckoning to her.Shang Xiaoning also beckoned to him,immediately to go.

Wen Greenjade stopped her,"You haven't eaten yet.Ask him to come in and eat,and then go away."

"No,I want to go to the street with him to eat snacks,I want him to treat."Shang Xiaoning said that she changed her pajamas,put on a shirt and jeans and ran out.

Wen Greenjade left her mouth behind,a face of helplessness.

On the car,Shang Xiaoning asked Jiao Liang,"How did you come so early?"

"Did I wake you up?I hardly slept all night."

'What is it?

"Excited.I'm so excited at the thought of being alone with you,how can I sleep?"

"It's not that dramatic,is it?Shang Xiaoning is a little embarrassed.

The car started.Jiao Liang asked again,"Why did you get up so early?"Did you lose sleep?"

"No,how come?I usually get up early.But because you are coming,I am afraid that you will have to wait if you come early,so I will get up early and get ready to go as soon as you come."

Jiao Liang smiled,"At least you don't hate me,and you hope to see me soon,right?"

"Oh,what a man you are."

"Okay,okay,don't talk about that,talk about something else..."

When Shang Xiaoning asked him to ask her to eat snacks,Jiao Liang was very happy and immediately drove the car to one of the most upscale hotels. Shang Xiaoning resolutely refused,must eat street snacks.Jiao Liang had to obey her.Found a quiet side street,sat in front of a stall,two people together to eat pot paste,oyster cake,fish balls.The edge of the pot is boiled water in the pot,and then use the soaked rice to grind the pulp,scoop it with a small bowl,pour it down the side of the pot,and wait for the cooked edge of the pot to shovel into the pot,the pot of soup put celery,flower clams,squid,and then into two bowls.Oyster cake is made with a shallow spoon,put some batter in it,add oyster and cabbage,pour some batter over it,fry it in a pan,wait for it to form,and then fry it in a pan of oil until golden.Fish balls are wrapped in the core of fish balls,the outer skin is fish pulp and sweet potato powder,the inside is pork filling.Jiao Liang didn't eat breakfast either.They enjoyed the meal very much.

85

Less than 7 o'clock,Jiao Liang is ready to take Shang Xiaoning around,Shang Xiaoning's mobile phone rang.It's a White Chrysanthemum.

"Are you up?I'm already up.Come here."

"So early?Not disturbing you?"Shang Xiaoning said.

"Oh,what's the trouble?Come on,come on,come on."

"Yes,yes,I'm coming,I'm already up."

When the car came to the residence of the White Chrysanthemum,that is,Li Whitejade 's home,the White Chrysanthemum was waiting at the door.

"Hurry in,I haven't eaten yet.We'll eat and talk."

White Chrysanthemum is very eager,but at the same time do not forget to look at Jiao Liang.Judging from her expression,she was satisfied.She and Shang Xiaoning exchanged a look,secretly nodded.Shang Xiaoning smiled and pretended to be confused.They followed White Chrysanthemum into Li Whitejade's house,and the rest of her family was not up yet.

"You have to eat,what's so urgent?"Don't rush to play."Shang Xiaoning said, she sat to the table,also greet Jiao Liang sit down.

White Chrysanthemum scooped a bowl of lean preserved egg porridge and chatted with them while eating.

"Well,I was busy last night and didn't have time to tell you."

"Busy for what?Busy falling in love?"

"Hee hee."

"Who chased who?"

"He chased me."

"You liked him too,and then you got together?"

"Yes, that's it."

"What does he do?"

"The model. I met him at the dance floor the other day when I met him. He was the first person to dance with me."

"You don't know him, and you're together?"

"Of course I do. Get along, get to know. If we don't get along, how can we understand?"

"What was the result?"

"Not bad, of course."

"So I'm going to eat wedding candy soon?"

"Hey, not so fast."

"Aren't you in a hurry?" Jiao Liang saw them talking, reminding them on the side.

86

"Oh oh, let's get down to business. As soon as I came to this country, I became very interested in this country, and I wanted to know everything about it. Hey, I am not just thinking about love, but also consider life and death, the national economy and people's livelihood. I thought, since it's not a dream, it's real, and it's not on the map, there must be some secret. I tremble with excitement at the thought of it.

"I asked Li Whitejade, but she knew so little about it that she could hardly explain why. I looked in the library again, but there was nothing in it. I had to ask Li Whitejade to help me find the relevant people to ask, the result she found a reporter, the reporter looked for someone, and finally found a famous master of Chinese studies. Do you know what Guoxue is? It is the knowledge that specializes in studying the history, humanities, folk customs and so on of this country. Isn't that what I need?

"I'm so happy. I immediately wanted to find this master of Chinese studies. However, Li Whitejade said, this master of Chinese studies in general people do not see, especially the ugly of the opposite sex. I said I look OK, he should like it?"Li Whitejade said,"What are you talking about? She's a woman. She only sees handsome young men.

"I said, what can I do? Where are we going to catch them?"

"Just ask your boyfriend. He must be young and handsome." Shang Xiaoning said

"Oh, no, I'm not sure yet. Besides, she's gone. What's her excuse? If the reporters go, they'll be interviewing her. We tracked down this reporter and tried to get her to think again. The reporter herself turned out to be young and handsome."

"You're not seeing her again,are you?"Shang Xiaoning said with a smile.

"Hey,I'm not that flirtatious,am I?I'm always the same,unless I'm not wanted.It's the same with you.And I said,you take us there.The reporter said that she had not met me and had to contact met o ask for my opinion.

"When contacted,the master of Chinese studies first asked,Are you handsome?The reporter said,should be OK?"No one around she ever told she was ugly,and a lot of girls chased her.The master of Chinese studies asked,what's your own evaluation?The reporter said that so far,I have not found any young man more handsome than me.The master agreed immediately.She agreed to meet at 8:00 this morning.Take me with you.Of course I must take you with me,and you should know something about this country.I just wanted to ask Li Whitejade's dry mother to find you.Li Whitejade's dry mother is also a female captain.Maybe she knows your female captain."

"What's this reporter's name?Perhaps I do?"Jiao Liang said.

"Yes,you are also a journalist,you should recognize him.

'What's the matter?Do you know?He's dead,in someone's bed..."

"I recognized him.His name was Gold Pingmei."

"Huh?"White Chrysanthemum surprised to open the mouth,half a day can not close;The bowl in his hand also fell onto the table,"He was with us yesterday,and it was only yesterday that we got in touch with the master of Chinese studies..."

"So he couldn't have died soon after contact?"Shang Xiaoning said.

"They say he died of an asthma attack."Jiao Liang said.

"Then why not stay at home?"White Chrysanthemum asked.

87

"They're talking about work.They are superiors and subordinates."Jiao Liang said seriously.

"Talk of work and bed?"Shang Xiaoning .gave him a white look.

"Leaders work hard all day,and when they go home,they have to talk about work with their subordinates.Of course,they are tired."

"It is not the leader who is in bed,it is the subordinate who is in bed."Shang Xiaoning said.

"It's easy to explain.The leader also understands the hard work of his subordinates.After work,but also to the leader's home run,report work.The leader told him to go to bed with him."

"Why aren't you wearing any clothes?"Shang Xiaoning would not let go.

"The leader must have found that he had an asthma attack and gave him first aid.Then you have to do a heart massage,and it only works when they're naked.And mouth-to-mouth resuscitation.He died in the end."

White Chrysanthemum suddenly could not help but burst out laughing,"Sister Shang Xiaonings ,you do not listen to him,he is telling jokes,you are still serious with him.I didn't know he was so funny..."

"Huh?Is he telling a joke?"

"No,that's what the leader told the doctors and the police."Jiao Liang still did not smile.

"Then perhaps it is so?The leader is also kind."Shang Xiaoning said.

"Oh,Sister Shang Xiaoning.Even if the leader really said so,it is not necessarily the truth.What else would he say?There has to be an explanation."

"Oh,I thought it was true."

"Then you can't meet the master of Chinese studies?"Jiao Liang asked.

"Oh,yes.What can we do?I managed to get in touch with her..."White Chrysanthemum chagrin said.

"Is that enough?What else can you do?"Shang Xiaoning said.

White Chrysanthemum frowns and thinks for a while,her eyes light up and she says,

"Yes.Well,first of all,the master of Chinese studies had never seen the reporter;If I had met her,I wouldn't have asked if I handsome when I heard her name.Who could forget such a handsome man?Especially someone like her.That way,even if she watches the news,she won't know that the person looking for her is the deceased."

"Then you want him to go?You can't ask a dead man to take you."

"Well,that is the worst policy,that is to say that the master of Chinese studies will die immediately.I'm telling reporters not to die."

"What else can you do to revive the dead?"Shang Xiaoning said.

"I won't say it now ,to leave it in suspense.Well,I'll finish this meal and then we'll go."

"Where are we going?To the chief's house to get the body?"Shang Xiaoning asked.

"And carry bodies?That's already in the morgue.You need us?Besides,I don't have the guts.I can't look at the dead body.It's so scary."

"Then where are you going?"

"We'll see."

88

White Chrysanthemum ready to take up the rice bowl, a look at the rice bowl on the table has been overturned, just fell from her hands, she did not care.

"Oh, no, let's go."

Or sit in a bright car, White Chrysanthemum command the direction, "this way, this way...Turn right Yes, go around..."

"You have become a living map, and you have to command the locals." Shang Xiaoning said.

"Native! More local than I've traveled in the last few days? I know them all by heart. You think I just fall in love and don't ask anything? As I talked, I learned about the place, I explored it. Every inch of this land has left my footprints and sweat."

"It's hard enough, so people say that people who fall in love are crazy." Shang Xiaoning said.

"You don't want to say that early, I can see you. You'll be crazier than I am." White Chrysanthemum point Shang Xiaoning with fingers.

The car under the command of White Chrysanthemum, came to a small mansion. The party got out of the car. The White Chrysanthemum looked at the door number carefully again and said,

"Yes, this is it. 518 Champs Elysees."

"How can you remember it so well?" Shang Xiaoning asked.

"It's hard to remember?'Want to thank you for what?'I'm going to send. Ha ha ha..."

"This area is very expensive. Only the richest people live here." Jiao Liang said.

"Today I'm going to show you the richest people.

Shang Xiaoning think White Chrysanthemum has changed a lot.People are beautiful,foreign gas,skin is good,but also smart,lively.Not at all like the original. Oh,the sweetness of love.Shang Xiaoning dont know if she will become her in the future.It all depends on the focus.Shang Xiaoning can not help but look at Jiao Liang.

The White Chrysanthemum rang the doorbell,and a handsome young servant came to the gate of the courtyard and asked:

"Who are you looking for?

"Well,we have an appointment with Ms.Zhu Xishou,and she asked us to come at eight o'clock.We're here to interview her."White Chrysanthemum reached out to look at the watch,"It is just 8 o'clock."

Shang Xiaoning has not seen this watch,and again,White Chrysanthemum now has a mobile phone,also do not need a watch,the watch must be sent by her boyfriend.Shang Xiaoning envy her,when can she get such a gift?

"Oh,I heard Monsieur.She asked me to wait here for you.Come on in."The servant opened the gate and let them in,then closed the door and led them into the house.He led them to a living room filled with antique mahogany furniture,paintings and calligraphy on the walls,and POTS of orchids in the corner.

'I'll inform Sir.She works upstairs.'

'She works so early?"White Chrysanthemum said.

"She gets up at 5am every day and reads,writes and draws,even on weekends.""Said the servant.

89

After the male servant left,Shang Xiaoning said,"What was famous favour hendsame reporter?"I know him.I've seen him on TV."

"What was your impression?"White Chrysanthemum asked.

Shang Xiaoning skimmed his mouth,"Not good.You are 70 or 80 years old,and you are still so promiscuous."

"That old?Then she must know a lot.She's still working so hard.'White Chrysanthemum said.

"I don't like any more learning."Shang Xiaoning said.

"Now it's not about liking,it's about getting what we need."

They stopped talking at the clump of the stairs.Before Zhu Xishou, entered the door,a warm call rang out first.

"Ah,here comes our most handsome young men.My heart is racing."

Zhu Xishou than walked in.White Chrysanthemum greeted her and shook hands with her. White Chrysanthemum thin but with eyes looking for great beauty.When she saw the only male,Jiao Liang threw off the White Chrysanthemum's hand and said unceremoniously,then.

"Just you?No one has surpassed you?Look on the street.What's not better than you?No one is uglier than you,are they?"

White Chrysanthemum quickly explained,"a gentleman it is like this.The great beauty is on me way,the great beauty,my good friend,I didn't know?they called me just now.The car broke down on the road,and asked to come first. Because I knews how much admire you and how much you want to hear from you I was a big fan of yours.It is a great pleasure to meet you,and I have many things to ask you that I do not understand."

Zhu Xishou's face softened,"I can't see ordinary people,how can I teach children?If you want to learn,you can go to the library or school to learn."

"I went to all the libraries,but I couldn't find what I wanted.This is something only you have here.It's all in your belly."

"Oh?What's that?"Wish I thin to interest.

"About the origin of the Kingdom of women,and everything about it."

"Who are you?Why are you interested in this?Wish I thin alert."

"We are foreigners.But I love it here.I love everything about it.I'm going to live here in the future,so I'm very interested to know what kind of country it is."

"Alas,"Zhu Xishou sighed and blinked his eyes,as if he were going to cry.

"What's the problem,old woman?"White Chrysanthemum asked nervously.

Zhu Xishou shook her head,her voice choked and said,"I am happy...Yes. Come on,sit down."

90

Everyone was a little puzzled,looked at each other,and sat down.Then the servant boy brought tea and put it in front of everyone.Zhu Xishou took the tea,drank a few sips,put it down,and said:

"I'm really excited today,I really am.No one has ever been interested in the history of this country or wanted to study it.My own children are not like that,my grandchildren do too.How long do I have?My belly of knowledge is going to my coffin."

"If you write a book about it,can't you keep it?"White Chrysanthemum said.

"Who is it for?They don't even have history in school.We only study the history of the world and the history of mankind,not our own history.5,000 years of civilization,just like China.My research results can only be published in academic journals.But no one reads it.It's impossible to sell.So I published the article,and not only did I not get paid,but the publication asked me to pay 400 bucks.They can't sell magazines,they have no income,and they have to wait for us writers'money to pay them.Where is the reason?"

"Then who writes articles?"

"Do not write,evaluation of the title to the paper.With a title,there is money and status.So people are willing to spend money.Some people don't even write,they go directly to the editor of the journal,ask them to write and distribute on behalf of them,and give money,which is also 400 yuan."

"Huh?How did that happen?Then write a book."

"Write a book!No one wants to publish my book,the publishers don't want to publish it,they say they can't sell it,they want me to pay for it.I printed a thousand copies and brought them back,and they are still piled up in the cellar."

"You give it to me,I want it."White Chrysanthemum said excitedly.

"Yes,you can have them all,as long as you like."Zhu Xishou winked again,"I can't even recruit graduate students,and now I'm disqualified."

"I'll be your graduate student,I'm interested,do you want it?"White Chrysanthemum said quickly.

"Really?Are you serious?"Zhu XIshou open childlike naive eyes.

"Really,I just don't know if I'm going to get it.Don't know what classes to take?"

"Don't test anything,no one has signed up yet."Since I am studying Chinese culture,I will follow the old etiquette and take students.Just bow down to the master."

"Really?"White Chrysanthemum shouted in surprise,immediately jumped up from the chair,fell down and worshipped,and said:"Please be a disciple."

Zhu Xishou hurriedly get up,help up the White Chrysanthemum:"Son,please get up."

After they both sat down,Zhu Xishou said with relief:

"I didn't expect to receive students at my age,which is really God's eye."Now I have a successor,and I will die in peace."

Then the old woman spoke passionately about the ins and outs of the country.

Three hundred years ago,dozens of women off the coast of Fujian,China,stole the family boat at night and went out to sea together.They want to go to Penglai fairy Island,fairy into the road.They're all self-grooming girls.

91

At that time,the men of the sea had to go out to sea to fish,and the women stayed at home to farm,take care of the children,and serve the in-laws. It's hard for a woman to be alone at her husband's house.Mother-in-law,uncle,none of them are easy to serve.Moreover,the sea is also dangerous,and the husband may not return at any time.Sometimes to serve old,become a lifelong slave;Some will be sold by in-laws.

Many girls are afraid of marriage and do not want to marry at all.It's better to stay in her mother's house,wait on her parents,and get hurt than to be a widow all her life,serving people who don't have blood relations.Therefore,when many girls reach the age of marriage,they comb their hair into the style of married women,indicating that they will never marry.It's called a self-grooming girl.

These self-grooming women want to run away from home because they can't stand the gossip of their older siblings,younger siblings,and even their parents.However,the sea of people,where to make a home?What do them live for?And it's inconvenient for women to be out there.As soon as the proposal was put forward,it was unanimously approved by everyone.So,one night,after the men had all returned from the sea,they all got into some boats,and when the tide came in,the boats were lifted by the water,and they set out.

But no one had ever been out to sea,nor knew how to get there.Just vaguely heard the man at home said the boat,do not know where Penglai fairy Island.But since it is the fairy Island,it must be people have not been to,it must be far away. So they sailed to the opposite side of the coast.They believe it will arrive one day.

However,she do not know how far they went,nor do they know how many days they went,until the things on the ship were all eaten,and they did not see the shadow of Penglai Fairy Island,surrounded by a vast sea.That's when they panicked.Many of them were crying,they didn't want to die,they were young.

Someone found fishing gear on the boat,but they don't cast nets,they don't draw nets.So everyone immediately saw hope.After that,they taught them to fish and eat.At first they can cook it,but at the end,they have to eat it raw.

Just when they were almost desperate and almost exhausted,another storm came and nearly capsized the boat.After the storm had passed,and they thought they were safe,an even worse thing happened.In a split second,the ship suddenly disintegrated into pieces of wood.They all fell into the water.Fortunately,they all grew up on the beach and could swim when they were very young,so they all fell onto the board before swimming twice.

Now they were utterly despairing and thought they were going to die at sea. Some began to cry,others regretted going to sea.But the desire to survive keeps them from giving up.When they could hold on no longer and were about to slip into the sea,land appeared ahead.

"Ah,here,Penglai Fairy Island has arrived."

The cry brought everyone to life.They all looked forward together,and sure enough they saw land.Then the girls were crying and screaming and laughing and Shouting and it was all a mess.

92

"Everybody row over there,quick."

This sentence reminds everyone,and everyone is holding the board,rowing with their hands and pushing off with their feet.And the current goes that way. At last they all made it to the shore,and lay there for a long time.They gathered wild fruits,shells and snails from cracks in the rocks,and live fish,shrimps and crabs from puddles.

Tthey do not know how many days and nights they slept,and when they woke up,they went to the beach to find something to eat,and then brought something back.

When they had recovered their strength,they began to walk farther,hoping to find the gods.

Hard work pays off,they really saw the"fairy".That is a house in the distance.They cried and jumped and ran to the house.However,to their great disappointment,the house was not only shabby and simple,but also the four people who came out of it did not look like fairies.They were all tattered and thin.

They were very surprised to see who was coming,and then they all shouted and cried to meet them.When they reached the front,they only heard them say:"Now there is salvation,we can go home."

Everyone suddenly cold down,are these people also drowned in the sea?Asked,sure enough.Everyone was eager to ask where the gods were.They say where are the gods?They've been all over this place.It was an island,large,with no one and no land around it.

Everyone was shocked.It was a desert island!It's not a Penglai fairy island at all.Once again,everyone lost hope,and suddenly all had no strength,no idea,and sat down softly on the ground.When the four"immortals"learned of their situation,they began to cry with sorrow:

"Oh,our lives are so hard,and we still can't go back when people come..."

It turns out they were Taiwanese,just kids.One day,seeing an empty boat,an older boy sneaked them onto the boat.Together they played the game of weighing the anchor,not wanting the tide to rise,and the boat floated away.There was no use in their crying and Shouting,as the boat went further and further away.In the end,they were fishing,too.The boy was very capable.Itheydo not know how long it took,but also encountered a storm,and came here.

At first they thought they could find him,and when they couldn't,the boy built the house and carried all the things off the ship.But soon after,the boy had a stomachache and died.They've been living with each other until now.For exactly 20 years.

"Your ships didn't break up?"

"No,there are some things on it we still use today.But the clothes are long gone,and we are very torn,you see."

"What have you been eating for 20 years?"

93

"What else is there to eat?Eat some wild fruits,and some things from the sea."

"Is the ship still there?"

"It's long gone.I don't know where it drifted."

"We will settle where we come.In fact,it's quite good here,although we can't be immortal,but we can be free people,isn't that what we want?"

When one said this,everyone was happy again.The room was too small to squeeze in,and some people stayed outside.

Because there was only one boy in the family,and sickly,the family raised her as a boy.Her father was a boat builder and often took her with her and she was like to follow him.So she's good with her hands.She uses all kinds of tools. After examining the tools in the room,she said happily,"Yes,there are axes,saws, knives,hammers,flint,nails,and compasses."

The nail was wrapped in tarpaulin and didn't rust much.The tools are always in use,and the ones that aren't are oiled and unrusted.

She led the group to cultivate wild fruits,collect a large number of food,dry,in case the weather can not go out.The house was later built properly. She even made a small boat out of floating planks that could take two people out to sea and catch a lot of fish.Then they found Ma,and she made a loom,and then she led them to build a real boat.

She said she had to feel her way out.If a boat can come in intact,it can go out intact.You have to do business with people on the outside,or life will be bad. There are so many things missing here,it's impossible to live.

She sent some wise,capable men who were good swimmers,tied logs to their bodies,and went out in small boats to look for them.If the boat breaks up,they can swim back.She patrolled her ship around the island not very far,and when anyone fell into the water,she would rescue them,listen to their stories,and carve the location on a piece of wood.

    She slowly learned to use the compass,which she learned from the four"gods,"who also learned from the boys.She uses her own incense,which is made of sawdust and gum and dried.That way,she could pinpoint exactly where the boat was going,how long it was going,and what happened.

    After years of groping,they finally got a very strange route,like walking in a maze.Only in this line,the ship will not break up.

    But out of the sea,she still didn't know which way to go.Every time she walks,record it.When the food is almost gone,she'll be back.

94

In this way,after many explorations,one day they finally met a merchant ship,also a Chinese ship.In addition,she also learned a lot of sailing knowledge, understand the location of some countries,specialties and so on.

Here,women are the biggest,they don't need to dress up,it's no one men. She also sent four"immortals"back to Taiwan during her second business. Since then,the women's country has not broken ties with China,and has been developing in parallel with China.When everyone wanted to preserve the country,leaving behind children became their strongest desire.

All she recruited were thin,small,and weak;Let's get some self-grooming girls on board who want to escape.When they arrived in the land of women,the men realized that the ship was full of women.Women are the biggest on the island,which is the complete opposite of other countries.Men have to dress like women and do women's things.Men are complaining,but there is no way,they have to accept.In this way,the country of women has marriage and the next generation.After a certain number of people are reached,no more people are admitted.

The route map is a top secret handed down from generation to generation. No man can get out of here,or they'll all be gone.So,even if the man steals the ship and it breaks up,he will fall into the sea and die.Or be sent back by the waves.

Later,when the old man died,the man did not know what the outside world was like.Gradually,society was shaped in this way and became what it is now. Women are strong,outside the Lord,men are weak,inside the Lord.In those days,women could have three wives.Anyway,what the men out there do,the women out there do.

During the Second World War,they did not do business,it was difficult.After China's reform and opening up,they have to import some things from China,and China's things are cheap.

It's like any other country now.But when they go out to do business,they do not say that they are women's country,afraid of trouble.No one can get in,but the technology is so advanced,it could be flattened one day.Is there any place in the world that no one has ever been?When they go to other countries,they say they are from China;when they go to Hong Kong and Taiwan,they say they are from the mainland;when they go to the mainland,they say they are from Hong Kong and Taiwan.They have bank accounts in all these places where they can deposit money and then buy what they need.

They also used simplified Chinese characters,which they learned from the overseas editions of Chinese newspapers.They also learn all kinds of languages,and have all kinds of education,in short,she has all the things a country should have.

"How can men not know about the outside world when communication is so advanced?There's the Internet,there's TV,there's books."White Chrysanthemum said.

"You forgot?The boat passed by and they all scattered."

"What's that got to do with the ship breaking up?"

"Have you ever heard of Greek mythology?There was an island where there were monsters with women's heads and birds singing beautiful songs,and they called them Sirens.Come,come,stay,the monster sang.Those who heard this song immediately lost their souls and wanted to come and stay on this island.But as soon as we got near the island,all the nails were sucked out of the ship,and the ship broke up."

95

"Is that true?I know the story."

"You know the Bermuda Triangle?All the ships,all the planes came here and the instruments went down and disappeared.Some of the boats are still there.The people are gone.Where do people go?They have all come to the land of women."

"Huh?So the satellite can't see you?"

"Of course,it interferes with the signal.What the satellite sees is a vast ocean.Scientists wanted to investigate,but couldn't.How do we communicate with the outside world?"

"What about books?Books will do."

"The books are processed by us.The books we buy are sold as they are if there is no discernable male or female rank;If it's serious,turn the gender around,publish it and sell it.So they still see the same world as they do.For example,Jia Goodjade,we changed him to a woman and Lin Blackjade to a man."

"Oh--no wonder her name is Li Whitejade,after'woman'."

"Who is it?Who is Li Whitejade?"

"A friend of mine.I'm staying at her house right now...So Confucius is also a woman?"

"Yes,because he said that only women and small people are difficult to raise,and they are not inferior when they are near,and they are resentful when they are far away."We change it to be that men and small men are difficult to raise,that they are not inferior when near,and that they are resentful when far away."

"Oh,ha ha,this is so interesting that I can learn for the rest of my life."

"In fact,in nature,all males are beautiful,why?Because he wants to attract the female,curry favor with the female.That is,they are female-centered,and the females are big and powerful.Because it wants to reproduce,it must be able to protect young animals.And their own body is good,and the offspring are healthy,which is conducive to the evolution of the species.

"You see,bees,ants,which social animal is not the female boss?It's really big.How much bigger it is.Elephant,grassland hyena,which is not matriarchal society?Also,praying mantises,females are bigger than males,and so are eagles. And the egg and the sperm,one is 200 microns,the other is 6 microns,and the sperm plus the tail is 66 microns.

"Let's talk about people,they were also matriarchal in the beginning. Later,because men have no ability,only eat and do not do,and good fighting,simple mind,think about problems are straight,and will not take children and educate children,will not take care of people,say a word can choke,so they sent them to do some simple physical work,do not do no food.They had to do it.

"You think,how can a man be healthy when he has half a chromosome less than a woman?In particular,personality and thinking become difficult for ordinary people to understand.You know,people can't live without one chromosome.He lost half a bone,and as a result,he lost a tendon.Do you think the memory in a computer is better at 120 or 360?Of course 360 is good.Women have a chromosome called the X chromosome,which is forked;When a man loses half a root,he becomes Y-shaped,called the Y chromosome.

96

"But after this goes on,there is another disadvantage,that is,men do some physical work every day,and are outdoors,basking in the sun,breathing the fresh air,the body has been exercised,the physical strength has been enhanced;And women do meticulous work,brain work,education,management,long-term no exercise,physical strength has declined.After men can finally defeat women by force,the suffering of women comes,and they live like slaves.The world that follows is the world that you see.But it's much better now.It's not as good as it was in ancient times."

"Oh--so I see."Shang Xiaoning kept nodding,and then said admiringly,"You are really learned,how can you know so much?I've never heard any of this before?"

"Who will tell you?A man?Don't we tell the men here about the man world out there now?It's the same thing.Human physique is largely the result of social selection.Why are women big boobs in the outside world?It's the result of thousands of years of men's choices.They all define what kind of woman is a beautiful woman by their own likes and dislikes.A woman can't work,can't study,depends on her husband to support her,of course,she must curry favor with him and do what he wants.

"You see monkeys,orangutans,the female has no breasts,people still have milk,children still enough to eat.In my country,too,the women are flat chested and the children are well fed.On the contrary,the men here have a larger Adam's apple,a larger lower body,but a small waist,good skin,and a gentle personality. This is the result of women's social choices.Those people's things are small,their temper is bad,their body is bad,their skin is bad,no one wants them,they can't get married,they can't keep their offspring,and they become extinct."

"Well,it's nice to be here,where women really roll over and take charge."White Chrysanthemum said.

"We are going to reverse the history that has been reversed.No way for a man to get involved in politics.But now there is more tolerance,and each department has stipulated a certain number of men,so that women can be equal."

"And how do you know that?Since there are no books?"White Chrysanthemum asked.

"This is learning.What good is a book?I speculated from a lot of data,from the data of the data to find clues,and then tell you in the way of a story.Just like translating oracle bones,translating codes,archaeology,you have to find your own way.My files are all over the world.From the disappearance of their ships,satellite positioning,trade manifests,bits and pieces from history books,hearsay,myth,etc. My books and papers,they have to be based on real evidence,otherwise who will believe you?Even you don't believe in yourself."

Zhu Xishou has been talking so much that she forgot the handsome male reporter.Jiao Liang has not interrupted,with his male power fighter style,he will jump up and argue with her.But now,the more he says that men are bad,the more he has to show a gentleman's demeanor;And Shang Xiaoning is also around,he attacked a woman,it is equal to attacking her.He made up his mind not to say anything.

97

When it was time for lunch,they didn't realize that time was flying by.Zhu Xshoui must stay with them to eat,because she had not finished her speech.After dinner,she also said that she would tell the words of several lifetimes.Before she finished talking about dinner, ate dinner here .After a long talk,it was late when they went home.Zhu Xishou said White Chrysanthemum later can live in her home,her home only she and male servants two people,children do not live here. She'll have the house,too,and she'll see her as her successor,her granddaughter.

The very next day,however,something happened.

White Chrysanthemum's boyfriend, Daylily ,told her that someone had reported that reporter Jiao Liang was a spy,and that he was communicating with people to subvert the country.The person to contact is Shang Xiaoning.Now the country has decided that if Shang Xiaoning can settle down,it will be OK,if she wants to go,she must be and Jiao Liang according to the spy.

"What kind of singing is that?Who's so immoral?Who reported this?"

"It's the Swan Shaw."

"That wicked woman."

Last night on the way back,Shang Xiaoning put her with Swan swan said,also made the white Chrysanthemum laugh,but she can not laugh now,but also gnashing teeth to hate it.So she told Shang Xiaoning this story to Daylily. listen.After listening to Daylily thoughtful.

"Huh?How do you know the inside story?"

"I also heard from a friend,which is supposed to be a state secret."Because he is very friendly with me and knows that you are from a foreign country,he told me quietly,and I will tell you quietly now.You can only tell the person concerned,and you must not spread it outside."

Urgent,White Chrysanthemum immediately Shang Xiaoning out secret talk,talk after,and called Jiao Liang,hope he can come up with some ideas.Jiao Liang asked Shang Xiaoning:

"Would you rather stay here?"

"No.Everything is fine here,but there is no son."

"A son can be born again later."

"But it wasn't the other one.It was the other one."

"That's hard."Jiao Liang also have no point.

"Or you'll both run away."White Chrysanthemum said.

"What about you?"

"Here I am,dying here and not going back."Is my heart not broken over there?"

"What about your family?"

98

"Why not?But you can write a letter,I can say I am in what country,just ask the female captain to take the letter to China and post it?Or just send it to another country.You can take some money and some photos.It's like you were already dead.If I had killed myself,wouldn't my family still have never seen me?This is my paradise,how can I come back to earth?"

"Local people have to give birth to children only let out,and must come back,if not come back to the female captain is to ask."Jiao Liang said.

"Isn't that easy?When I get married and have children,I can go back."White Chrysanthemum said.

"Men can't go out.If they go out,they can't come back."Jiao Liang said.

"That's for sure.If I were a man,I wouldn't come back."

"Foreigners have to take a medicine before they go out,and when they take it,they will forget what happened here.If you do not forget,you will be killed."Jiao Liang said again.

"So scary?Forget it,I don't want to come anyway."Shang Xiaoning said.

"How can we escape?"Jiao Liang asked.

"Ask for the female captain.If she can take us here,she can take you away."White Chrysanthemum said.

"Didn't you say it was confidential and you couldn't tell anyone?"Jiao Liang said again.

"Now it is time to say no,you must flee.And I think the female captain is very righteous and prudent,should not go to snitch or leak information?"White Chrysanthemum said.

"That's who she is.Talk to her.It's okay."

The three person went back to the female captain's house and discussed the matter with the female captain.The female captain immediately said,"I told you that Swan Swan was a bad woman.""How can you benefit yourself at the expense of others?I hate it when people make false accusations.I'm gonna do you a favor. I had to send you away.It pissed her off.I'm sailing the day after tomorrow.'

"But how?Someone must have looked into it."Shang Xiaoning said worried.

"I didn't check it before,but I was the gatekeeper here.I need to see a certificate that says you can get out,promise to come back.The number of crew members going out and coming back is the same,and the photos and names must be matched,and the office will be fine.The proof must also be submitted.The proof is at the public Security Bureau."

"That's pretty strict."

"This is called strict?We had all been trained and brainwashed to be absolutely faithful,absolutely reliable in character,and it would take a long time to study,until we were married and had children,before we could be female captains and take ships out.We must ensure that the female captain does not smuggle,do not smuggle,do not take bribes,and that she can come back and be managed without mercy."

"So you didn't hurt your character by helping us?"Shang Xiaoning asked.

"Then there is no way,all have children,who does not want to home?"Of course I won't say anything to anyone,for my own protection.If I don't tell you,we'll go in secret.Who knows.Just how to go in secret?There are so many people on board,and they might want to send someone to check.That's a problem."

99

They are hiding in Shang Xiaoning's bedroom to discuss,then Tang Comesinster but opened the door,reached into the head and said:"I have a way,but you have to promise to take me away."Take me away,and I'll speak."

"This kid,he's still eavesdropping."'said the female captain.

"Come in and let me see what you have in mind."White Chrysanthemum said.

Tang Comesinster opened the door and walked in.

"You didn't want a home when you were so young?Don't want your mother and father?"'asked the female captain.

"My family is not good.I heard Aunt Shang Xiaoning say that their boys can go to school,they can be scientists,they can be leaders,they can be astronauts and presidents.Maybe I'll be president."

What the little boy said made everyone laugh.

"And your mother and father are reluctant to let you go?"'said the female captain.

"Shede,when I was born,they were going to throw me away and kill me,and now they are like I am dead."

"Well,this little fellow is not easy to talk about,and he will do great things in the future."Shang Xiaoning praised.

"What's the best way to do that?"'said the female captain.

"One more,I will go with you,and one of you will be my mother and one of you will be my father.You promised."

This Shang Xiaoning and Jiao Liang face said red.

"What are you talking about?"Shang Xiaoning said.

"It's not nonsense,it's true.If I go with you,and you don't want me,and you throw me away,won't I be the same as I am now?"Said the little fellow,and began to cry.

Shang Xiaoning quickly comfort him:"Good,I promise,promise,swear.Now stop crying,and tell me your way."

Tang Comesinstersmiled through tears,he said:"They check,must be checking your boat people,right?"Search your ship,they leave when they can't find anyone.Then you sail away,and everyone will be all right."

"What about us?Where are we?"White Chrysanthemum asked.

"We're on the other boat."

"How do I get up there?"

"Because they must only be looking at this ship,and we all live here,so they must all know."They thought we were going to take this boat,but we didn't."

"Then other people's ships also need those certificates,we do not have,a check will not expose the target?"Shang Xiaoning said.

100

"That's right.The female captain first asked which ship was going to the nearest country,and then asked them to take us with them,saying that I had a serious illness and my mother and father were going to take me to see a doctor.You have the proof.You're a day or two late for something.You'll be there to bring us back,and it won't affect them."

"Hey,this little guy is not simple.Well,do as you like."said the female captain.

"But when we go,we'd better go in the middle of the night,without anyone seeing us."Tang Comesinster said.

"Of course we are.We're not fools."said the female captain.

All the arrangements were in order,and in the evening the female captain opened the door,piled suitcases and many other things in front of it,turned off the light and the door,and drove from the garage to his own door,just enough to cover it.Then he opened the door,and by the faint light of the street lamp,she opened the trunk and put the luggage in one piece.

Just as she pulled up to the door to block it,the lower part of the door was quietly opened,which had been made into a movable door.It was also Tang Comesinster's idea.People climbed out and climbed into the car.They all lay down under the seats when they got in the car.Jiao Liang also spent the night here.

When the female captain's luggage was finished,the female captain got into her car and started.Drove straight to her boat,dropped off her luggage,drove back,drove halfway,turned to another dock,and went straight to the boat she had contacted.But before boarding the ship,the female captain stopped the car and, after carefully observing that there was no one around, told them all to take their seats and not to run away. The child must also pretend to be seriously ill, and the parents must also show anxiety and sadness.

That female captain was waiting at the entr.nce of the ship. Then she took them to female captain's cabin and rhe female captain said, 'The child is very ill. Stay with me, quiet and undisturbed.' The female captain was also afraid of being seen, and it was safer for her to know alone. After all, it was not entirely legal, but she could not force people to produce a certificate, they did not intend to hand over people to her, just let her take a day early, save people. It has nothing to do with her. Even if they run away, it's not about her.

The female captain arranged them all and drove back. Halfway there, she wondered if she would go back to her boat and look at her luggage. She looked, and sure enough, the luggage had been moved. Does she still hide people in boxes? It's stupid, too. It's worse than a kid.

But now she is more relieved, someone followed her here, and went inside to look for her luggage, which indicates that at least no one followed her later, and her whereabouts are unknown. She pretended to forget something, shuffled the box here and there, put something in it from her arms, took something out again, put it in her pocket, and then drove home.

The next day that ship sailed on time, and the that female captain spoke to the female   captain. Tte female captain was relieved to have dropped a stone to the ground. She had a very leisurely day, and after saying a warm farewell to her family, she drove to the dock, parked her car in the dock garage, and boarded the boat.

101

  The female captain went to her room,and before he had a chance to rest,suddenly the mobile phone rang,which startled her.Who's gonna call?It won't be family.It won't be anyone on that boat.Everything's going well.What do they need to contact?Something bad must be going on.The captain's heart rose in her throat,his hands trembled,and she dared not answer the telephone.

  She coughed dry,calm the mood,then opened the mobile phone,a look is the White Chrysanthemum phone.Suddenly decided in her heart a lot,she will have what?Did she drive the boat?General concern,of course,has something to do with that.

  But when she heard what was said,she suddenly became nervous again.The original White Chrysanthemum boyfriend Daylily these days a little mysterious,often can not find him.When she found him,she asked him where he went,why he turned off his phone,and he did not answer,and he hesitated and said that he was not comprehensive.Especially this morning,when he disappeared and couldn't be reached.White Chrysanthemum will go to his house,he must have a good friend,she is ready to catch them both in bed.However,before she arrived at his house,he came out in a hurry,and the White Chrysanthemum quickly hid in the side to see where he was going.He wound up zigzagging all the way to the dock,straight to the boat.He showed the guard some kind of ID,and the guard let him in.

  Is his new love on board?The White Chrysanthemums are on board,too.But the security guard stopped her and she took out her ID card,which she had already obtained and which only permanent residents can receive.But the security guard said no.White Chrysanthemum said,how did the person in front get in?The security guard said he was CIA.She was shocked.Has she been dating an agent?How does he pretend to be so good?Oh her.

White Chrysanthemum in retrospect on the number,no wonder someone reported Jiao Liang,Shang Xiaoning.Turns out he's an agent.White Chrysanthemum scared out of a cold sweat,fortunately she did not put their escape plan to tell him,they all have to die.Think here,White Chrysanthemum heart Tuk Tuk straight jump.

But,with the ship about to sail,why isn't he leaving?If they follow the ship,they find out the secret,and the captain's family will suffer.White chrysanthemum was so anxious to call the captain.

When the captain heard this,he was frightened out of his wits and rushed out of the captain's cabin.Have you seen a man come up?They said they didn't see him.The female captain said,"Bad,he's a terrorist,he's got a bomb.I want you to search it,and I want you to find him.The ship has been delayed.'

People scattered and looked everywhere.After a while,she heard someone shout,found it,found it.The captain rushed over and saw that this man was tall and beautiful,but his skill was extraordinary,and all the people were not his opponents.

When the female captain came,the man said,"I will not leave until I find the man.I will sail with you."The female captain was so anxious that he wished he had a pistol in his hand to shoot him.Just then,someone hit her behind,she looked back,it was the first mate.The first mate gave her a wink,which meant that the first mate was circling behind him,and the female captain was drawing her attention from the front.The female captain nodded to herself.

102

The female captain said,"I don't understand what you're saying.Who are you searching for?"

"You know who you are,I don't need to tell you."

"I don't know,all I know is that you're a terrorist with a bomb on you."

"Hey hey,joke,you say I am a terrorist,where is the proof?I have proof of my identity."

"Your certificate is fake,otherwise how can you cheat and get in here?"

"I'll show you." Daylily said to pick his pockets,and to move forward.At that moment,the first mate suddenly raised the fire extinguisher behind him and threw it at his head. Daylily fell,did not have time to hum.

The female captain,all limp and dripping with sweat,leaned against the post.The first mate came over and the female captain put his arms around her and said,"Thank you,you saved everyone's lives."Then he took a few breaths and said to everyone,"Get him off the boat and let's go."

Several of the crew carried the Daylily off the ship and handed it over to the guard,and said so and so again.The security guard looked surprised. White Chrysanthemum is still there,did not go,see Daylily was carried off the ship,face flesh and blood,crying up,she beat her head.There was no time to call an ambulance,she only stopped a taxi,had him carried up,and followed the car,crying.

Some of the crew came back and asked the female captain,"Shall we call the police?"

The female captain said:"the men was a CIA,so we knock down him and leave him off ship.

White Chrysanthemum all the way crying,a hand aro.und Daylily ,to the hospital,the doctor immediately launched a rescue.The doctor asked,"How did you get hurt?"White Chrysanthemum a leng,said upstairs fell a brick hit."The doctor is giving Daylily examination, Daylily woke up,he saw White Chrysanthemum is crying,he asked her with difficulty:

"Where am I?What the hell happened?"

"You don't remember?A brick fell upstairs and hit you on the head."

"Oh..." Daylily nodded weakly,"I have something to say to you...Put your head here."

"Don't say anything now."White Chrysanthemum cried and said.

"No,I must say...I can't go into a coffin with a lie...I'm afraid I can't...Just let me say the truth for once..."The mouth of the Daylily moved,and no sound was heard.White Chrysanthemum had to put his ear to his mouth,"I am an agent...008...Specialized in investigating the entry and exit of personnel at home and abroad...The letter came to me first...The superiors don't know that The reason I tell you...I want you to inform them."

"Then why are you looking?"

103

"I'm going to die anyway...Not afraid to say...I was taking this opportunity to sneak out...Because you make it sound so beautiful...If I find them...I would have looked the other way...But I didn't find them...That means they're still here...But I pretended I had to find them and go sailing with them...You need to tell the female captain...Tell her not to be afraid...I'm not a bad person..."

"Can you just leave me?"

"Can't bear to...I'm in pain too...But I long for heaven on earth...Men liberate If for freedom...Either can be thrown..."

"Are you so cruel,and value freedom so much?Doesn't love mean anything to you?"

"It makes sense...Great significance Now I regret it...But it was too late...Life is precious...Love is so precious...But I can't get it...Nothing is more precious than what is lost...When I die...Don't be sad...And find a good...Have a good life...Let me say one last thing...I love you...I will marry you in the next life..."

"You will be fine,I will wait for you,and marry you in the next life..."Whoo..."The White Chrysanthemum cried and shouted.

But Daylily could not hear anything,he closed his eyes.The heartbeat on the EKG machine also showed a straight line.White Chrysanthemum burst into tears,how to shake him he did not move.The doctor hurriedly pushed her away and began to save him.

Besides,everything went well there,but when they came to the ship,the female captain insisted that they eat the medicine,that is,the medicine that can forget the daughter's country.Shang Xiaoning said:

"We won't tell,on my character."

"And I promise I won't.My word is my word."Tang Comesinster said.

"I can't even tell you.It's embarrassing."Jiao Liang said.

"That's your business,my business is to tell every foreigner to take medicine when they go."It's easy,it's painless,it has no side effects,so why make it hard on me?It's for everyone's own good.What do you want to remember about our country?It could get you killed.Come on,eat.You have to eat.For you and for me."

Shang Xiaoning they had to eat.

When the female captain took them on board,he simply said to the people on board that this was the people on the ship,and got off the ship to see a doctor. He's not looking any better.She need to come over here.The ship will not come here for the time being,let them take them,the formalities are over there.They'll pick them up later.No one on board said anything,and no one paid any attention to it.Everyone went about their business.

After eating the medicine,Shang Xiaoning still remember the things of the women's country,she thought,may not have the medicine,she dare not say no effect;If it doesn't work,doesn't it get she killed?All three were silent,lying quietly on the railing and looking at the sea.The female captain is busy.

Suddenly,Shang Xiaoning cried out:

"This is the fishing boat I came from,I recognize it,it is still there,that means the people on it are still alive...Ah--"Shang Xiaoning shouted and waved to each other.The boat was close enough to make out the faces of the men on it.

104

To stay closer,the people on the boat also seemed to see Shang Xiaoning, recognized her,and waved to her.Shang Xiaoning jumped up with joy.The female captain came over and asked:

'What is it?So happy?"

"This is the boat that took us out to sea,from which we fell.They're still here,the boat's still here,I'm so happy."

"Really?I'm happy for you,too.In that case,since someone has come,you can go back in their ship,and we won't send them."

'Why?Shang Xiaoning asked in surprise.

"Because you have not yet reached the medicine,you still remember the things of our country,once we meet with them,you will inevitably introduce it,and you will leak your mouth.You go in a boat,and that's when the medicine kicks in.They ask you,and all you say is,Iyoudon't remember anything,you just remember the boat saving you.And now I'm back."

Speaking of this,Shang Xiaoning is not good to say what.With tears in her eyes,she embraced the female captain:

"How can I thank you in this life?"

"You're welcome,as long as your life is good."The two hugged for a long time,and the female captain abruptly withdrew Shang Xiaoning and said:

"Farewell."The female captain choked back tears and hugged Tang Comesinster again,"I'll miss you."Finally she waved her hand and said,"I wish you happiness."

Jiao Liang also had tears in his eyes and said:"Thank you for your great kindness."

"All you have to do is be nice to her."

"I will,don't worry."

"Well,then,go away.I'll miss you."The female captain turned and shouted,"Let the boat go and send them across."

Shang Xiaoning they got on the boat,to the sea,turned around and waved goodbye to the female captain,but see the female captain in wiping tears.

After boarding the Chinese ship,Shang Xiaoning still remembers everything.They stood on the deck and watched the ship go away.When the women's ship sailed away,Tang Comesinster suddenly said:"This medicine is fake."Fortunately,the men and women on board had gone to the bridge and did not hear.

"SHH-"Shang Xiaoning said,covering his lips with her forefinger,"we don't remember anything,except that the boat saved us and now it's bringing us back. That makes it safe."Shang Xiaoning blinked his eyes again.

"Now that the medicine is working,I don't remember anything."Tang Comesinster said with a grimace.

All three burst into laughter.

After a while,Tang Comesinster asked again:"Can men here go on board?"

"Haven't you forgotten everything already?Remember,everything you see is the other way around,okay?Stop making such a fuss."

105

"Yeah, I see."

The female captain received a call from White Chrysanthemum, who told her about Daylily. The female captain suddenly felt very sorry, why hit a good man?

"And how is he now?" Listen to white Chrysanthemum talk like he's still alive. She'd never forgive herself for killing him.

Sure enough, White Chrysanthemum said, "Now it's okay, I'm recuperating." But thank you for the dozen. If you don't, he's still working as an agent and sneaking around. Now he has forgotten everything and can no longer work. But he didn't forget life. He didn't forget love."

"That's good. You don't dislike him, do you?"

"How can that be? Love is too late." Then White Chrysanthemum lowered her voice again and said, "He is pretending." Only you know this, top secret."

"Oh, of course, what am I? When will we drink your wedding wine?"

"Soon, soon."

The female captain's heart was full of happiness, and everything was so perfect.

www.ingramcontent.com/pod-product-compliance
Lightning Source LLC
Chambersburg PA
CBHW081152070526
44583CB00021B/2799